Simon Parkes is the founder of the Brixton Academy,
which he owned and operated for fifteen years.

JS Rafaeli is a writer and musician based in London.

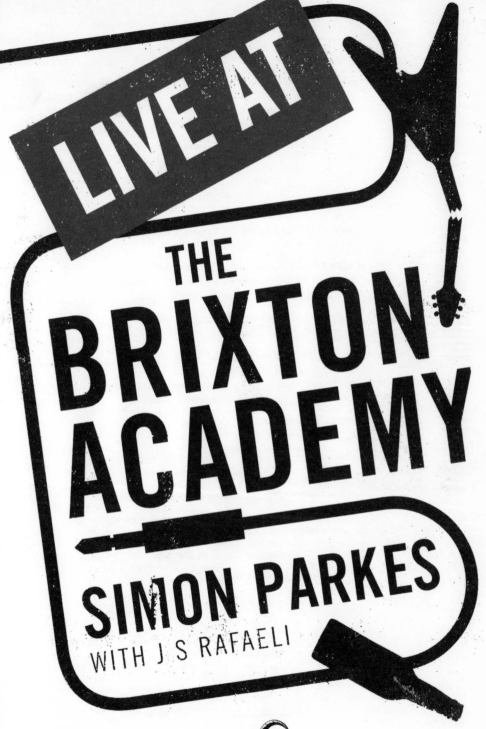

LIVE AT

THE
BRIXTON
ACADEMY

SIMON PARKES

WITH J S RAFAELI

SERPENT'S TAIL

A complete catalogue record for this book can be
obtained from the British Library on request

The right of Simon Parkes and JS Rafaeli to be identified as the
authors of this work has been asserted by them in accordance
with the Copyright, Designs and Patents Act 1988

First published in 2014 by Serpent's Tail,
an imprint of Profile Books Ltd
3A Exmouth House
Pine Street
London EC1R 0JH
www.serpentstail.com

ISBN 978 1 84668 955 0
eISBN 978 1 84765 993 4

Designed and typeset by Tetragon, London

Printed by Clays, Bungay, Suffolk

10 9 8 7 6 5 4 3 2 1

FSC
www.fsc.org
MIX
Paper from
responsible sources
FSC® C018072

*Dedicated to all the musicians,
fans, and everyone who has ever
partied at the Brixton Academy*

CONTENTS

INTRO: THE GUY BEHIND THE GUY

The guy was cracking up.

It was all there: the fretful pacing, the darting eyes and flighty hands, the split-second switches between obsequious pleading and frustrated rage. All the telltale signs of a cocaine addict in need of a score.

Inspiral Carpets had just finished their soundcheck. The band were laughing and fooling around as the roadies cleared the stage for the support act. I was backstage with some of my own crew, ensuring everything was in its right place, and that the soundcheck changeovers were running smoothly.

That's when the guy decided to make his move.

'Umm ... hello mate ... uhhh ... you're Simon, right? The venue owner?'

'Yeah, that's me. What can I do for you?' I asked, as if I didn't know.

He leaned in close, his voice dropping to that guttural, agitated hush that drug addicts mistake for discretion. 'Well ... it's just ... I was wondering ... could you, y'know ... sort us out?'

'Sort you out with what?' I asked, deliberately making my voice boom in faux naivety. At the very least, I could have some fun with this.

The guy cringed in druggie paranoia, his eyes shooting around the room, as if at any moment black-clad spooks were going to burst in and punish him for trying to score a bit of gear.

'I was just after ... y'know ... maybe, a couple grams of coke ... I just thought, ... y'know ... perhaps you could help me out?' he whispered in desperation.

I looked the guy up and down. To me, he had just marked himself out as a chump. I liked to party as much as anyone; I ran a rock 'n' roll venue, after all. But the rule was never to mix business and pleasure. I didn't even drink on the job; and I certainly never got high with other industry players while working a gig. It was unprofessional but, much more important, it left you vulnerable.

Still, you don't get very far in the music business without the ability to spot an opportunity. The guy may have made a tacky move, but played correctly, I could turn this to my advantage. He would get his coke. But he'd have to wait until I had him exactly where I wanted him.

I gave him a wink. 'Yeah, I think I can help you. I'll call someone I know. It may take a little while, but I'll sort you out.'

Those were the magic words. All those tiny muscles behind the guy's eyes, which had been so rigidly tensed in grinding junkie anxiety, seemed to relax simultaneously. He broke into a broad smile, clasped my hand, and thanked me effusively.

I may have kept work and fun separate, but I wasn't an idiot.

I knew exactly what went on. I knew how it functioned, and who made it happen. If you've got a problem with people getting their kicks however they do it, then rock 'n' roll probably isn't the job for you. I always made sure none of my own team got involved with dealing, but I knew who to talk to.

He liked to refer to himself as 'The Doctor'. We just called him Doc. He was tall and wiry, with glasses, long straggly hair, and a nervous disposition. Doc was a constant fixture at the Academy, always wandering around in the same torn jeans and grubby military surplus jacket. He must have had an arrangement with someone to get backstage passes, on the understanding that he would find the bands, and their crews, whatever they needed to stay happy.

'Listen Doc,' I whispered, pulling him aside, 'you see that guy?' I pointed out our mark. Doc glanced over quickly; then turned back to me, nodding.

'In a little while, you're going to give that guy two grams of Charlie. It's on me. But here's the thing: you're not to do anything at all, until I give you the signal. You got it?'

Doc nodded again. He understood I was up to something, even if he couldn't figure out exactly what. He would do what I told him; he had to. His entire livelihood was based on my tolerating his presence in the venue. One word from me, and very quickly there would be some other geek supplying dope to bands at the Brixton Academy.

I glanced back over at the guy, still pacing anxiously in the corner. I hadn't met him before, but I was aware of who he was. He was involved, at a fairly high level, with quite a few of the Manchester bands that had carved themselves a niche in the British charts of the past few years.

There was business to be done here. It was just a matter of timing.

I watched as the guy became progressively more and more impatient. Every few minutes his eyes would flick over to me and I would give him a nod, or a little wave, as if to say, No worries, mate, the gear's on its way.

All the while Doc stood at the opposite corner of the room, the product stashed safely in his pocket.

After about an hour the poor guy couldn't stand it any more and shuffled up to me. 'Sorry mate ... I just ... uhhh ... don't suppose there's any sign of your fella, is there?'

'Oh yeah,' I replied cheerily, pretending not to register the desperation in his voice. 'He says he's on his way. Shouldn't be too long.'

'Yeah ... uhhh ... great. Cheers.' He slouched away again in disappointment.

It was crucial I didn't let him get his stuff too soon. I had to let him get just frantic enough.

I let him stew for another hour. Doc did his part, never moving from his spot. We watched the dude's addict pangs get progressively worse. He was feeling it bad now: slumped in a chair, sweating and fidgeting so bad it looked like he was about to climb the walls.

Perfect.

He shot up in his seat as I walked over, his eyes tracking my every move.

'All right mate, the bloke's almost here,' I breezed.

His eyes lit up with joy.

'There's just one thing I wanted to talk to you about,' I continued.

The guy's face froze in terror. Was I about to say something to jeopardize his score?

'I've been thinking about getting Black Grape down for some gigs here. What do you say we do three nights at the Academy over the next few months?'

I had timed it perfectly. By this point, the guy would have agreed to anything. He nodded furiously and jabbered his assent.

We shook on the deal, and I turned and gave Doc the nod. The guy's eyes showed a momentary flicker of incomprehension, as some part of his brain registered that Doc had been standing in the same room as him the whole time. But he was so happy get his couple of grams that he either chose to ignore the thought or just didn't care. I, in turn, whipped £100 out of one of our bar tills, stuck an IOU in its place, and handed the cash to Doc. Not a bad evening's work.

And we did end up getting our three nights of Black Grape. They had just gone massive, riding high on the success of their first single, 'Reverend Black Grape'. A legion of ex-Happy Mondays fans descended on the Academy, following their madcap heroes, and we sold out all three nights. The shows themselves were storming, one of them even featuring a very random onstage cameo by Michael Hutchence of INXS. The combination of baggy Manchester psychedelia and slick, Australian cock rock took everyone by surprise, but somehow it seemed to work. And after the shows, there was a magnificent party backstage with Shaun Ryder, Bez, and the rest of the Black Grape crew, and I'm fairly sure Doc's services were in high demand once again.

But there is a melancholy coda to this story.

This was late 1995. By now I had already sold the Brixton Academy to a publicly limited company, but had agreed to stick around and keep running things for a year or so, to show them how the place worked.

A few weeks after the last of the Black Grape shows, I was going over some paperwork with one of the company accountants. Out of nowhere he pulled out the IOU for Doc's money that I had stuck in the cash till.

'And what is this?' he enquired.

I smirked to myself on seeing that crumpled piece of paper again. I'd forgotten all about it.

'Oh yeah,' I sniggered. 'That has to do with extra expenses involved in securing Black Grape.'

The accountant looked at me in blank incomprehension. 'What do you mean, *extra expenses?*' he asked.

Oh God. Was I really going to have to explain to the company accountant that I'd had to bribe some dope-head music-biz player with two grams of coke?

'You know ... *extra expenses.*' I winked. 'As in *hospitality expenses.*' Come on, he must get it now ... or at least have enough understanding to get from my tone that he shouldn't ask questions he might not like the answers to.

'I'm sorry, I don't follow,' the accountant continued brusquely. 'I'm going to have to mark this down as something, or the numbers won't add up.'

Over the course of those three Black Grape shows, we must have taken somewhere around £140,000 on the bar alone, plus the hall hire for the gigs themselves: not at all bad for a £100 investment. But here I was, being forced to quibble with this pencil-pusher over chump change.

I sighed. This seemed to be the way things were going. Since selling the Academy, I had found myself enduring more and more of these utter failures of communication. I was surrounded by suits. The businessmen who had taken over just didn't seem to speak the same language as me, or any of the rock 'n' rollers that I had had so much fun dealing with over the past 15 years.

'Mr Parkes, how do you wish to proceed over this matter?' the accountant asked in his clipped, businesslike tone.

Jesus, I thought to myself, did he really just ask me that? Where does this guy think he is? This isn't some bloody insurance company. In the old days someone using that kind of dry management-speak would have been laughed out of the room.

I could see from his face there was going to be no breaking through. I had got to know this kind of brick wall all too well. I sighed to myself again, grabbed my chequebook from the table, and scribbled out a £100 cheque to the company. That's how things seemed to work in this brave new, corporate world. There was nothing else to do.

It wasn't the hundred quid that bothered me. I couldn't give a fuck about that. It was the idea that the people I now worked with, the people who now owned the Academy that I loved so much, wouldn't understand that in the rock 'n' roll biz, one might have to write an IOU for £100 in order to book gigs that would bring in several hundred thousand. It's just how the game worked. Or at least, it's how my game worked. But it seemed that my style of play wasn't suited to the realm of corporate lawyers and graphpaper-brained financiers. Apparently, there was a new game in town.

I had built the Academy from nothing with my blood, sweat and love. It had been a grand adventure: often terrifying, always exhilarating. I had survived through a combination of quick thinking, gritty determination, and blind luck. The one thing it had never been, though, was boring.

Not for the first time, I was forced to ask myself if the suits who seemed to be taking over not just my venue but the entire industry actually had any feeling for the swing, pulse, and danger of what the music business was. What was to become of my beloved Academy with *these* people in charge?

Oh rock 'n' roll, what have they done to you?

PART ONE

LONDON CALLING

SCRAPPER

It was Mac, my father's bodyguard, who first warned me.

'Listen Simon, at some point tomorrow, some older boys are going to come after you. They'll be from the year above. Anyone older than that won't bother with young uns like you, and the kids in your year will be just as new and confused as you are.'

'But', he continued, 'the boys from the year above: they'll have something to prove. And they'll pick on you. It doesn't mean you've done anything wrong. It's just because you're different. That's how kids are.'

It was strange being told I was 'different'. I mean, obviously by this point I had realized there was a significant distinction between my two brothers and me: they each had two arms, and I only had one. But in our home, I had never been allowed to view myself as different. I didn't get any special privileges, I had to do all the same chores, and I was certainly never, ever, allowed to consider myself 'disabled'.

Some older kids are going to come after you. It's a tough thing for a ten-year-old to hear before his first day at a new prep school. But even at that age, I had learned that when Mac spoke, you listened. Mac had been around. He was a tough old nut and knew how things worked.

'So kiddo, here's what you do,' he went on. 'There will be three or four them, maybe five. One of them will be the leader. You identify who that is, and you put him on his arse. It doesn't matter how big he is, or how many of them there are, you just go after the leader, and make damn sure you put him down. Just remember what I showed you.'

Mac had spent the last six months teaching me how to throw a mean hook with my good right arm, and a few dirtier tricks besides.

'The important thing, Simon, is never let yourself be threatened. Not by anyone. Not ever. The moment you let someone threaten you or push you around, you're done for. If you get a good shot in first, no matter what else happens, at least you'll have stood up for yourself. They'll respect you.'

I nodded attentively, taking it all in.

'Now show me what you've got,' Mac commanded, holding up the palm of his large, calloused left hand. I let out a zinger, enjoying the sound of the meaty thwack as it connected.

Mac winced and shook his hand out, mugging it up a bit. 'That's it kiddo, you'll do just fine.'

Sure enough, the next day, during my first lunch break at the new school, up sauntered four boys: all from the year above. Blimey, I thought as they surrounded me, old Mac really does know what he's on about.

'Well, look at this, a one-armed spastic,' giggled one of the lads to his mates.

Right then. Leader identified.

'What are you doing in proper school, little spastic?' the boy continued.

My answer was to head-butt him square in the nose. He fell backwards, and the other three were so shocked, that I'd decked two of them before they had even registered what was going on. The last one jumped on me, trying to get me in a headlock, but I wriggled out of it and decked him too.

One of the lads wore glasses and ended up having to get five stitches, so of course I was hauled in front of the headmaster. It was all a bit dramatic for the first day of the school year.

'They called me a one-armed spastic, sir,' I explained.

What could the guy do? He gave us all a warning and sent us on our way. But the job was done; no one at that school messed with me again, and I earned the nickname Scrapper, which I wore with some pride.

I never forgot the lesson that old Mac taught me back in 1969. Throughout my life, in all my strange adventures in the music industry and beyond, it's been a key personal maxim: never to let myself be threatened or pushed around. I treat everyone with absolute respect, and can get along with just about anyone; but if you try to intimidate me, then we'll have problems. It's a philosophy that has steered me clear of a fair few sticky situations in my time. It's probably got me into quite a number as well, but something must have worked: I'm still around to tell the tale.

Mum was a committed campaigner for animal welfare. Dad shot pheasant. They were an odd couple in many ways. When she fostered some kids from Liverpool and they ended up running off with a load of her jewellery, my old man was for hanging. Her response was 'Well, they probably need it more than I do.'

Trying to see the good in people was very important to my mother. She had a religious, or at least a spiritual, aspect to her character. It was her golden rule that one should never make judgements on people or situations based on appearances or prejudice. You have one arm? OK. You're black, white, rich, poor? Fine. That's what you are, not *who* you are.

She drilled the belief into me from an early age. Along with Mac's lesson about not letting myself be threatened, my mum's belief in people, that if you treat them right and avoid casting the first stone, then they'll be all right with you, became the guiding principle of my life. Living by it has opened up countless opportunities that I might well have passed over, had I been of a more judgemental mindset.

And judgemental thinking could so easily have become a problem for me, considering where I came from.

You see, this story is about rock 'n' roll, but it all began with fish.

My great-grandfather founded a company called Boston Deep Sea Fisheries, which grew to be the largest privately owned fishing fleet in the world. By the time my granddad, the grandly named Sir Basil Parkes, took the reins, they had something like 186 deep-sea trawlers, 700 inshore fishing boats, fish processing factories, shipbuilding plants, and chains of butchers to supply the meat to shops: the lot. They were all over the UK: Aberdeen, Grimsby, Hull, and further afield from Boulogne to Nova Scotia. I remember my granddad saying things like, 'There's not a fish that lands on a table in a school or hospital anywhere south of Newcastle that hasn't come through us.'

Using the proceeds from the fishing, they had bought up a lot of farmland around Lincolnshire, and started a shipping business. There's a funny old family photo of me as a young child, standing in front of a giant tanker ship named after me. The shipping company was called Hull Gates, so 'my' ship was called the *Simon Gates*. My brothers each had one too, the *Benjamin Gates* and the *Frederick Gates*.

I guess having ships named after us should give you the idea. The family wasn't skint. We grew up in what can only be described

My brothers and me messing about in an Aston
Martin in Cannes. I'm the driver, naturally

as extraordinary privilege, living in a big old house up on the farm in Lincolnshire, and never wanting for anything. I don't consider all this as anything to brag about, but nor have I ever taken for it for granted. Like I say, I was raised to judge people on who they are, not the family they come from.

And while the family was wealthy, and my brothers and I grew up in considerable luxury, we were absolutely never allowed to become spoilt. My grandfather was a flinty Yorkshire man who wouldn't tolerate any nonsense, and had no truck with idleness. It was never an option for us to become lay-about rich kids; it just wasn't part of the family ethos. Business was serious; you were expected to work hard; money was never to be taken for granted. I remember my grandfather coming to London when I was much older, and being so shocked at the price of beer that he would only

'A very big house in the country':
The family home in Lincolnshire

order a half-pint, despite having been dropped off in his chauffeur-driven Rolls-Royce. It was just the hardbitten Northern tradition he came from.

It was with this same no-nonsense attitude that I was taught to approach my arm.

During the late 1950s, the German pharmaceutical company Grünenthal launched the medicine Thalidomide, marketing it as a new wonder drug that could act as a sedative, painkiller, and anti-nausea solution, as well as helping with coughs and colds.

The new drug was primarily targeted at pregnant women, as a palliative for morning sickness.

Unfortunately, the pre-launch testing by Grünenthal was disgracefully inadequate. What they missed was that, when taken by pregnant women, the molecules that comprise Thalidomide pass through to the still-developing foetus, where they bind to, and inactivate, a protein called cereblon, fundamental to the development of healthy limbs. So thousands of babies were born with malformed legs and arms; some were missing ears or other parts. The vast majority died within months of birth. By the time the drug was finally removed from the market in 1962, over 10,000 babies across 46 countries had been born with severe defects, or phocomelia.

The official drug classification of Thalidomide is that it is a teratogen. The word *teratogen* is derived from the Latin *gen*: to create or beget, as in *generate*; and the Greek *teras*, which can mean either 'monster' or 'marvel'. I've always rather fancied myself as the latter, but a strict pharmacological reading of the word means that the company produced and sold a drug that created monsters. It wasn't until August 2012, fifty years after the fact, that Grünenthal issued even the most meagre, equivocal apology.

As it happened, my mother was recommended this shit while pregnant with me, and I popped out missing half my left arm. So there was never any hope of me playing upside-down, restrung guitar like Jimi Hendrix. It was just one of those things.

As I say, the attitude towards all this at home was very much 'just get on with it'. I never got any special treatment; I just had to figure out my own ways of doing things. And if you look at the course of my life, I think it's fair to say I did. In fact, by the standards of Thalidomide, I've always considered myself fairly lucky: at least I had the one arm; many victims of the drug were far more severely impaired.

But no matter how down-to-earth and no-nonsense the attitude at home, having one arm as a kid is always going to force you to fight that little bit harder, to have that little bit more to prove. I think that's probably why I got so heavily into sports.

My first love was rugby. I started playing in a Yorkshire Colliery Sunday League team. Yorkshire miners' sons playing rugby have their own very special kind of toughness. They don't care whether you've got one arm like me, or eight like some Hindu god: they'll hit you, and they'll hit you hard. I loved it.

I also became a long-reigning regional champion in modern pentathlon. And here is where I have to confess getting a bit of mischievous joy out of rocking up, seeing the looks of disbelief on my competitors' faces – 'What's this one-armed guy doing here?' – and then absolutely trouncing them. It was the same every time; I knew those dismissive glances so well. And I knew how to deal with them.

The swimming is where it got really funny. We'd all be called out one by one, and do our walk up to the diving blocks. Everyone would cheer the other guys, in their fancy goggles and swimming hats. Then the announcer would say, 'Simon Parkes'. Out I'd stroll with no goggles or hat, just giving everyone a big grin and a wave with my one arm. You could palpably hear the whole place fall silent, as everyone thought to themselves, Wait a second, that guy's just going to go around in circles.

But what they didn't know was that, thanks to Boston Deep Sea Fisheries, I had grown up with a pool at home. I may not have had exactly proper technique, but I was a total water baby, and had figured out my own unique way of getting to the other side. I always managed to do well enough to maintain my lead from the other events, and to wipe the patronizing smiles off people's faces.

I suppose sport was just a good opportunity for me to prove I could keep up, and even excel. It was certainly my main outlet when I was a kid. At least until I discovered the existence of girls, booze, and rock 'n' roll. But that was still a little ways off.

First, there was Gordonstoun.

ROLL OVER BEETHOVEN

Gordonstoun School is set in the grounds of a 17th-century estate in Morayshire, Scotland. I suppose, after places like Eton and Harrow, it must be one of the poshest public schools in the country. Three generations of royalty have passed through the place, including the Duke of Edinburgh, Prince Charles, and when I wound up there, Prince Andrew, who sat a few desks over from me.

Yet, for all its Hogwarts looks and royal connections, life at Gordonstoun was no fairy tale. A fierce, spartan ethic prevailed. We began each day with a long run and a cold shower, and while the cane had been retired a few years earlier, any infraction of the tight disciplinary code could be punished with Penalty Drill, usually involving several laps round the school grounds or other physical training.

I got to Gordonstoun in 1972. The Rolling Stones had just released *Exile on Main Street*, young music fans were bewitched by David Bowie's transformation into Ziggy Stardust, and Alice Cooper had kids the world over singing, 'School's Out for Summer'. But I was still a little young for all that, and somehow the message never reached Gordonstoun.

Being an energetic, sporty kid, I didn't really mind the physical discipline. But I did have a lot of trouble with the rigid hierarchical structure of prefects, house masters, and all the rest of that claptrap. I've simply never liked people telling me what to do. It wasn't long

My brothers and me with the Rolls. I'm the one
pretending to neck the champagne

before I had gathered together a little gang, and we had made a
reputation for ourselves as upstarts and troublemakers who didn't
know our place in the school pecking order.

And Gordonstoun didn't like that. They operated in the fine old
tradition of the British public school system, whereby older pupils
are inherently superior, and mercilessly cruel, to the younger boys
in their charge.

It was only a matter of time before my group's cocky attitude,
combined with all the usual nonsense of being a one-armed-
kid-at-a-new-school, meant I had to establish my reputation as a
'Scrapper' all over again. It didn't take much. The thing that those
older boys at Gordonstoun didn't realize is that if somebody is
missing an arm, the other arm has to do double the work, and
can become very strong. After a few sixth formers ended up with

black eyes, people soon learned where the boundaries lay. There was always Old Mac's voice in my head, 'Don't let yourself be pushed around.'

All that aside, I did well in my schoolwork, pretty much first class across the board, and apart from my anti-authoritarian streak, I settled at Gordonstoun fairly well.

Then the mid-teenage phase kicked in and I discovered rock 'n' roll.

One of the few fragments of popular culture we were permitted at Gordonstoun was keeping record players in our rooms. I'm not sure exactly when it first clicked, but by fifteen I was hooked.

I remember most of the lads would quickly section themselves off into musical tribes: there were the rockers with their Led Zeppelin and Black Sabbath, the funk kids prancing around to James Brown and Sly Stone, a few stalwarts holding on to the 60s and religiously pumping out their Beatles, Stones, and Pink Floyd, and a small sect of blues purists who looked down on anyone who listened to anything after Robert Johnson and Skip James.

I didn't buy into any of that crap. I loved it all. As long as I could hear some real soul and fire, some deep feeling or badass attitude, I didn't give a toss about genre. Every record seemed to me a window into an incredible new world. I soaked it all up, much to the detriment of my studies. Every time someone brought in a new LP I would hold it like a talisman, a sacred object, as if all the excitement of life had been solidified into this circular black disk and its mesmerizing cardboard sleeve.

At the beginning of term, kids returning from holidays would smuggle in copies of *Melody Maker* and the *New Musical Express*, which would get passed hand to hand around the school. We would read in awe about these magical things called *gigs* where you could actually be dancing in the same room as these amazing musicians. Actually in the same room! The idea was almost too exciting to believe.

In the later years at Gordonstoun we were allowed home for half-term breaks and long weekends. Back in Lincolnshire I had my own car. The guys in the local pubs knew me and I could get served, and I began to realize that, while blokes might try to make fun of a guy with one arm, it was a great way to start conversations with girls. So I was popping down to Lincoln every few weeks where I enjoyed complete freedom, and then coming back to the incredibly strict environment of the school. It was a recipe for trouble.

My grades dropped and I became a right terror for my teachers. There's got to be one in every school, and I did my best to fill the role: smoking smuggled cigarettes with my gang around the back of the science rooms; necking the odd bottle of wine or whisky lifted from some posh family's cellar on the weekend; and the music, always the music.

There were a couple of masters at Gordonstoun who were classic 1970s, right-on types with beards and left-wing pretensions. Yet, here they were teaching at this ultra-elite school full of royals and the heirs to industrial fortunes. What precocious little smart-arse like me could have resisted twisting the knife a little? People who have grown used to being addressed as 'Sir' can get a little tetchy when suddenly greeted with a cheery 'Good morning, Comrade!'

It was the poor harassed careers advisor who probably got it worst. 'Well, Simon,' he asked at our first meeting, 'have you given any thought to your future? You know this school has wonderful connections with both medicine and the law.'

'No, sir.' I winked back. 'I'm going to be an international playboy.'
The conversation only went downhill from there.

Then, when I was about sixteen, perhaps inspired by some Bob
Dylan record about lonesome ramblers or one of those Lou Reed
songs about the big bad city, I decided to have an adventure.

I phoned home that Friday: 'Hi Mum, I think I'm going to go
and stay with Charlie this bank holiday; he wants me to play in a
football match with him on Sunday.'

'OK dear, see you next week.'

Step one. Easy.

I left school early that Friday, boarding the train as if going home
for the long weekend as usual. But at Edinburgh station, instead of
changing over to the Grimsby train, I crossed the platform, walked
up to the ticket booth, and said the magic words: 'One weekend
return to London please.'

As the train pulled away and I watched Arthur's Seat whizz
by on my left, my heart was in my throat. Clutched in my hands
were a scrap of paper, with the phone number of some friend of
Charlie's who had a flat in London where I could supposedly stay,
and the battered copy of *Melody Maker* where I had first seen the
small advert for Chuck Berry in concert, and had come up with
this crazy idea.

I stepped out of Finsbury Park station into pissing rain and a surging crowd. It wasn't hard to figure out where the venue was; I just
followed the small groups of long-haired guys in jeans. I felt a little

surge of pride that some of them were holding the same issue of *Melody Maker* as me, though none seemed also to be carrying an overnight bag with their school badge stitched into it.

I was in a state of feverish excitement as I saw the Rainbow Theatre looming before me, its neon sign flashing through the rain, like some temple to a religion I'd been waiting my whole life to discover. I walked ecstatically up to the lady behind the little window marked Box Office, money in my hand.

'Sorry love, it's sold out. Been sold out for months.'

Those were probably the most crushing words I had ever heard. I couldn't believe it. I had travelled all this way, had built this night up so much in my mind. I had never even considered the possibility of this turn of events. 'But I've come all the way from Scotland,' I pleaded.

'Sorry love, nothing to be done,' the lady snapped, picking up her magazine. Then she paused, looking me up and down. At first I was seized by terror that she was going to start asking questions about my age, but then her face seemed to soften. 'Look darling, why don't you try just walking round the corner?'

I had no idea what she was talking about. What possible good was *walking around the corner* going to do? Was this some weird London insult, a way of saying 'Get lost'? At this point I was too upset to care. I turned and walked slowly away, wondering what the hell I was going to tell everyone back at school.

I stopped after about fifteen yards, pausing in a whirl of teenage self-pity, and searching my pockets for the scrap of paper with Charlie's friend's number on it.

'All right mate,' came a gravelly voice just behind me. I turned to see this huge guy looming over me, wearing a long black leather coat and fingerless gloves. I froze. This was just what I didn't need. Scrapping with bigger kids at school was one thing, fighting off London muggers something else entirely. I clenched my fist instinctively.

Then the guy said something amazing. 'Looking for a ticket, mate?'

'Whu ... whu ... What?' I stammered.

'A ticket for tonight. For Chuck Berry,' he said, jerking his head in the direction of the venue.

'What? To buy?' I asked, not quite believing what was happening.

'No, for bloody Christmas,' the guy shot back, shaking his head in disbelief. 'It's a fiver. You want one or not?'

Tickets at the box office were £3. I didn't care. After making it all the way down from Scotland, I wasn't going to quibble over two quid. I held out the cash, my hand almost shaking, and the geezer handed over a colourful, rectangular piece of card that for me was the key to the kingdom.

The guy walked away. It was only as my eyes followed him that I registered about five other big fellas, all dressed in long leather coats, walking up and down the street, leaning in close to random punters, and offering tickets for the show. I had had my first experience of a real live ticket tout! As I strode triumphantly back along the outside wall of the Rainbow, I realized that I had actually walked just around the corner from the box office. So *that's* what the lady behind the window had meant.

I marched up to the doors; the security guy tore my ticket, and I was through. The band was already playing as I entered the auditorium. I was hit with a wall of heat and noise. I bobbed and weaved trying to get a better view, eventually gathering the courage to push through the crowd towards the front. The band was tearing through a blistering version of 'No Particular Place to Go' and I was in awe. The sheer power of the sound; the feeling of having 2,500 people packed together with all their attention focused on this one event happening onstage. I had never felt anything so powerful. The rest of the show was a blur. I threw myself into it utterly and completely, letting myself be swept up in the magic. Chuck did his manic duck-walk guitar solos, and they played all the hits: 'Maybelline', 'Rock 'n' Roll Music', 'Roll Over Beethoven', 'You Never Can Tell'. They saved 'Johnny B. Goode' for the encore, at which point the whole place exploded. I left that night dripping with sweat, with my ears ringing and a feeling of having been religiously transported.

Needless to say, when I got back to Gordonstoun and told everyone, I became something of a living god. I convinced my friends to join me on a few more of these adventures, before almost getting everyone expelled when we snuck off to see Bob Dylan, Eric Clapton, and Joan Armatrading at Blackbushe, the biggest gig ever staged in mainland Britain. Luckily, by then our exams were finished, and we escaped with a stern warning and some serious Penalty Drill.

But my time at Gordonstoun was coming to an end anyway, and a new phase about to begin.

ONE WAY OR ANOTHER

I don't think the question was ever actually asked. No one ever said, 'Simon, do you think the family business is for you?' It was just assumed that I, along with my brothers, would go into the firm and carry the torch from one generation to another.

It was my granddad who sat me down and laid it out. 'All right boy, you've been through school. Well done. Now, if you're to take this business over one day, you need to learn it. You can't just go to some poncy business school then swan into management. If you want to lead people, you need their respect. And if you want respect, you go and earn it.'

I nodded. I could see where this was going, but you didn't interrupt Granddad Parkes.

'We've arranged some jobs for you. You begin next Monday.' And that was that.

So at 4.30 a.m. on the appointed Monday, I dutifully clocked in for my first shift lumping fish at a processing plant on the Grimsby docks. Obviously, the blokes down at the plant weren't supposed to know I was the boss's son, so I signed in as John Richards. I thought a cross between John Lennon and Keith Richards could suit me fine for a while.

I cleaned fish, I gutted fish, I chopped fish, and I packed fish: every stage of the industrial process. The only thing I didn't do for a few months was eat fish. Trust me, you'd be sick of the smell of it too. This was cold, tiring, slimy work. But I finished each week knowing that I had definitely earned my £38.40.

After a few months they rotated me from the docks to the farm. I ascended from fish guts to pig shit. The company had bought up a load of new land, and wanted to convert it from pork farming to raising crops. The only thing that stood in the way was thirty years' worth of manure. On my first day, my boss handed me a shovel, pointed to a series of red-brick structures stretching uninterrupted for about a mile and a half, and said in his broad Lincolnshire accent, 'See them sties? They need mucking. Get to.' The shit needed to be shovelled, and I shovelled it. For months.

It was tough work, but I was out of school and free. Which meant that every weekend I was straight down to London for gigs. Many of my friends from school had inevitably wound up in London, and being the elite, coddled kids they were, had got themselves quite cushy set-ups down there. There was always a flat to stay in, and some party to crash. I tactfully didn't mention to these posh kids in their Holland Park pads that I had spent the week shovelling shit up in Lincolnshire; I was there to have a good time, drink their booze, and chat up their girls.

But what I was most interested in was going to rock 'n' roll shows. Punk had exploded and blown the whole music scene wide open. I saw Iggy Pop tour his incredible album *The Idiot*, with David Bowie on keyboards, and Talking Heads closing their set with 'Psycho Killer'. I saw Bob Marley giving one of the most true and heartfelt performances I have ever experienced back up at the Rainbow, and Eric Clapton jam with Muddy Waters on 'Got My Mojo Working' at the Hammersmith Odeon. All these shows just blew my mind.

I had learned from my Chuck Berry experience. Ticket touts became my lifeline. This was the late 70s, well before the days of instant information and Internet credit card booking. If you wanted to buy a ticket for a show, you still had to go to the venue's box office, or at least to one of the cooler record stores. And first you had to know that a gig was even happening. This was one thing if you lived down in London; but up north, by the time I had heard of a decent concert, it would have long since sold out. So touts were my only option. Without them I would have missed out on so much. I'll always have a soft spot for ticket scalpers: I think they provide, or at least provided, a seriously valuable service for real music fans. And the ones I eventually got to know well had a damn sight more soul than any online ticket booking system.

While I was busy yoyo-ing between hard toil in Lincolnshire, and hard partying in London, things had been slowly going haywire in my family life. My mother and father went through a drawn-out and acrimonious divorce. I didn't think my old man behaved like a complete gentleman through all this, which put considerable strain on our relationship. Then my granddad got seriously ill, and perhaps thinking of the £50 million odd quid that his death duties would entail, he packed up and moved to the Isle of Man.

All this resulted in the family company being chopped up and divided. It went something along the lines of my brothers and I keeping 53 per cent, my dad getting 47 per cent and running some of the shipping and farming, with the whole thing being managed by trustees. While all this was going down, I was too young, and too busy finishing school and learning to gut fish, to have been made aware of the deals that were being knitted together. Looking back, I wonder how differently things might have turned out if I had been even two years older and able to exert a measure of control over what happened. Because, as things transpired, these arrangements would come to have a profound impact on the course of my life.

But for now at least, my destiny seemed set. I was to go into the family firm. So, having done my time at the sharp end of the industry, I was packed off to business college in London.

This was a dream come true. The company owned a plush flat in Cadogan Gardens, complete with maid and drinks cabinet. I had a great pad, money in my pocket, and the world at my feet. What young man wouldn't be happy?

Besides, while there is a whole book to be written on the joys and dangers of Lincolnshire farmers' daughters, I had been getting

As a teenager on a boat

a bit of a reputation up there. Mothers had begun to shut the door in my face when I came to call. London was a whole new world.

The business course wasn't overly demanding. I found I could breeze my way through it fairly easily. Each day I'd swing by the college at Elephant and Castle, making sure to park my sharp little sports car away from the badlands of the Walworth Road, kill a few hours in classes, then hit the town.

The partying took a minor setback when my dad saw the booze bill. The flat in Cadogan Gardens was meant for entertaining foreign clients and partners who came through town. Hence, part of the housekeeper's job was to keep the liquor cabinet fully stocked at all times. Well, my friends and I had a very good time with that one. After a few months a message went through from the company accountant to my old man, and I got my marching orders in no uncertain terms.

So I moved in with a friend on the King's Road, just above the original Boy shop, and just turned up the volume on my lifestyle.

This was when I started going to music shows in earnest. I remember Tina Turner stalking the stage of the Venue in Victoria, then seeming to almost drape herself over the microphone stand. She had a preternatural control over her band, making them go so quiet that the audience was driven half crazy with anticipation, before leading them into yet another furious crescendo. There was a raw, humming eroticism that seemed to emanate from deep within her. Few performances have ever matched that for pure sexuality.

This was also the heyday of the Sunday punk shows at the Lyceum. I saw all the greats at their filthy best: The Damned, The Slits, The Adverts. Those shows had a menace to them that made your pulse race. When Poly Styrene screamed, my god did you stand up and pay attention. And I got completely swept up with the two-tone explosion, catching the raucous, no-bullshit energy of early gigs by The Selecter and The Specials.

It was through going to shows like these that I began to get a sense for the different venues on the London circuit. The Lyceum and the Hammersmith Palais were all right, but I got frustrated with the Albert Hall, and even more so with the Hammersmith Odeon, which for some reason seemed to be the hottest concert hall in town. I didn't get what people saw in it. First off, the gigs were seated. Ludicrous! Who wants to sit down at a concert? And, the décor was all pastel carpets and popcorn machines. It might as well have been a family cinema in 1950s Blackpool. Now, I've got nothing against Blackpool cinema proprietors, but it's not what you want for a rock 'n' roll show. But for some reason, i.e. money, it was where all the best bands would play. So I ended up there a lot.

Eventually the business course finished, and I emerged ready to fulfil my ordained destiny and take my place in the family empire. Only to find the empire no longer existed.

Somewhere along the line the trustees, amongst whom the various family companies had been divided, had sacked my father from his portion of the business. There had been some legal drama, and amidst the ensuing fallout, owing to a noxious mix of incompetence, neglect, and, dare I say it, avarice and perfidy, the company and its assets had been dismembered, dissected, and frittered away. We were by no means destitute, but there was definitely no certain, gilded future before me; and more immediately, no cast-iron job. Two years of dead fish and pig shit for this?

I was at a loose end, cut somewhat adrift. I headed back up to Lincoln for a bit. We still had the farm; perhaps I could have thrown myself into that. But I'd been in London. I had the bug. Rock 'n' roll had taken me down to the crossroads like Robert Johnson, and there was no way I was sticking around the country. My brothers could handle the farming; I headed back to the city. I was searching for something.

'Do you think she's wearing knickers?'

'I bet she isn't.'

'Her. No way. You know she's got nothing on under there.'

The band were just coming onstage, picking up their instruments, tuning, and letting out the odd little riff to check the sound. *She* was standing motionless as a statue, holding the mic stand, and fixing the crowd with an aloof, icy stare that was pure, concentrated sexual charisma.

'Goddamn, she's so hot.'

'Hot? Mate, hot doesn't even begin to cover it. That's *Debbie Harry*.'

Blondie were in the house.

My friends and I were sitting towards the back of the Hammersmith Odeon. We'd been waiting for this gig for weeks, and had spent most of the afternoon getting in the mood with bourbon on the rocks, and big spliffs full of the Lebanese hash that was so ubiquitous in London at the time. By the time those razor-sharp New Yorkers strolled onto the stage, we were very much in the zone.

'I'll bet you fifty quid she's got no knickers on under there.'

My mates weren't going to let this go. Suddenly, through the haze and fug of my addled state, I realized exactly what I needed to do.

'Only one way to find out,' I said, and I was off.

I sprinted straight towards the stage, racing down the causeway between the neat little blocks where the crowd was sitting. God, I hated these seated gigs.

Unconscious memories of all my yomping through pentathlon courses were ricocheting through my mind. I had it all planned perfectly. I would vault onto the barrier that separated the band from the crowd; from there I could launch myself onto the stage. I knew, of course, it was too far for me to get there on my feet, but my plan was to land on my side, execute a perfect roll to the right, and end up on my back just by the microphone stand: the perfect position to verify the relative state of Debbie Harry's intimate undress, and put this important question to rest.

Propelled by the explosive opening riff of 'One Way or Another', I saw the seated punters whizzing by in a blur out of the corner of my eye. I felt like a young god. I wasn't going to sit there like some placid, bovine schmuck. I was at a rock 'n' roll show: I wanted some movement, some action!

I timed it flawlessly: one jump up, somehow managing to maintain my balance on the narrow ledge of the stage barrier. Then, with adrenaline coursing through my veins, and blood and Blondie pounding in my ears, I launched myself like Icarus towards the stage.

I never even landed.

There was that special, unfamiliar weightlessness of being caught in mid-flight, and I found myself in the strong grip of several burly, and thoroughly unamused, security guards. These guys were pros: within seconds, four of them had me by the legs and shoulders. I didn't touch the ground till I hit the pavement. They opened the double doors with my head, and gave me the old heave-ho.

I landed hard on my back and burst into hysterics. Rock 'n' roll indeed; I'd only seen about forty seconds of the band!

I was actually pretty used to this by now. Over the past few months, since my return to London, I had turned into something of a hellraiser. I'd lost my initial awe of music shows, and now always wanted to be part of the action. My friends and I pushed our luck consistently, and by that point the Odeon was the only venue left in London that I had never been physically thrown out of. Now I could cross it off my list. It had only ever been a question of time.

Funnily enough, about twenty years later I was in Los Angeles suffering from a nuclear-powered stinker of a hangover, when who should step into the elevator with me but Debbie Harry. My god, I thought to myself, recalling my ignominious ejection from the Odeon all those years before, what I wouldn't have done to be stuck in a lift with you two decades ago. That morning, though, she was looking fairly rough herself, and I decided against asking her, just for the record, if she was wearing underwear.

ASTORIA

These were good times for me. I had enough money to get by, and spent most of my time tearing around town and going crazy at gigs. Somewhere in the back of my mind I knew that sooner or later I would have to start thinking about things like 'real life', and a 'career', but that time definitely wasn't now.

This was also a very exciting period for live music. In 1979 Britain had been through its 'winter of discontent'; the television was full of class war and race riots. There was a palpable feeling of tension and danger in the air. I was, of course, cushioned from the sharp end of all this. I had enough to live on, at least in the short term, but I picked up on that menacing, revolutionary atmosphere just like everyone else. When you went out to a show, especially the punk and ska bands, you truly never knew how the night would end up. Anything could happen. It was wild.

It was amidst all this that one day, as I was lying around a girl-friend's flat, a call came in for me.

'All right Simon,' trilled a cut-glass, Edinburgh Scottish accent. 'It's Drew Macphearson here. I've got a wee proposition I want to bend your ear about.'

Drew was a guy I had known at school, one of the native Scots at Gordonstoun. He had never been part of my close gang, but I remembered him as being someone who would usually lend you a hard-to-get-hold-of record if you asked.

It turned out that Drew had started a small promotion company up in Edinburgh. Now an opportunity had come up to buy a venue called the Edinburgh Playhouse. Since he remembered me being 'a guy that loved his music', he wondered if I might be interested in going into business, and taking it over it with him.

Now, I've never considered myself a particularly acute businessman. In fact I've generally erred towards being overly naive and trusting, especially when I was young. But even I know a shakedown when I see one. I realized right away that Drew had only got in touch because people at school knew my family had a lot of money. But I was intrigued, and I wasn't about to let on that all the cash was gone.

What the hell? At the very worst I figured I'd have a nice weekend up north and check in with some old mates.

So I hopped on a train, cruised up to Scotland, and Drew and I went to check out the Playhouse. I thought it was a cool place, but the guys showing us around took about ten seconds to clock that we weren't serious buyers. 'Just a couple of wankers' was the phrase I thought I heard one of them mutter to the other under his breath. And, to be fair, you didn't need to be too sharp an operator to work out that Drew, with his Laird of the Glen brogue, and I, not just a toff but an *English* toff, had no place in the hard-scrabble, cut-throat underworld of the Scottish music business.

Though the potential deal fizzled out, I did have a great weekend and I returned to London with the seed of an idea planted in my mind. If music shows were what I truly enjoyed, why not make them my business? But for now it was just a daydream. There didn't seem to be any way simply to pick up and get a start in the music industry. So I forgot about it and got back to concentrating on the important things in life, like chasing girls, and going to see The Specials every chance I got.

A few months later the phone rang again. 'All right Simon, it's Drew. There's some venue down in south London that might be up for grabs. I'm not about, but do you want to go have a look?' Once again I thought, What the hell? I was living in Battersea at this point, it was only around the corner.

I walked into the Brixton Astoria and fell in love.

It was incredible: a moment I shall never, ever forget. Walking through the dilapidated elegance of that art deco foyer and into the huge, dark expanse of the main auditorium, I felt this momentous excitement churning in the pit of my stomach. *This was it.* This was what I had been waiting for. What a space! What a stage! It seemed to go on forever. Even as a virtually derelict building, currently used only to store chairs, I could sense the incredible potential of this place. I could almost see the bands moving on that stage, feel the crowd pressing up close, hear the music booming through the hall. Store chairs here? You must be crazy. This was the venue that London had been missing all along. I could make this place glorious.

But beyond the amazing building, at that moment I felt something change within myself. All my casual fly-by-the-seat-of-my-pants nonchalance vanished in an instant, replaced with one burning, intensely focused desire. I *had* to get this venue. I didn't care about anything else. I just knew this place could be magic for gigs. All my frustration with the other venues in London welled up. Bollocks to them with their seated concerts and cheesy cinema décor. If I could get this place, I could change everything. I knew somewhere deep in my soul that I would do something new here, something truly wild.

Looking back, I can only laugh at how much my incendiary

enthusiasm was based on utter naivety. This was 1982: Brixton was still smouldering from the riots that had torn the community apart the previous year. The area was pockmarked with burned-out buildings. During this era if you even mentioned the word 'Brixton' to any white, middle-class Londoner, there would usually be an audible intake of breath. Brixton meant the badlands down south. Best avoided, probably never even talked about, except in the context of some horror story on the news: the place where sensible, upstanding people feared to tread. In short, it was still just a rough, violent, poverty-stricken, West Indian neighbourhood. Any real businessman, any real Londoner, would have run a mile.

But I wasn't a businessman. And I wasn't from London. I came from rural Lincolnshire, and simply didn't know any of this stuff. I carried none of those prejudices. All I saw was a place where I knew I could put on amazing gigs, the wild, passionate, anarchic gigs that you couldn't do somewhere like the Odeon: the gigs I had been longing for all this time.

The Astoria itself was an easy building to fall in love with. Originally built as a grand Atmospheric Cinema in 1929, it had retained almost all the beautiful art deco touches that made it famous in its day. Atmospheric Cinemas were conceived in 1920s America as giant 'movie palaces', where the masses would come not just to see a film, but to have an extraordinary, glamorous experience. As such, they were designed purely for luxurious escapism, with all the facilities for live performances to accompany the movies. Most were modelled on some exotic foreign theme such as the *Arabian Nights* or the Taj Mahal.

It was the entertainment entrepreneur Arthur Segal who imported the concept to London, hiring T. R. Somerford and Edward Albert Stone to build four 'super cinemas' in the Atmospheric style. Aside from Brixton, he also built theatres in Streatham and on the

Old Kent Road, and, funnily enough, the Rainbow in Finsbury Park. But the Brixton Astoria, as it was originally known, was always the jewel in the crown. In its time, it was the biggest cinema in Britain, known as 'Brixton's wonder theatre'.

The original theme of the cinema was the 'Mediterranean Night'. So the whole building, down to the smallest details, is modelled after the Italian Renaissance. From the grand half-cupola that domes the exterior entrance to the proscenium arch – modelled on the Rialto Bridge in Venice – that frames the stage; from the beautiful, patterned marble floors of the foyer to the original plasterwork by Marc Henri, the entire building is a strange and wondrous thing. Not many people actually notice it, but the ceiling of the main auditorium is decorated with twinkling stars, originally meant to give cinema audiences an impression of sitting beneath the Venetian night sky. A bit of Venice in south London, who'd have ever thought it?

But that was all in the distant past. By now the building had been standing empty for years, and had fallen into total disrepair. There were holes in the walls, and pools of water all over the floor from leaks. As I walked through the building, kicking up thick clouds of dust, door handles would come off in my hand, my foot would go through floorboards, and there was a powerful smell of the damp and mould that had set in. The place seemed so woefully neglected, with a Janis Joplin-ish air of ragged, frayed beauty in its abandonment.

Of course, I didn't know the history at the time. It was only over the years that I became lovingly attached to every brick of the place, eventually becoming quite a geek about theatre architecture and art deco design. At first, all I saw was a beautiful old building with a romantic air of faded glory, and an amazing space where I knew bands would put on mind-blowing shows.

The lease on the building was held by the brewery Watney Combe and Reid. However, it was only used by Rank, the landlord, and coincidentally owners and operators of the Hammersmith Odeon, as a storage space.

A year earlier a couple of guys had opened the place briefly as a music venue called the Fair Deal. As it happened, Fair Deal could not have been a less appropriate name. These guys proved to be as crooked as they come, doing a runner with UB40's box office takings, a very expensive sound desk, and £120,000 borrowed from Watney's to set the place up. The stigma of the location, along with the scandal of the Fair Deal fiasco made this a tarnished venture from the start. No sensible businessman would have touched it with a barge pole. But something, some would say hubris, a few might say vision, told me I could make this work.

Over the next few weeks I became like Captain Ahab, totally fixated on the idea of this venue. I had to get it. But how? I swung between wild enthusiasm and pessimistic despair. The words of those guys up in Edinburgh rang in my ears: 'just a couple of wankers'. I was twenty-three years old and had no track record in the music business. Why would anyone trust me with a huge new rock venue? On the other hand, the building was standing empty and disused. It was a burden to Watney's, not an asset, and there didn't seem to be a queue of people lining up to take it over. Maybe, just maybe, I could pull this off? My young man's reckless, naive confidence wasn't going to let anything stand in the way. I had to make this happen.

'I'LL GIVE YOU A QUID FOR IT'

The guy I spoke to at Watney's on the phone sounded very excited that they might have found someone to take the Astoria off their hands. I could picture him at the other end of the line, his hand over the receiver, whispering to his office, 'We've got some mug here that wants to take on that place in Brixton!' They were very forthcoming, inviting me down to Watney's head office at the Mortlake Brewery to talk things over.

I walked into the room and I could see their faces fall: this guy isn't serious, it's just some kid.

Jim Millar and Bob Scaddon, the two men in charge of all this for Watney's, made a funny double act. They were like Laurel and Hardy: Bob, a tall, gruff cockney, sharp-featured, no-nonsense, and bald as a coot; and Jim, short, softly spoken and Scottish, with a mischievous grin and a glint in his eye. Over the years these two guys would become trusted friends and advisers, but that was all still a long way off. I had a lot of convincing to do.

I may have been only twenty-three, but I was bright and could think on my feet. I had been to business school and could speak that language, and I had a devil-may-care confidence that slowly began to win Bob and Jim over, helping them take me more seriously.

I think there is something in the British public school system that can take people one of two ways. It can either breed a sense of smug entitlement that is one of the most revoltingly unattractive aspects of human character you will ever encounter. Or, at its best, it can instil an understated self-assurance that actually has a lot going for it. I like to think I fit more in the latter category, and as they gave me a tour of the brewery and we made small talk, I could sense the two older guys beginning to warm to me.

From the conversation, I also began to get a feeling of just how uninterested Watney's were in holding on to this venue in Brixton. They were in the business of selling beer: and with the building standing empty, they weren't selling any. They also let slip that aside from the crooks behind Fair Deal, I was the first person in two years to express any interest in the place. I suddenly felt a little surge of daring. Maybe I could make this happen?

We walked back to their office and got down to brass tacks. I presented the first parts of my business plan. If I started with 40 gigs in the first year, we could expect 60 in the second, then moving up to over 100: generating an expected return of so-and-so many pounds, over so-and-so many years. Almost to my amazement Bob and Jim seemed to take it all very seriously, asking probing questions about my plans and how I had worked out the numbers.

I started thinking, They must really want to get rid of this place, if they've let a schmuck like me get this far. Luckily I had done my homework, and was able to bat most of their questions away fairly and honestly.

Then it happened. Jim Millar leaned over and said, 'Well Simon, having listened to your proposal, we think you have a handle on the figures involved, and we're prepared to sell you the lease on the building for £120,000.'

I was simultaneously elated and crushed. It was incredible that they took me seriously enough to actually make an offer; that in itself was huge. But I did not have £120,000. I understood what Bob and Jim were trying to do. They just wanted to make up the loss they had incurred through the Fair Deal scam. Fair enough. I also knew I definitely couldn't let on that I didn't have that kind of capital or, in reality, any capital. In the back of my mind I was thinking that I might be able to borrow that kind of figure, but my main concern was to keep the conversation going. Just keep them talking, and who knows what could happen?

'And what would the exact terms of the lease involve?' I asked, in my best unimpressed-and-businesslike voice.

They started to list all the usual things, rent structures, insurance, et cetera. Then Bob Scaddon cut in and said something that would change the course of my life. 'And obviously, you'll be responsible for all repairs and improvements at the end of the lease term.'

That's when the penny dropped. Suddenly it all became so clear. It wasn't just that Watney's were frustrated with the venue standing idle; it was that at the end of the fifteen-year lease they would have to take care of all the repairs on the building. Rank were going to take them to the cleaners. It could run to millions of pounds. Jim and Bob were in charge of all this for the company, and were terrified. If Watney's ended up paying through the nose for an empty building, it was their heads on the block.

This changed everything. I realized in an instant that as badly as I *wanted* to get hold of the Astoria, they *needed* to get rid of it. And as I had learned early on from Jagger and Richards, *need* trumps *want* any day of the week.

The whole dynamic of the conversation flipped in my mind. I did some extremely fast mental calculations, and weighed up my options. Then I paused. This was the moment of truth. All or nothing. I could risk everything or play it safe.

'Let me make you another offer,' I replied.

I leaned forward in my chair, looked the two men up and down, and said, 'I'll give you a quid for it.'

Jim and Bob blinked, looked at each other, then back at me. From their expressions, I might as well have started jabbering at them in Mandarin. They obviously thought I had lost my mind.

Jim responded with a phrase that, when delivered in a particular way that only a certain type of British character can achieve, cuts like razor wire.

'I beg your pardon.'

He might as well have said, 'You sir, are a raving lunatic with no right to civilized society.'

I continued, totally unfazed. 'Listen: you sign the lease over to me for one pound, and I'll sign an exclusive deal to sell only your beer for ten years. If I'm eventually doing upwards of 150 gigs annually, with 5,000 people at each show, that's a lot of pints you're going to sell.'

I paused for effect.

'And', I continued, 'I take on the responsibility for the works at the end of it all.'

Now it was their turn to do some mental calculations. Throwing in that last line about the works was just to let them know they had given their position away. The exclusive beer deal, on the other hand, was a serious offer. I'd just thought it up on the spur of the moment, but they potentially stood to do very well out of it. I could see the wheels turning in their heads as they did the arithmetic. Their expressions softened as they realized that perhaps they might have underestimated me.

They started to throw more questions at me on the details, but now I was in full flow. I abandoned my entire carefully prepared business plan, just making it up as I went along.

I'm still not sure if I had so wrong-footed Jim and Bob with my crazy offer, or they just realized that they didn't have any other options on the table, but they decided to take a punt on the loony kid in front of them. We finished the meeting with a smile, a handshake, and a promise that the lawyers would be in touch.

I had bought the Brixton Astoria for a pound.

I managed to maintain my composure as we walked out to the brewery entrance. I shook hands with Bob and Jim one more time, and the gates clanged shut. The second I was out of sight, I collapsed against a wall and let out a mighty whoop. I couldn't believe it. My head was spinning. I had done it. I had actually pulled it off! I don't think I felt a rush like that again until the birth of my first child.

Over the next few weeks, however, I came back down to earth in an avalanche of paperwork and legal documents. It was a heavy-duty crash course in licensing, regulations, property law, insurance policies, and all the assorted bureaucracy of showbiz. Immensely excited as I was, starting a major new venue was never going to be simple. I quickly learned that, as one might expect with a building of such varied history, the financial arrangements surrounding the Astoria were Byzantine. And I spotted one major obstacle I had to clear before I even got going: Rank.

The Astoria's finances broke down like this: the freehold on the building was owned by an old, landed family that had no role whatsoever in running the place. They leased the property to that venerable institution of British entertainment, the Rank Organisation. Rank, in turn, had created a sublease to Watney's, who had then sold it on to me for a quid.

Now, Rank's deal with the freeholders was quite a special thing. This is one of the many unbelievable-but-true facts about the venue: the rent for the entire building is only £50 a week.

The Astoria was originally built in 1929, opening about two months before the Wall Street Crash. Crucially, the original lease on the property included no provision for rent reviews. Thus, the rent for the entire Astoria building was set, and locked, at £2,600 a year. It was probably a significant figure back in 1929. Obviously, even by the 80s, it was absurdly cheap. This ludicrous arrangement still holds, and will until the year 2029. The current owners, Academy Music Group, will probably get quite a shock on the morning of 1 January 2030; till then, they're absolutely laughing.

Back in 1982, however, I had a problem. I wasn't at all happy about the idea that my new landlord was also going to be the owner and operator of my primary rival, the Hammersmith Odeon. It didn't take a financial wizard to work out that this was not a workable position for a rookie venue owner.

To my mind, the solution was simple: I had to persuade Rank to sell me their own lease on the property.

The initial meeting was a nightmare. The guy Rank sent to deal with me was named Penfold, and the poor man looked and sounded exactly like the character Penfold from the cartoon *Danger Mouse*. It was terrible; every time he opened his mouth to speak I almost broke down in hysterics.

While there was no question of trying another 'I'll give you a quid for it' gambit here, Penfold proved willing to sell me Rank's lease for £150,000.

I was almost surprised at how ready Rank were to part with it. To me it was astounding how they had missed the potential of the Astoria as a venue for all these years. But as our contact progressed, I began to understand just how much jobsworths like

Penfold represented the spirit of what Rank had become. They were a big, established company, and suffered from the blinkered malaise and institutional complacency that afflicts so many big, established companies. There was a palpable sense of arrogance in the way they dealt with people. Exactly the kind of snobbish attitude guaranteed to drive me crazy.

Well, if Rank couldn't see the diamond-in-the-rough they were holding, I was more than happy to take it off their hands. And if they were too arrogant and disconnected to see the threat I represented, then more fool them.

The only problem being, how was a 23-year old kid, with no track record and no collateral, supposed to raise a hundred and fifty grand?

This was one of the very few occasions when I have to confess to shamelessly deploying the old school tie to my advantage. I threw on my suit, whipped up another slick presentation, and marched down to my local branch of Midland Bank.

The choice was crucial: Midland was where my father and grandfather did their banking. The manager listened politely to my proposal, and I made sure to pepper the conversation with the words 'Gordonstoun' and 'Boston Deep Sea Fisheries'. I knew the second I walked out the door, he would be right on the phone to their branch in Hull asking 'So, who is this Parkes fellow?'

I knew the manager of the Hull branch would assure him that 'Sir Basil's grandson' was a 'good chap from a fine family'. Nowadays, of course, this smoke-and-mirrors bullshit would never fly: your name goes into a computer, and up comes the file. But back then it was a different world. I got the loan.

I marched into the Rank offices buzzing with confidence. As we signed the papers I couldn't resist shooting Penfold a wink and grinning, 'Bye-bye, Hammersmith Odeon.'

Penfold just squinted at me, and with the most smug, patronising sneer replied, 'Yeah, good luck, son.'

This was probably the worst possible thing he could have said. I'm the type of guy that if you tell me I can't do something, I won't rest till I've done it twice over. It's just how I am. At that moment I silently vowed that within ten years I would take the Odeon's crown and make my place in Brixton the premier venue in London.

In the end, it only took me about four.

But it wasn't going to be easy.

ACADEMY

In late 1983, a few weeks shy of my 24th birthday, I was handed the keys to the Brixton Astoria.

There have been few feelings in my life like unlocking those doors and letting myself in for the first time. Running my hand over the beautiful, but filthy, marble of the foyer, and looking up at the domed ceiling of the entrance, I started laughing to myself almost maniacally. I couldn't believe this was actually mine. Then, pushing open the heavy doors, I walked through into the dank stillness of the main auditorium. And I got a serious shock.

There were about ten or eleven people in there, standing in a semicircle staring at me. They were dressed in a ragged collection of combat fatigues, punk leathers, dreadlocks, and tattoos. It was an even mix of black and white; young guys and girls, and one Alsatian dog on a string. I guess today this gang would be described as 'crusties'; back then I didn't even know the word.

What I did know was that there was a bunch of fairly threatening-looking people all giving me the silent death stare. Who were these guys? What the fuck were they doing in my venue? And were they about to stab me?

I decided to play it cool and friendly. 'Hi, I'm Simon.' I flashed them all a nice, big grin.

Silence.

Hmmm. Perhaps this was trouble? I got ready to make a sprint back through the double doors behind me, trying to plan the best escape route.

Then one of the gang, a tough-looking rocker with long, greasy hair and leather biker trousers, broke the stand-off and began walking slowly towards me. He stopped midway between his group and myself.

'So you're the crazy fucker who bought this place.'

OK, at least they knew who I was. I don't know why, but that seemed to take the situation's murder potential down a little.

'Yeah, that's me,' I replied. 'I'm Simon Parkes. You must be the welcoming committee. How nice of Rank, I never knew they cared.' I thought a joke might help break the ice.

More silence. Shit. Maybe I'd played that wrong.

The rocker guy narrowed his eyes, sizing me up as if we were facing off in a Clint Eastwood western. There was a moment in which everything seemed to hang in the balance.

Then, some invisible force shifted, and his face broke into a crooked smile. 'Well then, I'd say this calls for a drink,' he said, stretching out his hand. 'Mike Henley at your service.'

As I shook his hand the rest of his gang seemed visibly to relax. Whatever unspoken initiation had just occurred, I had evidently passed it.

Mike Henley grinned. 'We've been, um, looking after the place, while it was, shall we say, otherwise unoccupied.'

OK, they were squatters. I had suspected as much; but they seemed like an all right bunch to me.

'Come on, let me show you around,' Mike Henley said, slapping me on the shoulder. 'But first, let's see about that drink.'

Mike led me over to the bar. The others seemed to lose interest and drift away.

'I reckon what we need are a couple of Henley Specials.' He smiled, pulling out two pint glasses. 'They're serious drinks, but just right for a big moment like this. You game?'

I wasn't about to let myself be shown up in my own venue. 'Sounds great, lay it on me.'

Mike reached below the bar, coming up with a couple of cans of stout and a bottle of brandy. He filled the glasses three-quarters full of the stout, topped the rest up with the brandy, and slid a glass along the bar. 'There you go, a Henley Special. It'll put hairs on your arsehole, that will.'

It was 10 a.m.

'Here's to rock 'n' roll.' Mike grinned, and necked about half his drink. I gave mine a sip. It was vile, burning horror in a pint glass, but I managed not to grimace too obviously.

'It's quite a special place you've got yourself here, mate,' said Mike, looking me up and down. 'I mean, you must be off your fucking head to try and start a venue in Brixton, but there's nowhere else like it, that's for sure; and I've seen them all. Drink up and I'll show you.'

I took another swig, and Mike led me towards the centre of the auditorium. 'See that stage,' he said, gesturing towards the front of house, 'it's got thirty-six load bars, that stage does, thirty-six!'

I nodded, making a show of being impressed that I hoped would convince Mike that I knew what a load bar was.

'See, it was built for full-scale theatrical productions,' Mike continued. 'You can lift anything with those things: scenery, curtains, whatever you want. You could do a fucking full-scale opera here if you wanted.'

Ah, so that's what he was on about. As I was to learn later, load bars are the pulley system that theatres use to lift and manoeuvre heavy props and curtains. Images of sandbags on ropes from old slapstick movies flashed through my mind. So I had thirty-six of the things, and apparently that was impressive. Rock 'n' roll.

'You know something?' asked Mike, as he hopped up to the stage itself. 'You've got the second-biggest theatrical stage in Britain here. The only one bigger is Drury Lane. Pretty cool, huh? Britain's second-biggest stage hidden all the way down in Brixton.'

Mike reached into his pocket, pulling out a silver hip flask. 'Drink?' he offered. I looked down to see the glass in my hand was empty. How had that happened? Well, what the hell, I grabbed the flask and took a swig.

'But here's the best bit, come look at this.' Mike guided me backstage.

'Look,' he said. 'There's your back doors, right? They're only twenty-five feet from the stage. At Wembley Arena there's a fifty-metre load-in, and you have to go up and down all these bloody ramps; it's a giant arsehole of a ball-ache. But here, you open the back door and you're twenty-five feet from the stage: all on one level, in and out, no bother. And you know what that means?'

He paused, passing me the hip flask again. I shrugged.

'It means the road crews are going to fucking love you. They can do their thing in half the time they can anywhere else.' Mike leaned in conspiratorially. 'And those are the guys you need to get in with. You want to make it in music, you'd better make damn sure the roadies like you: because, secretly, they run the whole fucking show.'

I took another swig from the flask. I was loving this. Not only was this exactly the knowledge I needed about the venue, but he was confirming all my instincts about how great this place was. Then a question occurred to me.

'Mike,' I asked, 'how do you know all this stuff?'

'Oh, I've tour-managed bands all over the world, mate,' he replied. 'I've just come off two years on the road with Rush. I've worked every great venue from Norfolk to New Orleans, and all the shittiest ones to boot. I know a good concert hall when I see one.'

A real live rock 'n' roll 'road man'. This was fantastic.

Mike led me around the rest of the venue, making much of the ten dressing rooms, five production offices, and catering facilities that could do fifty at a sitting: all the stuff that road crews, the real soldiers of the music industry, care about. We polished off Mike's hip flask and walked back down to the bar for a couple more Henley Specials. I was pretty sozzled by now, but feeling very good about the whole venture. I was learning about my venue, and I liked Mike Henley from the get-go. He was obviously fond of his drink, but his passion for music was written all over him and, most of all, I could tell he saw the potential of this building. In those early days it meant a lot to me that an industry veteran like Mike could share my vision of the place.

'So I have to ask,' he said, pouring another round, 'how can a kid like you afford to buy a venue like this? All respect and everything, but you don't seem like a gangster. Your dad have money or something?'

'Oh,' I said nonchalantly, putting my feet up on the bar, 'I only paid a quid for it.'

Mike's drink sputtered all over the bar as he burst out laughing. 'How's that?'

'Yeah, they asked for a hundred and twenty grand. I offered them a quid, and they went for it.'

I was pissed, but I played it as cool as I could.

Mike raised his eyebrows. He looked me up and down once again, and nodded in slow approval. 'Fucking hell, I knew you were off your head, but I didn't realize you were *that* fucking nuts. You must have some balls on you. Keep going like that, and maybe you'll actually be able to make something work here. Here's to you.'

We clinked glasses and drank. I liked this guy, something told me he was all right. Through the haze of booze an idea came to me. I didn't think twice.

'Well man,' I said leaning over the bar, 'why don't you stick around and help make it happen?'

'How do you mean?' he asked, pausing with his glass halfway to his mouth.

'Well, look, I'm going to need a stage manager. You understand the business, and you already know the building inside out. How about it?'

Mike took a long, contemplative swig, then set his glass down and wiped his lips.

'Well, it's a grand old place, and I already know the local pubs. I suppose it'd be nice to get off the road and stay put for a while.' He spat onto the palm of his right hand and held it out. 'What the fuck? You're on.'

I smiled and spat on my own hand. We shook. I'd started to put my team together.

I turned up the next morning with a stinking hangover, but ready to make things happen. Mike Henley met me at the doors. It was impossible to tell if he'd been to bed or not.

The rest of his gang of squatters had melted away overnight with all their gear. What remained was several years' worth of junk and neglect. There was cleaning to be done.

Oh well, if I can muck out pigsties, I can tidy my own venue.

We got to it: moving out the half-broken detritus of all the venue's previous incarnations, fixing dozens of leaking toilets, rehanging doors, replastering walls, and scrubbing. Constant bloody scrubbing. There always seemed to be more dust, more dirt, more grime, to wipe away. In those first few weeks it was usually just Mike and me. Occasionally he would get some of his local cronies to come and help out for a bit of cash, but most of the time it was just the two of us making the place workable, inch by slow inch.

Of course, along with all the manual labour, I was also having to slog my way through mountains of paperwork. Licensing, insurance, financing: the lot. It wasn't quite the fast life of rock 'n' roll mayhem I had envisaged, but at least my business course was proving useful for something. 'Just keep going,' I kept repeating to myself. 'Motown wasn't built in a day.'

Mike and I were painting backstage when, out of the blue, he popped the question. We had stopped for a cigarette break, when he turned and said, 'So, Simon, what are you going to call this place, anyway?'

I hadn't even thought about this. In my head it had always just been 'the great venue in Brixton'.

'I don't know man. I love the name Astoria, but I guess there's already one of those in the West End. But I like that Roman sound to it, I'd like to keep to something along those lines.'

'I know what you mean' agreed Mike, 'there's rock tradition there, like the Coliseum in LA.'

'Exactly, or the Harlem Apollo.'

The Apollo was the one for me. That was always the model for what I wanted to do with my venue in Brixton. A historic theatre,

helping to restore a run-down black neighbourhood through legendary gigs: it made sense.

'It's a shame we can't call it the Brixton Apollo. I would if I
could.'

'Yeah' laughed Mike, 'I don't think old Guy Fisher would look
too kindly on that.'

At the time, Guy Fisher was the owner and operator of the Apollo
in New York. He was also a notorious, high-ranking member of
the African-American heroin cartel The Council. The following
year he would be imprisoned for life without parole on multiple
counts of racketeering. Not a man you wanted to annoy by nicking
his venue name.

'So,' Mike continued, 'something like the Apollo, but not the
Apollo. Hmm.'

We paused for a moment.

'How about the Academy?' I asked.

I have no idea where the idea came from. I just liked the sound
of the word. It had multiple syllables and began with A. Astoria;
Apollo; Academy. It had a nice grandeur to it.

'The Academy,' Mike repeated thoughtfully. 'The Brixton
Academy. It's good. I like it.'

So that was that: the Brixton Academy was born. I wish I could
say there was some dramatic flash of divine inspiration, but it was
just Mike Henley and me on a cigarette break.

We picked up our paintbrushes and got back to work.

Gradually things started to come together. I figured out an arrangement for occasional licences with the council, and we patched up
the place enough so that you could walk along the balcony without

worrying that your foot was about to go through the floorboards. It was time to start booking some gigs.

The conversation usually went something like this:

'Hi, this is Simon Parkes, from the Brixton Academy.'

'The what?'

'The Brixton Academy. It's a great new venue on Stockwell Road.'

'What, the old Fair Deal place?'

'Yes, but it's relaunched. We've got new management, a whole new vibe. It's a fantastic concert hall.'

'Umm, yeah, thanks, I think we'll pass.'

'Well OK, but maybe you just want to come down and have a look. We've got five thousand capacity, it's a beautiful old restored theatre.'

'I'm sure it is. It's just ... it's not really our demographic around there, if you know what I mean?'

'Listen, when people see this place, they'll want to come to shows here.'

'Mate, I'm not trying to be funny, but there's no way you're *ever* going to get a rock band to come and play in Brixton. It's just not going to happen. Anyway, we've got an ongoing relationship with the Hammersmith Odeon.'

And so on...

I don't know how many times I must have heard that bloody line: 'you'll never get a rock band to play in Brixton'.

I had this unshakeable certainty that as soon as bands started to perform here, they would do amazing gigs. But the agents, the ones who ran the business, didn't want to know. They weren't interested in new ideas, no matter how good. They had a system that worked: bands came to town, they went to the Odeon. Why should they rock the boat?

To me, of course, it all sounded just like the complacency I found so boring and irritating in organizations like Rank. I hate it. People get too comfortable, they stop looking for new ideas, and, invariably, it's their undoing. There was also the old Simon Parkes bull-headedness. The more they told me I couldn't do it, the more determined I became that I would. But how?

It was Mike Henley who cracked it.

I had just hung up the phone on yet another dead-end conversation, with yet another imagination-deficient agent, when he tapped me on the shoulder.

'If they won't send their rock bands down here because they're worried about their demographic, we'll serve the demographic that's already here. We're in Brixton, let's do some bloody reggae gigs. It'll get things started. We'll bring the mountain to Mohammed.'

Of course. Sometimes you realize the answer has been right in front of you the whole time.

'All right, Mike, great idea. You got any thoughts on who I should call?'

'It just so happens I do.'

Mike scribbled a number down on a scrap of paper and handed it to me. 'There's only one person who can crack the reggae scene for a white boy like you. You need to speak to Sweaty Betty.'

BIM BIM BIDDY BONG BONG

It was a strange mixture of relief and disappointment when Sweaty Betty didn't turn out to be an overweight Jamaican prostitute, but in fact the agent David Betteridge.

The history of popular music is threaded through with stories of sharp hip Jewish kids hooking up with innovative black talent to create magic. From Phil and Leonard Chess at Chess Records, to Jerry Wexler at Atlantic, and all the way through to Lyor Cohen and Russ Simmons at Def Jam: no one knows why this particular combination works, it just does. It's the bricks and mortar from which the rock 'n' roll business was built.

Dave Betteridge was a shining example. He'd come up with Chris Blackwell at Island Records, from when Blackwell first moved the company from Jamaica to London and was selling ska records from the back of his car on the Harrow Road. Dave had gone on to become the driving force behind the iconic Trojan Records, the label that broke ska and reggae to a mass audience. He probably knew more about reggae than any white guy alive.

He also sweated profusely. Hence the nickname. No one knew why he sweated so much, he certainly wasn't fat; but he was always to be found, backstage at a gig, constantly wiping his forehead with a handkerchief.

When I thought about it, if I ever found myself in some of the situations that Dave regularly, and fearlessly, put himself in, I'd probably have been sweating too. Dave was the only white agent who would deal with most of the black promoters and artists. He had the experience to know how to handle himself in that scene. Most of the other London industry guys had had their fingers burned too many times. Because, as I was soon to learn, doing business with Jamaican artists and their crews meant doing business the Jamaican way: it was messy, chaotic, and often violent.

Promoters would regularly sell half the tickets to a show, then disappear, leaving the agent to pay off the balance of the band's fee. Or the band itself would take half the deposit from the promoter and then just decide not to show up. Sometimes an artist's management would neglect to sort out the appropriate work permits, so a band would get turned away at customs, leaving the agent and the promoter to confront a few thousand Jamaican music fans who weren't going to get the artist they'd paid for. Anyone would need nerves of steel to work in that environment. As a five-and-a-half foot tall white guy you needed balls of brass. Dave had both. He kept doing it because he loved the music, but no bloody wonder he got the sweats.

I always admired old Sweaty Betty. He was a damn good businessman, and saw the potential immediately. A 5,000-capacity venue in the middle of Brixton? It was perfect for him. Dave was just the type to take a chance on something new and untried, that's what made him great.

'All right,' he said, after about five minutes looking around the building. 'I've got Eek-A-Mouse coming through Europe on tour soon. His record's doing well. How about we do it here?'

Those were the magic words I'd been waiting for. I'd booked my first gig.

I had always imagined our debut show at the Academy would be a flawlessly organized, perfectly executed, glittering night of music magic. I wish I could say that's how it actually went down.

We were still patching the place up the night before the gig. There always seemed to be another fire officer to show around, another licence to apply for, another insurance form to fill in. At the last minute we hired in a local security firm, did an eleventh-hour sweep of the building, and got ready to christen our new venue.

We hadn't sold a lot of tickets in advance, but that didn't worry us. Dave Betteridge assured us that with reggae gigs, you always did most of your business on the night of the show at the box office.

We were expecting a good crowd. Eek-A-Mouse was one of those ludicrous, one-of-a-kind eccentrics of the Lee 'Scratch' Perry school, that only reggae could produce. Though a committed Rastafarian, he would often perform in a full cowboy outfit, complete with rhinestones and Stetson hat. It takes something special to pull that combination off, and Eek-A-Mouse nailed it.

In 1981 he'd had a big hit with a song called 'Wa-Do-Dem', which had broken his unique 'biddy bong bong' vocal style to an international audience. This tour was to support his new album *The Mouse and the Man*, which had been preceded by the big single 'Ganja Smuggling'. Brixton was perfect for him. Word of the show spread around the area, and we knew people were hyped for it.

On the day of the gig I didn't have time to get nervous, or even that excited. Between getting the building ready, sorting out the inevitable last-minute hiccups, and making sure the band were taken care of, it was just a matter of getting things done. I was flat out all day, right up to when we unlocked the door and the first

63

punters started streaming in. Then I forced myself to pause, take a moment, and just watch. This was it. People were queuing up, having their tickets torn, and walking into my venue. *My venue.* For the first time those words sounded real.

Eventually we got Eek-A-Mouse onstage, and he started straight into his 'bim bim biddy bong bong' routine, over a classic fat dub bassline. The hall was filling up nicely, and everyone seemed in high spirits, in every meaning of the word. I thought I could take a minute to relax and enjoy my first gig.

I hadn't yet learned that it's when you think you can relax that everything falls apart.

One of the local kids we had taken on as a runner came sprinting up and frantically pulled me by the sleeve. 'Simon, Simon, it's all fucked, you gotta come.'

My blood went cold, but I tried to keep cool. 'All right, don't panic. Show me what's up.' The kid led me over to the corridor on the side of the auditorium, and I saw exactly what he was talking about.

Some clever fucker had managed to jimmy open one of the venue's side doors, and people were streaming through this new entrance without having paid for their tickets. No wonder the crowd was in such a good mood, half of them had got in free! I raced over, fighting my way through the oncoming flow of punters, and slammed the door shut amidst the angry shouts of those who hadn't yet snuck in. They'd just have to pay their £3.50. I stood guard over that door for the rest of the night, sending out regular patrols to the other entrances.

The rest of the show passed off well, with Eek-A-Mouse at his loony best. But after the gig finished and the audience filed out, I had to count up our loss on the box office from that side door fiasco. I was distraught. We had lost about a third of our sales and were down thousands of pounds on the night. Most of all I was hugely pissed off with myself that I could have made such a schoolboy error, overlooking something so obvious.

David Betteridge and Mike Henley, with their vast shared experience of the music business, took a much more relaxed view. 'Look Simon, no one got shot, the building didn't burn down ... all in all you got off pretty lightly.'

I found these words only half reassuring.

There wasn't any time to hang around moping though. The next morning we were in bright and early to get the venue cleaned up and ready for the next bit of action. In those days we didn't have cleaners. Once again, it was just Mike Henley, myself, and a couple of helpers sweeping, mopping, and polishing the bars.

Mike could see I was still furious about what had happened the previous night.

'Listen Simon,' he said, pausing to lean on his mop, 'it's fine. We just need to sort out our security situation.' He took a long, 9 a.m. swig on his hip flask, 'I know just the guy you should talk to.'

Within 48 hours the meeting was set.

'Simon, meet Mad Mick Murphy. I think he can help us with our security issue.'

'Hi Mick, good to meet you.'

'It's Mad Mick. Not Mick. *Mad Mick*. And don't you forget it,' thundered the six foot three, seventeen-stone monster in front of me.

Right then.

'Sorry mate, I didn't realize. It's good to meet you Mad Mick, I'm Simon. We need some help on our door.'

'Aye, around these parts you'll need help with a lot more than your doors.'

Mad Mick warmed up a bit after our rocky start. It turned out he and Mike Henley had met on a gruelling tour with Siouxsie and the Banshees. Mike had been tour manager, and Mad Mick head of security. As they swapped war stories, and Mike kept the drinks flowing, the camaraderie between them was obvious. It was funny considering how different the two were. Though both were big guys, Mike was a cowboy-booted rocker, with a certain 70s glam campness to his mannerisms; Mad Mick was Brian Blessed on steroids. A giant bruiser of a man, with a shock of wild hair, a biker's beard, and an unhinged glint in his eye: you didn't ask where he got his nickname, but you could hazard a guess.

But if Mike trusted this guy, that was good enough for me. We ended the meeting with a bone-crushing handshake, and Mad Mick thundering, 'Aye, no problems here. I'll get the boys together and we'll take care of the place. It'll be nice to hear a bit of music again.'

POLICE AND THIEVES

I popped up to Lincolnshire for a weekend to see my family. It was hard to communicate all that I was experiencing down in Brixton. The two worlds were so wildly different. I spoke at a thousand miles a minute, trying to get it all across, ' ... and then there were about two thousand Rastafarians, all sneaking in through the side door; but it's ok, because we've got this great guy called Mad Mick Murphy who's going to sort out the security for us.'

My siblings looked at me with such utter incomprehension that for a moment I did stop and think, What if Mike is right: what if I am actually off my fucking head?

But I didn't have time for contemplation. It was straight back into the action. Dennis Brown was coming to Brixton.

Dennis Brown: the 'crown prince of reggae', the man Bob Marley identified as his favourite singer, the guy who basically invented the whole 'lovers rock' style. This was just the gig to raise our profile.

Mad Mick Murphy was as good as his word; he had indeed got 'the boys' together. Before the gig I was introduced to a group of the scariest-looking people I had ever seen. Mad Mick went down the line: 'Simon, this is Pete the Mercenary, Black Nigel, Big John, Gary the Fireman, and Pat.'

Pete the Mercenary was a lean, heavily tattooed human weapon of bone and muscle; I don't think there was an ounce of fat on him.

The whispered story you didn't ask too much about was that he had been a commando, before using those transferable skills for private gain in various exotic locations around the world. Black Nigel was built like Evander Holyfield in his prime and, as it turned out, had been a promising boxer before pursuing 'other career paths'. But even that former heavyweight looked like a pipsqueak next to Big John. The guy was huge, and I mean planetary. He wasn't what you would call fit and trim, but if he wedged himself in a doorway, there was no way anyone was getting through. I never found out where Gary the Fireman earned his sobriquet, but I doubt it was from saving kittens stuck up trees.

Then there was Pat.

I remembered my first difficult introduction to Mad Mick; I didn't want to offend anyone again by forgetting their hard-earned nickname, especially not guys like this.

'Pat the what?' I asked.

Mad Mick furrowed his eyebrows in incomprehension, 'What the fuck are you on about?' he snapped testily.

'Well, you're Mad Mick, he's Pete the Mercenary, he's Black Nigel, and he's Big John, but you didn't tell me Pat's other name.'

'No mate,' replied Mad Mick. 'That's Pat. Pat don't need no other name. Pat's just Pat.'

I looked over. While no one was quite as spectacularly enormous as Big John, Pat was huge, with a profoundly intimidating presence. He looked most like Brutus out of the Popeye cartoons, a thick black beard sitting atop 270 pounds of solid muscle. The kind of guy that makes brick shithouses shit bricks.

'Good to meet you, Pat.'

'All right, boss,' the big guy nodded.

Well, I'd survived the introductions. I didn't know it at that point, but over the next few years these guys would become my most trusted team, and good friends as well, saving my life more than once. But that was all to come. First we had a gig to get through.

Things started well. The band showed up, the crowd queued outside, and Mad Mick's team made sure the side doors remained shut and that people actually paid for their tickets.

Then, just as the hall was getting nicely full, with the pre-gig DJs pumping out feelgood reggae, and little puffs of smoke starting to rise up from the crowd, Mike Henley came running up. 'Simon, we've got a problem. The police are downstairs.'

Shit. What could have gone wrong? My mind flashed through every scenario. I had filled in every form, passed every inspection; what could I have forgotten? I walked down to the foyer with my heart in my throat.

Waiting for me were two plainclothes detectives, standing out like very white, suited sore thumbs, in a sea of dreadlocked Rastafari red, yellow, and green.

'Are you Simon Parkes, proprietor of this venue?'

'Yes. Can I help you?

'Do you have one Dennis Emmanuel Brown performing tonight?'

'Yes. Why? What's going on?'

'We have here a warrant for the arrest of Mr Brown for non-payment of alimony.'

They held out a paper for my inspection. 'Please take us to where we can find him.'

Jesus Christ. Non-payment of alimony, what the hell was going on? And, more important, how was I going to play this?

On the one hand, I had a venue full of heavy Brixton reggae fans that had paid to see a show. If they didn't get Dennis Brown tonight, it could all seriously kick off. And, even more important, if it got out around Brixton that I had led the police straight to a reggae legend, that would be the end of the Academy before it even started. I didn't want to become 'the guy that grassed up Dennis Brown'.

On the other hand, I also didn't want to get done for Obstruction of Justice, and I couldn't afford to alienate the Brixton police. They could end the whole Academy adventure with the stroke of a pen. I had always known I would have to keep the cops onside, but I had never counted on a dilemma like this.

I needed to think fast.

'Look guys, let me show you something,' I said, motioning for the two cops to follow me.

I led them towards the backstage area, taking a long route round, and hoping that Mike Henley would have the presence of mind to race backstage and get everyone to clear away their ganja.

I walked the cops around the back of the stage till we were standing in the wings and could see out over the stage itself and into the auditorium.

'Look,' I turned to the two detectives, 'there are just under five thousand West Indian reggae fans out there, most of them are serious Rastas. They've paid to see Dennis Brown, and if you arrest their hero before he even comes on, there's going to be a riot.'

The use of the word *riot* was deliberate, but risky. Brixton police were still licking their wounds from the infamous riots of the previous year. And Brixton itself was still a tinderbox. You could feel it in the air, especially at big reggae gigs. One spark could set the whole thing off. The police couldn't afford to provoke the situation, but on the other hand they didn't want to appear weak.

The detectives looked doubtful.

'Here's what we should do,' I continued, seizing the initiative before they had a chance to respond.

I grabbed a piece of paper and started to scribble. 'This is the name and address of the hotel where I know Dennis Brown is staying with his road crew.' I held out the scrap of paper. 'He'll be going back there after the show tonight. You can pick him up there, *out of Brixton*, and we can all avoid any ... problematic situations.'

The two cops took another look out over the sea of faces in the auditorium. They must have been nervous; as police, they were deep behind enemy lines.

'All right, Mr Parkes,' said one, 'that sounds sensible. Thank you for your co-operation.'

The fuzz beat a quick retreat out of the building, and I made a beeline straight for Dennis Brown's tour manager.

'Look, mate, we need to talk,' I panted. 'The police are after your man Dennis Brown – some bullshit about unpaid alimony – I've just convinced them not to arrest him here, before the gig, but they're going to be waiting at your hotel tonight. Do not go back to that hotel!'

I was seriously worried that Brown's team were going to panic and pull the show in order to get their star out of there as quickly as possible. Or even worse, assume that I was working with the police, or somehow on their side. With the incendiary racial tensions in Brixton at the time, it was all too easy for any white guy to become identified as one of 'them'.

The tour manager seemed completely unperturbed. He pushed his dreads back, away from his face, and stroked his beard thoughtfully.

'Dem Babylon always afta I an' I,' he replied in lilting Jamaican patois. 'Dreadlocks stay wan step ahead always. Jah 'im send messenger like you for protec' I. Tank you frien', tank you.'

He held out his fist. I tapped it with my own, and that seemed the end of the business. We got on with the gig.

The show itself was great. Dennis Brown knew what the crowd wanted and gave it to them. There seemed to be a genuine *one love* atmosphere in the venue, and I was very relieved that I had managed to finesse a difficult situation without either pissing off the police or alienating the entire West Indian community. Dennis Brown's crew all seemed totally cool with what had gone down, trading jokes and enormous spliffs as they packed up their gear and bundled Brown off to some secret location to evade the law.

If only everyone had shown such good faith and professionalism.

As I was walking around backstage after the show I saw Mad Mick's guy Pat standing by the door of the promoter's office. He motioned me over, putting his finger to his lips to keep quiet.

Without saying a word, he motioned towards the door. He then put his hand on the handle and gave a little push. You wouldn't have thought a guy that big would be able to push that quietly and discreetly. The door didn't budge. Pat raised his eyebrows at me. This wasn't right. Only I had the keys to lock that door. Someone must have wedged something from the inside to keep it shut.

What was going on now? My heart started to beat a little faster.

Still staying as quiet as possible, Pat pointed twice at the door, silently asking 'Shall we go in?' I nodded my head nervously, readying myself for whatever might be happening in that office.

Taking two steps back, Pat put his fingers to his lips once again. Then, with a little run-up, he gave the door an almighty kick, putting all of his considerable body mass behind it. There was a huge crash and the door flew back, very nearly coming off its hinges.

Pat and I burst into the office, only to see the promoter of the show in the process of passing a bag to an accomplice out the window. Startled by the crash of the door, the guy whipped around to see Pat and me staring him down. He panicked, jumping up on a chair and trying desperately to scramble through the open window.

I don't blame the guy for trying to run. Confronted by an enraged man mountain like Pat, I would have scarpered too. He got about halfway through the window before Pat reached him. Pat grabbed the guy by the belt, hauled him back into the room, and slammed him up against the wall by the throat.

''Ere boss,' he snarled. 'Looks like Mr Promoter here doesn't want to pay his venue fees.'

'No, no, it's not like that guv,' honest,' the guy protested, somewhat pathetically after his escape attempt.

'SHUT IT,' roared Pat, leaning his face about an inch from the terrified promoter's nose.

The guy was visibly shaking. I would have been too. He had been caught red-handed. In Brixton trying to rip someone off like that would usually mean a savage beating, at the very least.

'What shall we do with him, Boss?' Pat turned to me, still holding the guy against the wall by his throat, about a foot off the ground.

'I don't know Pat, what do you think we should do with him?' I asked.

It may sound as if I was toying with the guy, like some kind of Bond villain talking to his henchman; actually it was a genuine question. I didn't have the faintest notion of how to handle a situation like this. Obviously I couldn't just let the guy go, it would make me look like a soft touch for every other petty-criminal-turned-music-promoter in Brixton. And I really did need the money he owed me. On the other hand, I wasn't about to break the guy's legs. That might have been how things operated in his world, and in Pat's, but it wasn't where I came from.

'I'll get you the money, guv, I'll get you the money. I'll come back tomorrow,' the guy pleaded. I could hear the terror in his voice.

'I said SHUT IT,' Pat bellowed again, giving him a shake.

Then, with his free hand, Pat reached into the guy's trouser pocket, felt around a bit, and fished out a set of car keys.

'Now you listen to me you little fuck,' said Pat, his voice dropping to a menacing south London rasp almost more terrifying than his shout. 'You drive that red Honda outside, don't you? I seen you drive up in it. Well, now that's my boss's red 'onda.'

Pat turned and tossed the keys towards me. My hand snapped out and caught them instinctively. He turned back to the promoter. 'You bring our money. You get your car back. You understand?'

The guy frantically nodded his head, as much as he could with Pat's giant hand still wrapped around his throat.

'Yes, guv, I'll bring the money. I promise guv.'

'Good,' said Pat, lowering the guy to the ground, 'and we'll know how much, so no fuckin' about. Now fuck off out of it.'

The promoter bolted out of the room, using the door this time, not believing his luck at still being able to walk.

He did actually come back the next day with the remainder of the money, and I did give him his car keys back. But that episode was a sharp lesson for me about exactly the kind of world I had begun to move in, about how things operated in Brixton. I wasn't in Lincolnshire any more; and these weren't lessons you could learn on a business course.

I would never in a month of Sundays have thought to take a guy's car keys as collateral. Yet, this was the perfect solution: tough, but avoiding unnecessary violence that could start a war should the guy turn out to have backup of his own. I wouldn't have even thought to scope out the car a promoter was driving, just on the off chance that information might become useful later. These were all Brixton lessons that I was going to have to learn very quickly.

As we cleared up the mess and counted up the money that remained, I turned to Pat. 'Pat, how did you even know there was something going on in here?'

'That bloke was a wrong un, boss,' he replied without hesitation. 'Sometimes blokes are just wrong uns. You got to keep your eyes on 'em. Me, I can spot a wrong un a mile off.'

Right then, that's how it worked. You just either needed to be able to spot the wrong uns, or make damn sure you had someone around you who could.

Over the next few years, Pat's ability to spot a 'wrong un' was to become an absolute lifeline for me, as I came to realize just how steep, and dangerous, Brixton's learning curve could be.

GANGSTERS

We were still scrambling to book gigs. Every one we managed to get in the diary was a small personal triumph for me. I knew the Academy would be great once bands started coming, but I was beginning to accept that it would take time. I just had to stay cool, and keep hustling until I got the break I needed.

I also knew that Lambeth Council was very politically left-leaning. In the midst of Thatcherism, and all the social, economic, and cultural conflicts of the time, they were desperate for anything that might help regenerate the area, or instil any kind of hope and community cohesion. So I managed to convince Lambeth and the Greater London Council to help finance bringing Fela Kuti over from Nigeria for a concert.

I half suspect the council paper-pushers may have agreed to this without doing their homework about just what putting on a Fela Kuti show entailed. In the end, we flew a 59-person entourage over from Lagos, roughly half of whom were registered as spouses of the main star.

It was absolute chaos, but a very joyous show. Fela danced and jerked his way across the stage with seemingly bound-less energy, his face daubed with streaks of white paint like an entranced shaman. His band blasted out four hours of their stomping afrobeat funk, and Fela's thirty wives joined him onstage in a powerful backing chorus. Watching the impact of that huge ensemble, I realized how right Mike had been,

For Fela Kuti's incredible stage show he brought 30 of his
wives over from Lagos to double as backing vocalists

just how special – unique – the Academy stage could be when properly used.

Obviously we didn't make a penny on the Fela gig, but it was a great night, and it raised our profile in the area.

In fact, it raised our profile so much, that we started coming to the attention of all the wrong people.

The punches started flying just as the show was about to start.

It was a few local hoods, outside the front door, at the precise moment when the queue was longest, and our box office busiest. Mad Mick's security guys moved straight in, using their uniquely persuasive powers to restore order as quickly as possible. I didn't think too much of it. These things happen in Brixton.

The rest of the gig was great. I think it was Yellowman, or another one of those middleweight stars of the early 80s reggae pantheon. But I remember a good vibe, a good performance, and no promoters trying to escape out the window with the money.

After the show, however, things became clear.

Just as we had finished packing up and were getting ready to lock the place down for the night, Black Nigel came up saying, 'Simon, there's a couple of geezers downstairs wanting to talk to you. I think you had better go and speak to them.' There was a strange tension in his voice as he delivered the message.

I walked into the foyer to see two guys nonchalantly lounging about. Both were Jamaican: one with shoulder-length dreadlocks, the other in a classic woven Rasta hat. Both were big, imposing characters.

'All right guys, I'm Simon, what can I do for you?' I asked.

'Me 'eard you had a little fight down 'ere before de show tonight,' the dreadlocked guy began. He spoke slowly and deliberately. 'We thought mebbe you could use some 'elp wit' your security. Mebbe our little firm could 'elp run the door for you; mek sure nuttin' like dat happen again.'

Fuck. This was a classic protection racket stunt. My mind started racing. Of course the fight this evening had been staged. It had been timed perfectly, just when we were busiest, to cause the maximum disruption. At a popular gig, the smallest interruption at the box office can disrupt the whole flow of the night, and spread jumpy, nervous energy through the crowd.

I had to figure out how to handle this. I had no idea about these guys. Were they random chancers, or was this the Yardie Vito Corleone I was speaking to? Was this an offer I could, or could not, refuse? My mind flashed back to the tension with which Black Nigel had said I 'had better' go speak to these two. Shit, this might be serious. If I let these guys take over the door, I was done for. If you control the front door of a venue, you control the venue; it's the key to the whole operation. On the other hand, these guys didn't come off like the type of characters you could say no to.

What could I do? My brain was doing somersaults trying to find the right thing to say.

In moments of stress, people tend to regress to where they come from, where they feel most comfortable. The response I stammered out was the lamest, least street-smart, *whitest* thing I could possibly have come up with.

'Well, uhhh, thank you for that. Umm, actually the contract has just been awarded, but we are on a three-month trial period; So if you drop your CV by our office then we will certainly call you for an interview when it comes up for tender.'

Oh god, had I seriously just asked a Yardie gangster to hand in his CV at the office?

The two big geezers stared at me in utter incomprehension. This wasn't the response they had been anticipating. I expect their business conversations generally consisted of people either begging them for mercy or reading them their rights. As much as I didn't know who they were, or how to deal with them, they could obviously make neither heads nor tails of me, with my talk about CVs and three-month trial periods. They just didn't know how to handle the evasive, impersonal language of business school.

'All right den, we see you in three months den.'

The two obviously confused would-be racketeers melted back into the Brixton night, and I breathed a long sigh of relief. I didn't quite understand what had just happened, but it seemed like the crossed wires of intercultural misunderstanding had averted some trouble, at least for now.

I hadn't meant to play a clever game with those guys, I'd just blurted out the first thing that came into my head. But it became yet another important lesson for me. There was no way I could stand up to people like that. Black Nigel filled me in after they left: those two were Rondall and Wilson, local heavies and known 'faces' around Brixton. I could never take them on at their own game, and I certainly had to avoid any kind of macho standoff. But if I played it right, then maybe my outsider status could keep me safe. I was so far removed from that world that perhaps I could avoid some of its nastier elements. If I couldn't fight these guys directly, at least I might be able to confuse them into submission with middle-class niceties.

It was a line I would have to walk a lot over the next few years. Sometimes it worked better than others. We certainly hadn't seen the last of Rondall and Wilson, or many other crooks of their type.

IT TAKES MORE THAN A LITTLE TEAR GAS

Over the next few months, as we put on more reggae shows, it became obvious we were being tested.

A small fight would break out at the door, staff would be followed after we locked up at night: small intimidations that, while not being immediately dangerous, contributed to an air of unease and tension.

We had become big enough that the local 'characters' had to start paying attention. They only had to do the math. If we had 5,000 people through the doors at a gig, plus the bar take, then there was money to be made. They wanted a piece of the action. It's extremely creepy when you know you're being watched, but you don't even know who exactly the predators are. It could have been Rondall and Wilson, or any other of a number of Brixton players; or all of them in turn. I just had to keep from panicking, and trust in Mad Mick and his boys to keep us safe.

It was my poor car that took the worst of it. Whoever had their eyes on us had obviously scoped me driving in one day. From then on it was a constant succession of having my tyres slashed, my paintwork keyed, or my windows broken.

It started to get really irritating. One Friday as I was leaving the Academy, planning to drive up to Lincolnshire for the weekend, I was confronted, yet again, with four slashed tyres. In absolute frustration I turned to the security guy next to me and stormed, 'Oh for fuck's sake, I have to get rid of this bloody car.'

When I returned on the Monday morning, having taken the train up north, the same security guy came up to me looking pleased with himself and said, ''Ello guv'nor, I got rid of that car like you asked.'

'You what?' I asked.

'That car outside. You said you wanted rid of it. Me and the boys took care of it for you.' He smiled at me, obviously very satisfied with his get-ahead attitude.

Bloody hell, my very own Henry II and Thomas Becket moment. They could at least have taken the radio out first!

That was a problem with some of Mad Mick's team: they were hard as granite, but could sometimes be fairly blunt instruments. This guy wasn't part of Mick's inner circle, but even with the core team, it took a while to convince them that they didn't *always* have to knock people's heads together.

But what could I do?

'Uhh thanks very much mate, nice work with that.'

I didn't bother getting a new car for a long time. It would only get done over again. I bought myself a bike, and began my tenure as the mad one-armed white-boy cyclist of the Stockwell Road.

Aside from these bits of trouble, the reggae gigs were doing well for us. The Academy's profile was rising, and I was learning a lot. Working with the Jamaican guys was fascinating, not just in terms of rough lessons in the music biz, but interesting cultural points, like how the Rastafarian artists were so particular about what they ate that they would fly their own chefs over from Jamaica to do the catering for their shows. Which was fantastic for me. I loved helping myself to their rice 'n' peas backstage.

But I knew that to really make things happen, we had to get the rock bands in. Reggae was great, but it was a niche market. Plus, from a venue owner's point of view, we never made any real money at the bar on reggae shows. All we got was the hassle of having to rotate our upstairs security every half-hour, before they got too spaced on the thick clouds of blue smoke rising up from the auditorium.

So I was overjoyed when a call came in from the promoter and music industry legend John Curd.

In the 60s, when the Rolling Stones still fancied themselves as the bad boys of pop, it was John Curd they went to when they needed someone to organize their huge Hyde Park concert. In the 70s and 80s he was the man who pushed the punk bands like The Damned and The Ramones. Later he was the first British industry player to take on the new hip-hop artists coming over from America. John was the guy who would take on the things that no one else would touch, who enjoyed the excitement of something new and dangerous. He's still in the game to this day, taking care of artists such as Eminem and the Red Hot Chilli Peppers.

John had a reputation as a fierce, old-school operator of the down-and-dirty British music biz. He wasn't one of the faceless, suited salarymen who run the industry today. If you crossed John you were as likely to wind up with a broken nose as with a solicitor's letter. There were countless stories about him head-butting some agent that tried to pull a fast one, or throwing some rival through a table in the middle of an awards ceremony. Even the truly huge players on the live music scene, the guys like Harvey Goldsmith, knew not to mess with John Curd.

I was happy even to get a call from a guy of John's stature. He said he wanted to bring Burning Spear down for a show at the Academy. It was another reggae gig, but a very good one, definitely a step up. I thought that once John actually saw the place, he would realize its potential for rock bands. This could be a good break for us.

The night of the gig we put on extra security. I wanted this to run absolutely smoothly, with no local Brixton nonsense to spoil John's impression of the venue. Mad Mick's guys brought down four huge Rottweilers to stand in the foyer, as an extra show of force.

We usually tried to organize the door traffic in a sort of funnel. There would be two queues outside: one for advanced ticket holders, and another one, much longer at reggae shows, for people paying at the door. The idea was that the crowd would be manoeuvred so that, when they actually came to pay at the box office and have their ticket torn, they would come in one by one, or at least in small groups. This made a sudden rush on the box office impossible, and the crowd generally easier to control.

I usually stood in the foyer, at the intersection point of the two streams of people. From here I could keep an eye on things, and my guys would know where to find me in case of an emergency backstage, or some other issue that only I could deal with.

So, on the night of the Burning Spear gig, as we got near to show time, I was standing with John Curd in my usual spot, watching the punters as they streamed in. Everything seemed to be running smoothly.

Then, out of nowhere, a small object, just bigger than a can of Coca-Cola, came sailing through the air. It bounced on the floor with a few clanging metallic thuds, and came to rest just under our box office window.

We all turned to look. As I did so, I suddenly felt the most extreme burning pain in my eyes; they began to stream uncontrollably, and the inside of my mouth and throat felt as if it was on fire. It was a fucking tear gas canister.

At that exact moment, there was a surge at the front doors as a couple of guys tried to barge their way into the building. Jesus Christ – we were in the middle of a robbery. There was a rush of frantic activity. My security guys and I slammed the big front doors shut. Through the pain in my throat, I desperately tried to maintain control over the situation, before everything collapsed into chaos.

Meanwhile, the four Rottweiler dogs all began to sneeze furiously. Looking back, it must have been pretty funny: all of us scrambling around to clear punters out of the way, as these fearsome beasts just blinked and sneezed.

John Curd had the absolute presence of mind to grab the keys off me and double-bolt the box office door. He had his priorities in order: that's where the money was.

There was pandemonium in the foyer as we tried to get the gas canister out and make sure audience members weren't injured, all while partially blinded by the gas. Eventually things calmed down a bit, and I was able to empty a water bottle over my face.

Then, with a shock, I remembered that our poor ticket girl, Plum, must still be locked inside the box office. There was no way John would have taken the time to get her out before making sure the ticket money was safe.

I threw open the door and found Plum lying on the floor, managing to keep below the gas as it rose up through the air. Smart girl. I'm not sure I would have thought of that. I helped her up and rushed her to the toilet, where we both plunged our faces into sinks of cold water, in order to at least partially get rid of the burning.

But I still had a gig to run. I ran back out to the foyer, my eyes still streaming. We managed to get the doors open, and the crowd back into a somewhat orderly formation. The rest of the show went well. I was disappointed not to catch much of Burning Spear, being more preoccupied with the fire still raging in my mouth and throat.

Inside though, I was burning with rage, not tear gas. Though the robbery attempt itself had been a non-starter, and we had shut it down fast, I was pissed off. Why did these arseholes have to choose tonight to pull this shit? My fear was that John would decide that Brixton was just more bother than it was worth.

I should have known better. It takes a lot more than a little tear gas to spook John Curd. In fact, John and I have been good mates for almost thirty years now, and have been through some extremely hairy moments together, and I still don't think I've ever seen him show a sign of fear.

As we were winding the night down after the gig he walked up, patted me on the back and said, 'Yeah, you've got a good place. I like it. I've just taken on a band called The Cult, let's do a gig.'

Inside, my heart leapt. We had broken out of the ghetto: we had booked a rock band.

DREAD MEETS PUNK ROCKERS UPTOWN

I learned a lot from John Curd from day one. For him the experience of a gig started the moment you bought your ticket. Every poster, ticket, and bit of paraphernalia was uniquely and lovingly designed, with passionate creativity and attention to detail. In the 60s and 70s he had worked extensively with the iconic graphic artist Barney Bubbles, who was involved in Hawkwind's psychedelic west London scene, and had directed the video for The Specials' 'Ghost Town'. Tragically, Barney had recently committed suicide.

The Bubbles spirit endured though, as John still made sure that every aspect of a gig experience was a little bit special. With him, it was never a matter of herding people through the door, then herding them out again. He was definitely a wily operator, and fierce as hell if you crossed him, but John had soul.

We became good friends over the years. But that first Cult show was a pretty rocky start.

This was the first time we were bringing a largely white audience down to Brixton. We needed to get it right. Yet again, Mad Mick and I doubled our security. We didn't think there would be another robbery attempt. With rock gigs, so many people bought tickets in advance that there was rarely enough money in the box office to make it worthwhile. Reggae shows ran on cash, and presented a much more tempting target. Even so, we knew that a lot of very nasty people had their eyes on us.

As it happened, the takeover attempt that night didn't come from Yardie gangsters, but from John Curd himself.

As we were setting up for the show, he approached me, saying that because of what had happened with Burning Spear, he had brought his own people to cover the front door security. A couple of his guys loomed behind him.

Shit. This was difficult. John Curd wasn't a guy you wanted to piss off, and at the moment he was the only promoter willing to bring rock bands our way. But there was no way I could give up my front door. If I let John run things tonight it would set a precedent: every other promoter would demand the same privilege.

Plus, Mike Henley had warned me about John Curd. He was rumoured to *over-capacitate* events. *Over-capacitating* is music biz speak for when a promoter sells too many tickets for a gig, and pockets the extra cash. If any capacity regulations are exceeded, it's the venue that is liable for the fine.

For a moment, I almost let inexperience get the better of me and let John have his way.

Then something snapped, and decided I wasn't having that kind of bullshit, no matter who was demanding it. I refused point blank.

John wasn't a man who liked hearing the word *no*. He got right up in my face till we were fronting off nose to nose. I could see his two heavies behind him. Mad Mick and Black Nigel stepped up on my side.

John was a huge bruiser of a man. In the back of my mind, though, there was always old Mac telling me not to let myself be pushed around. For a moment it looked like it was seriously about to kick off. My heart was pounding, but I was ready for a scrap if it came to it. I wasn't going to give up my front door.

After a few tense moments, John backed down. My guys would tear the tickets and keep the head count, his would keep a watchful eye on the queues outside. It was a compromise that allowed him to save face but left me in control of the important action. I guess John didn't fancy taking me on here on my home turf. I just wanted to make sure that it stayed my turf.

In the end, the gig was a great success. And by standing my ground I think I earned John's respect. He realized I was somebody to take seriously. Without the wary mutual admiration we established that night, I don't think we would ever have become actual friends.

That Cult gig seemed to open a little crack in the stony façade of the British music industry. As a band, they weren't yet the big success they would become, but we had put on a rock show in Brixton. People had made the journey down, had a good time, and made it home safely to tell the tale.

Another group of people, who were extremely important to me on a personal level, had also taken notice.

The call came out of the blue. 'Hi there, this is Tim Parsons from Midlands Concert Promotions. We're booking dates for The Clash, and the band have specifically asked that they do their London shows at the Brixton Academy.'

Tim Parsons was an important guy. In a couple of years he would co-promote Live Aid, and later Oasis's massive concerts at Knebworth. But the words that caught my ears were *The Clash*. They were only the most culturally significant British band of the past decade!

This was huge. And it made perfect sense. Those guys were always the ones to put themselves just at the edge: where others

Joe Strummer: no one meant it quite like The Clash

wouldn't go, where there was a little danger. And they loved reggae. I was sure that one of them had come down to a gig by Yellowman or Burning Spear and thought, Wait a second, we sing 'Guns of Brixton'. We should be playing here!'

I was massively excited. Not only was this a huge break for the Academy, but also I had seen all the great punk bands live, except for the big two: The Clash and The Sex Pistols. There wasn't much chance of getting the Pistols these days, though we did have an eventful night with Public Image Limited a few years later. I was chuffed. If you're going to see The Clash for the first time, you might as well have them down to your own gaff. We booked them in for a two-night run.

The week before the shows, Mad Mick Murphy came to see me saying that he was taking some time off to go on holiday and was leaving Pat in charge of security. It was a bit annoying, coming so soon before our biggest gigs yet, but I liked how Pat had dealt with that promoter trying to climb out the window, so I reluctantly agreed.

The gigs themselves were incendiary. There is nothing on earth like seeing The Clash bound onstage and bang straight into those staccato opening chords of 'London Calling'. The crowd went wild. It was a very different energy from the chilled vibes of the reggae shows. I stood up on the balcony and looked down at that heaving mass; all these hardcore fans throwing themselves about in total abandon, and I just thought, *yes!* This is what I set up the Academy for. This was my vision becoming reality before my eyes.

The poignant moment was interrupted when some spods from the council decided to run an unannounced building safety check, just as the gig was in full flow. As I was walking them through one of our upstairs landings, I spied Pat in the process of 'removing' an overenthusiastic Clash fan from the premises. It was a big fella, and he wasn't going quietly, kicking and struggling as hard as he could. Pat was literally carrying this guy by the face, his huge fingers wrapped around the man's head. I frantically turned and tried to distract the council box-tickers with some of the building's architectural curiosities: 'You see, what's wonderful is that we actually have all the original 1920s lampshades still in place. No really, take a closer look, please.'

As I forced the somewhat confused council guys to gather around our pretty art deco lampshades, my eyes caught Pat's. To his credit, he understood immediately what was going on, and tried to be as discreet as possible, creeping around the back of us while still carrying the struggling punk by the face. To my surprise, we got away with it. Pat 'gently escorted' the guy out the building, without drawing undue attention to the mayhem going on in the auditorium.

I was elated with the Clash gigs. We had put on one of the biggest bands in the country, and had pulled off a couple of great shows. It felt like we were proving ourselves, as if we were really getting somewhere.

So it was a bit of a knock when Pat came to me not long after saying, 'Umm, boss, I think we might 'ave a little problem.'

'Why, what's up, Pat?'

'Well, thing is, boss, this holiday that Mad Mick has been on wasn't, strictly speaking, just an 'oliday. He's been busted out in India, and it don't look like he'll be 'ome too quickly.'

Bloody hell.

It turned out that Mad Mick had indeed been caught with several pounds of high-grade dope in an Indian airport, and was staring down the barrel of a ten-year sentence out there.

As sorry as I felt for Mad Mick, I didn't hesitate for a second.

'OK, Pat, how would you like to be Head of Security for the Brixton Academy?'

It was a snap decision, but Pat had impressed me with how he'd handled things both with the dodgy promoter and with getting that Clash fan out of sight so discreetly. He was obviously hard as nails, but he had also shown that he had a head on his shoulders, that he could act with a bit of discretion and forethought. He wasn't the type of guy to scrap your car based on an off-hand remark. I knew I needed someone who could think ahead, as well as just crack heads together.

'Promoting' Pat turned out to be one of the best decisions I've ever made. And it wasn't long before he had to prove just how tough and resourceful he really was.

COOL RULER

We were well aware that we were being watched and tested by various underworld players. Perhaps it had always been inevitable, or perhaps the news that Mad Mick was out of the picture had spread around via the Brixton rumour mill, but somebody wasn't happy about my new arrangement with Pat at the Academy. They saw a moment of weakness, and they decided to make their move.

The team was getting ready for two nights of Gregory Isaacs, Cool Ruler himself. Unusually for a reggae gig, the shows had almost sold out in advance. Isaacs was launching a big comeback after doing six months in Jamaica for firearms offences, and we were expecting a couple of very lively nights.

Early on the evening of the first show, Pat was in position outside the main doors, supervising the queues, when a car screeched to a halt on the curb. Four huge guys jumped out and proceeded to pincushion him.

In south London parlance, to *pincushion* someone means to beat them to a bloody pulp using baseball bats with nails driven into them.

Everything went into meltdown. Pat was rushed to hospital; the rest of us had to pull together and lock the place down. This was a targeted hit. Whoever carried it out wanted Pat out of the way. With him gone, we were vulnerable. The follow-up attack could come at any minute. Thankfully, the assault had taken place out on the street, which meant a much heavier police presence than usual around the building. I'm sure that is the only reason why another, even heavier, raid didn't immediately follow.

Nevertheless, over that night and into the next morning you could feel the whole of Brixton crackle with tension.

Word had gone out on the street that Pat had been killed. Throughout the underground gambling dens of Railton Road and the squats of Coldharbour Lane, rumours were flying about what had gone down, and how it was going to play out. Who had pulled off the hit? Which 'boss' was going to make a move and take over the Academy?

Inside the venue we went into full siege mode. A couple of guys and I stayed in the building overnight, undertaking regular patrols in case the gangs tried anything while they thought the venue was empty.

Black Nigel and our guys at the Academy had their fingers on the pulse of the area. All the next day they were plugged into the chatter going around the bars and jerk chicken joints. It didn't sound good. Control of the Academy would be a huge prize for any of the local gang leaders. The whole area held its breath, waiting to see who blinked first. No one knew the exact score, but we were certain that whatever was going to happen, it was going down tonight.

The tension inside the Academy was like razor wire. It felt like the centre of some military operation, or the build-up to the last-stand shoot-out in a western. People were running in and out, frantically delivering messages, as we sat there in string vests, surrounded by cigarette butts and empty boxes of takeaway rice 'n' peas. We went over and over our defensive strategies, and tried to work out how to read the gossip coming in from the street.

But we were an army without a general. Our head of security was out of action, and I didn't know the first thing about Brixton gang warfare. I tried to maintain my composure, but inside I was genuinely worried. Whoever was after us meant business. This wasn't some boardroom coup. People were getting seriously hurt. My people. I could see the whole Academy dream being snatched from me by forces I could not control.

Then Pat showed up.

That's the thing these Brixton thugs didn't understand about Pat: he was carved out of rock. Whoever had delivered the beating hadn't managed to kill him, all they'd done was piss him off, snapping him into action. That afternoon he had walked himself out of the intensive care unit while the nurse wasn't looking. He strolled into our frantic little HQ at the Academy with a casual, 'All right, boss.'

Just when you think you're surrounded, the cavalry comes charging over hill!

Pat was back on the door for the second night of Gregory Isaacs, his foam neck brace hidden under a voluminous trench coat. This show of brass kick-started Pat's legendary reputation around Brixton for being indestructible, a reputation we traded on for the rest of our time at the Academy.

But that in itself wasn't enough of a message. What I learned that night was that as well as being tough and smart, Pat was heavily 'connected'. While he himself was no gangster, he had deep links with the heavy criminal firms of south London.

That evening Pat brought in his own backup.

As we prepared ourselves for the show that night, I was called down to the backstage area and introduced to a small army of about forty or so short, ruddy Irishmen. I had never met so many Seamuses and Patricks in one place before.

Now, this was a sold-out reggae gig on a humid May night in Brixton. People were dancing like it was carnival; the venue was seriously hot and sweaty. But during this particular gig, amidst the West Indian party vibe, at every doorway and corridor of the Academy stood a pair of these stocky, pale Irish guys: all pouring with sweat because they were wearing long, heavy Crombie coats to conceal their sawn-off shotguns.

With hindsight, the image is pretty hilarious. It could have come straight out of a movie like *Lock, Stock and Two Smoking Barrels*. But the night itself was knife-edge, pulse-racing tension. Everyone was on tenterhooks, fingers on the trigger, just waiting for someone to make a move.

I went from position to position around the building with Pete the Mercenary and Big John on either side of me for protection, and with my heart in my mouth. This was the first night I wore a flak jacket on a gig. It would become a disturbingly regular addition to my wardrobe over the next few years.

In the end, whoever had been eyeing a takeover of the Academy that night must have thought better of it when confronted with this kind of firepower. The concert went off without a hitch. Our show of strength had sent out the message that needed to be sent.

And, though I didn't really get to enjoy them, the Gregory Isaacs shows themselves were brilliant. The Cool Ruler came on in a sharp white suit and had the audience in the palm of his hand. They ended up releasing a live album and film of that gig that were both very successful, and are still available now. But I'm sure nobody dancing that night, or listening to the album later, ever realized the background atmosphere of menace to those shows, or just how dangerous the nights were. Not to mention how important to the story of the Brixton Academy.

What I personally learned from those nerve-wracking gigs was that Pat was worth his weight in diamonds. He really proved himself, and he went on to blossom with the responsibility that came with being head of security. Over the next few years Pat became my most trusted partner at the Academy, as well as one of my closest friends.

Following the unmistakable message he had sent with his private army, Pat went on to use his connections to negotiate a loose arrangement with the local hoods. Not only would they leave the building alone, but they wouldn't come down past the railway bridge on Brixton High Street, allowing Academy punters to and from the station in relative safety. This truce broadly held, with us being subjected to only the occasional shooting, armed robbery, and stabbing for the entire time I was at the Academy.

So we were safe. Relatively speaking, at least. Now all I had to do was get on with booking some gigs and building our rep, and maybe even starting to make some money.

MR LAWES

'Hello guv'nor, give us a job.'

It was always the same line.

Almost every day since I had first taken over the Academy, this character had been turning up at the back door. Always the same cheeky grin, always the same request. 'Hello guv'nor, give us a job.' Like clockwork.

Johnny Lawes was a young local Rastafarian: shoulder-length dreads usually tied back in a ponytail. He was one of those guys who have a twinkle in their eye and a supreme gift of the gab: a total, natural charmer.

But I didn't know any of that yet. For now, he was just that friendly geezer who turned up at our stage door every day looking for work.

After several months, it became obvious that this guy wasn't going anywhere. If nothing else, he certainly had tenacity. Plus, he always seemed to give off such a good vibe that one day I thought, oh, what the hell?

I turned to him point blank and asked, 'OK then, what can you actually do for me?'

Without blinking, Johnny replied, 'You tell me any band you want, and I'll go and get them for you.'

These were big words for a guy with seemingly no music biz experience or connections. I would know; I'd been struggling to book bands for months. But something in Johnny's easy, unassuming confidence impressed me. He seemed so sure of himself, so certain that he could make things happen. It was just the kind of spirit I thought our venue could use. So I thought I'd test him a bit.

'All right then, I want UB40.'

I'd been pursuing UB40 since we had opened. They would be an important *get* for the Academy. Not only were they a huge act at the time, but they bridged the black and white divide, in both their band members and their audience. We needed gigs that could appeal to both the reggae crowd and the pop fans. But, most important, they were the band that had been ripped off in the Fair Deal scam. If I could bring UB40 back to Brixton it would be hugely symbolic of a new beginning to everyone in the industry and beyond.

However, it was an almost comically massive ask for anyone who wasn't a professional music agent. The last thing I ever expected was for Johnny to respond, without a moment's hesitation, 'Yeah, OK, I know one of their horn players up in Birmingham. Give me the contracts and I'll go get them for you.'

This kid didn't miss a trick. If he was bluffing, he certainly had me fooled.

Then, before I had a chance to collect my thoughts and respond, Johnny continued, 'Only thing is, guv'nor, is how am I going to get up to Birmingham?'

'Tell you what,' he pushed on, 'lend us your car, and I'll drive up there and book them for you.'

I didn't know this guy from Adam. It was completely ludicrous. But Johnny was so charming and persuasive, I found myself agreeing to lend him my car, which I had only just bought after the last one got scrapped, for three days so that he could drive to Birmingham and back.

Then he pushed things even further, 'Thing is, guv'nor, I haven't got any money for petrol.'

Johnny Lawes, always the charmer

Any sensible businessman would have burst out laughing and told Johnny to get lost. But there was something about him that seemed genuinely cool, like he would do the right thing. Maybe it was the old childhood lessons about not judging, and looking for the best in people? I ignored my sensible side, trusted my instinct, and handed over £20.

With no further discussion, Johnny trundled off to Birmingham, in my car, to book UB40.

A day went by. Then another. I had heard nothing from Johnny, and I was starting to get nervous. These were still the dark ages before the mobile phone. I had no way of contacting him. More to the point, I had no idea who Johnny even was. I had no address for him, no phone number, not even a surname. As the third day passed I began to picture the interview with the police officer when I had to report my car stolen, 'So, let me get this straight: not only did you hand this guy your car keys, but you gave him twenty quid for petrol as well?' I began to feel very anxious, and very silly. That would teach me to trust random punters in Brixton.

Then, on the fourth day, out of nowhere, up rolled Johnny with the car intact and a big smile on his face. In his hands were the signed contracts. He had coaxed UB40 into giving Brixton a second chance. This guy had convinced me to give him my car, and persuaded a major band to return to a venue where they had been ripped off before. Whatever 'it' was, Johnny had it. The man could win over anyone to anything. I gave him a job then and there.

From that day on Johnny became my right-hand man. We formed a pretty funny double act in running the Academy: the Rasta and the one-armed white boy. Like Pat, Johnny became part of my inner team, and a close friend. To this day I've met very few people who could match him for sheer wit, charm, and can-do.

THE MIKE
HENLEY DENT

It was fortuitous that Johnny came along when he did. We began to need reinforcements just around then. Our inspirational stage manager Mike Henley was about to make a dramatic flight into rock mythology.

We were doing some maintenance on the stage: moving equipment around with the load bars, and all the while throwing around ideas about how to move things forward with the venue.

I was complaining about my frustrations with our progress. We had started to make some inroads, and putting on The Clash had been huge, but most of the agents remained unwilling to send their hot bands down to Brixton. They still had their relationships going with the Hammersmith Odeon, seeing it as the only place to play in London.

I'd already seen how performers responded to our space, and to our stage. I knew what a good gig felt like, and ours already had a much better vibe than the Odeon. But it wasn't the artists I had to convince. It was their agents, the guys who weren't concerned about the vibe of a show because they were usually in a back room somewhere counting the money.

I got so pissed off about this that I had a serious look at the piratical idea of booking out every weekend at the Odeon for a whole year. This would have forced bands to come to me, and I could use the money from those gigs to pay off the hall hire for keeping the Odeon empty. In the end the numbers didn't add up, but only by a few grand. I came very close to going for the plan just out of sheer contrariness.

So that afternoon, as we were trying to get things right with our load bar system, I was trying to drum up some ideas about how to make Brixton a more attractive option to the music biz players.

Yet again, it was Mike Henley who had the answer. Looking out across the huge, empty stage, his eyes only slightly glazed from the nips he'd been taking from his flask 'just to keep off the cold', he suddenly said, 'You know what we can do, Simon? We've got a big enough stage here that the big bands, the *really* huge bands – Dire Straits, Clapton, people like that – could use this place for production rehearsals for stadium tours.'

At first I was sceptical. I wanted bands to do gigs here, not bloody rehearsals. But as Mike kept talking, it started to sound better and better.

'See, all we need is for bands to get a look at this place. If a group gets on this stage they'll want to play on it with a crowd. And once the road crews get in here, they'll spread the word through the industry, trust me on that.'

He paused for a hit from his flask before continuing.

'And the managers will go for it too. It'll save them a packet compared to hiring out Pinewood film studios every bloody time.'

The more we chatted about the idea, the more sense it seemed to make. At the very least it would get bands coming through the place, not to mention providing a bit of turnover for the accounts books. I started letting my imagination run a bit, turning over how I could start putting these thoughts into action.

Then disaster struck.

Theatre load bars, or fly systems, work on a simple counterweight balance system. You rope the piece of kit, curtain, or scenery you want to move, to a bar hanging from the ceiling. You then balance the object's weight, and through a pulley one person can move, or 'fly', extremely heavy objects on- and offstage smoothly and easily. When used correctly, it's a very simple, elegant system.

At the Academy, the counterweights we used were metal cradles loaded with cast iron ingots, each weighing about 25 pounds. Depending on the weight of the object we were moving, each cradle could be loaded to weigh anything from 25 pounds to half a ton. If necessary, to make things easier we could link cradles together, and move two or more objects at once.

The lines we used for this system were old-fashioned Manila hemp ropes. After years of use, these ropes would get worn, start to sag, and need to be changed. Replacing and testing the new ropes was part of what we were doing that afternoon on the stage.

Mike, being the stage manager, and knowing the system better than anyone, was in charge. But Mike, being Mike, had not only been taking slugs from his flask all afternoon, but had spent the morning in the pub having a big pre-lunchtime session.

Now I've never been one to lecture people about booze or dope. But what happened next was definitely a lesson that it's best to listen when they warn you about not operating heavy machinery under the influence.

Mike was adjusting the weights in one of our cradles and testing the new rope. Everything was running just as it should. We took most of the ingots off the cradle we were working with, so that it weighed about 150 pounds, suspended by our pulley system high above the stage. Mike stood below, the rope wrapped around his wrist.

Mike was a strong guy; he could easily take the 150 pounds. However, in his half-cut haze, he had got careless. He had overlooked the fact that the cradle we were using was also roped up to another, fully loaded cradle. So when Mike kicked off the brakes thinking he was going to feel the pull of 150 pounds, what he actually felt was closer to 1,150 pounds.

To our horror, Mike shot straight up towards the ceiling, his wrist still wrapped in the Manila rope. He looked like Superman, one arm stretched in front of him, rocketing into the air.

He smacked straight into a concrete gantry about 40 feet above the stage. The impact tore his arm loose from the rope and he plummeted back down, crashing into the guardrail that ran around the edge of the stage. The impact put a huge bend in the iron bar at the top of the rail.

As I watched Mike fall through the air and strike that metal bar, there was no doubt in my mind that he was going to die. It was one of those moments in which you are aware that you are seeing something occur, but it seems absolutely, cartoonishly, unreal. There was a split second of silent shock, followed by panicked activity as people sprinted to call an ambulance.

But Mike didn't die. By some miracle there was a pile of empty boxes just where his head landed, breaking his fall and certainly saving his life. He hit the rail with his shoulder, shattering several bones. If he had landed inches to either one side or the other, his spinal chord would have snapped like a matchstick, leaving him paralysed.

Likewise, if Mike hadn't hit that gantry on the way up, he would have gone straight up to the ceiling, over 60 feet in the air. There would have been no surviving that. All things considered, he was unbelievably lucky to come away with two weeks in intensive care, followed by several months of recovery in hospital. Who knows, perhaps all that booze made him more relaxed on impact, cushioning the blow?

Even when he could walk again, Mike was never quite the same. It wasn't just that his arm never fully recovered. He had done some soul-searching in that hospital bed. Understandably, he was looking for a quieter life. There was never really a question of him coming back to work at the Academy.

I was immensely sorry to see him go. Mike was fantastic: a true eccentric and, in those early days of the Academy, the most knowledgeable guy around about the ins and outs of the music biz. He was one of the first people to really get what I was trying to do, and was always ready to muck in and get things done, even if he was often three sheets to the wind while doing so.

Mike's Superman impression became something of a backstage legend amongst the roadies and techs of London's live music industry. We never changed that guardrail, and the bend he put in it was forever known as 'the Mike Henley Dent'. I don't know if the current venue owners have now replaced it. Part of me hopes that little bit of Academy history is still there, as a testament to the great Mike Henley, and his drunken moment as the human birdman.

WHEN THE GOING GETS TOUGH

Even up to his last day with us, Mike was coming up with good ideas. The more I thought about it, the more his thought of offering the Academy during the day for production rehearsals seemed to make sense.

When huge groups go on their stadium tours, it's not just the four blokes in the band that need to get their chops together. There is a huge production team of soundmen, lighting guys, riggers, and roadies who all need to know exactly what they're doing. I am always amazed by the discipline and efficiency with which a high-quality, experienced road crew can operate. Anyone who ever caricatures roadies as the slow-witted oafs of the music business doesn't know what they're talking about. They may sometimes look like Neanderthals, but when those guys pack down a stage, and load up the trucks, they know down to the inch how to position each flight case to save space and time. It's always impressive to watch a well-drilled production team at work: to see how they are able constantly to think on their feet, finding solutions for all the wildly unexpected problems that rock 'n' roll touring always throws in your path.

That level of professionalism takes practice. In those days bands would usually rent out huge film studios like Pinewood for their production rehearsals. No venue had a stage big enough to simulate adequately an American stadium show.

But we did.

Johnny and I started putting out feelers to the industry, and the response was incredible. While bands' agents might have been too stuck in their ways to countenance the idea of their little darlings playing gigs in Brixton, their managers were more than happy to save themselves a load of money on rehearsals. I was only paying £50 a week rent; I could afford to undercut anyone else on a per-day rehearsal rate.

Before we knew it, we had The Police and AC/DC booked in for weeks at a time. It was fantastic, like having your own private concert in your living room. And it was also fascinating to see these mega rock stars in their own element, getting on with work, without the glitz and hangers-on of the big concerts. With The Police, it was a show in itself just to stand in the wings and listen to the bickering between the ever-charming but fiery Stuart Copeland and the icy aloof Sting, with the poor guitarist Andy Summers constantly caught in the middle as peacemaker.

Obviously, a group like The Police were far too big for us to try to book for a show. Like The Clash, they may have been influenced by reggae in their early days, but as a band their ethos was diametrically opposed to that of Joe Strummer and Mick Jones. Sting & Co. sold out stadium shows for 80,000 people, and their steely manager, Stuart's brother Miles Copeland, wasn't known for letting his talent play below their earning capacity.

As I always suspected, however, as soon as musicians stepped onto that stage, they immediately recognized how unique and special it was. And as Mike Henley had predicted, the road crews loved the convenience of our set-up. People started to talk.

Thanks to those rehearsals, word began to spread about us within the industry. Tour managers began to know the name Brixton Academy. Renting the venue for practices and video shoots became part of the lifeblood of running the Academy, right up through the 90s. Perhaps most important, it meant that I could speak directly to bands themselves, without constantly having to go through their agents.

I remember the first day of a week-long rehearsal booking we had for Page and Plant. I was desperate for them to play an Academy show. I thought if we could get the main guys from Led Zeppelin to play Brixton, then surely the other classic rock bands would have to follow suit. So that morning I spied an older roadie leaning on the bar smoking a roll-up cigarette. I sidled up to him and asked under my breath, 'Hey mate, listen, sorry to bother you, but do you know Robert Plant? Would you mind introducing me?'

The old guy raised his eyebrows. I was sure he looked unimpressed because he had probably been asked these same questions countless times before, though probably by overexcited schoolgirls, not hungover venue owners.

'Yeah, I actually know Robert quite well. I'll see what I can do.' We chatted a bit, then he stubbed out his cigarette and wandered off.

It was only when the band started rehearsing that I looked up at the stage and froze in my tracks. That was no roadie, it was Robert bloody Plant himself.

I must have been somewhat charming though, or perhaps the Academy just worked its usual magic, as Page and Plant did come and play a smashing gig with us not long after. And Plant was totally cool, laughing off my faux pas without a hint of rock-star divadom.

It's always nice when big stars turn out to be decent guys. When Dire Straits came in to rehearse, it was a pleasure to watch how straightforward and unassuming the two Knopfler brothers were, as they figured out who should stand where for which solo.

Likewise, Eric Clapton became one of our stalwarts. He had this souped-up Ferrari, with so much invested in its sound system that he had basically turned it into the world's fastest tape machine. We would open up the back gates so he could drive it straight in. You didn't want to be parking that little gem on the Stockwell Road.

There was no bullshit with Eric. He was always a straight shooter. There was an old-school greasy-spoon café across the street called Pete's. The security guys and I used to walk over for big English breakfasts. We called it Poison Pete's, as eating there always felt a bit like playing gastric Russian roulette. Clapton loved it. Every day he'd park the Ferrari, do a few hours' rehearsal, then saunter out for some egg and chips and a flip through the papers. It was great to watch all these builders and truckers just going, 'Morning Eric': totally cool, no big deal. Eventually Poison Pete couldn't resist asking for a photo for the café wall, and Clapton gracefully obliged.

My own favourite Clapton moment was when he did his celebrated annual 24-date stints at the Albert Hall. All these amazing guest musicians would get invited to take part, and most of them turned up at the Academy for the rehearsals. I sat up on the balcony on my own, watching guys like George Harrison, Carlos Santana, and Muddy Waters jamming with this incredible top-of-the-line band. It was mesmerizing.

These rehearsals also represented an opportunity for me to learn about how the Academy's sound functioned. Having been originally built as an Atmospheric Cinema, the auditorium was designed for the unamplified acts that would accompany the movies. The acoustics are absolutely extraordinary. When the space is empty, two people having a normal, speech-level conversation onstage will be audible at the sound desk, all the way at the back of the room. Johnny and I used to play a game, trying to count the echoes one got from a single clap; we lost track at 32.

When used correctly, the space has a wonderful and unique acoustic potential. The trick was always to convince people to use it correctly. The Academy itself doesn't have its own PA system. Every gig has different requirements, so each act brings in their own. I was forever labouring to disabuse both bands and sound crews of the erroneous assumption that huge stacks of speakers and amplifiers added inches to their genitalia. At the Academy, less is more. Play too loud, and you'll get a boomy mess. Much better to turn your amp down and let the venue do the work.

The only real problem with those early daytime sessions is that they were bloody cold. In those days there was no heating system at the Academy, and we used to lug around huge industrial blow heaters. But when there were people in the building we weren't allowed to use gas. So, on a gig day, we'd have the heaters on during the day, then wheel them outside when the concert started, relying on the punters jumping around to generate enough heat to keep themselves warm.

Of course, when we had rehearsals during the day we couldn't use the gas heaters, and there weren't any music fans to use as a central heating system. It was freezing. I remember Eric Clapton playing guitar with fingerless gloves, and seeing Angus Young's breath as he sang with AC/DC.

But I knew the musicians would warm up when they started playing. They could handle it. The only time I really worried was when we hired out the Academy for filming the video to Billy Ocean's song 'When the Going Gets Tough, the Tough Get Going'. The tune was meant for the soundtrack of the film *Jewel of the Nile*, and the movie's three stars flew over to appear in it. So there we were, with Michael Douglas, Kathleen Turner, and Danny DeVito on stage, and the temperature a steady zero all day. These guys were the absolute apex of the Hollywood A-list at the time, used to LA sun and glamorous Tinsel Town pampering. As I watched them pull up in their big, chauffeur-driven cars, I had no idea how they would react to shooting in a freezing, empty venue in south London.

In the end they were absolute professionals, and we made a really fun day of it. As I watched them miming along to the song, and messing about on stage, it made me wonder angrily how I could have three of the biggest movie stars in the world in my venue, all having a great time, but still be struggling to convince agents to let their bands play in Brixton.

The video was a huge smash in America, getting massive airplay on MTV, and making Billy Ocean the first black British artist to top the US charts. I, of course, had high hopes that the clip's success would help to spread the word about the Academy.

But nobody in Britain ever got to see it.

Halfway through the video, Danny DeVito grabs a saxophone and mimes along to the solo, as if swept up in some John Coltranesque surge of musical ecstasy. This was a wonderful flash of impromptu, spur-of-the-moment comedy. It was totally unexpected, and we were all in hysterics as we watched him go for it, spinning around the stage like a dervish, holding a sax about three-quarters his own size. He only pulled the gag once, as a joke, but it was a fantastic moment, and I was really pleased that it made the final cut.

The British Musicians' Union, however, in their omniscient wisdom claimed that, as the video showed a non-union member playing an instrument, it could not be shown on UK television. DeVito was only miming. It was hardly as if he was threatening the livelihoods of British sax players. It sounds ludicrous now, but the ban was upheld and the video was never shown in the UK. Those were the 80s; it was a different world in many ways.

In the end though, it was exactly that 80s cultural environment, and those particular political conflicts, that were to help me break down the walls of the music establishment and turn the Academy into the institution it became.

STRIKE!

In 1984 Britain was paralysed. At times during that year, the country seemed genuinely to teeter on the edge of major upheaval, if not outright civil war. All those social, economic, and political divides that were tearing the nation apart seemed to find their expression in one generation-defining conflict: the miners' strike.

In pursuit of her 'new Britain' of free-market, consumer-driven prosperity, Margaret Thatcher had announced plans to close twenty unprofitable coal mines, with the loss of twenty thousand jobs across Scotland, Wales, and northern England. The National Union of Miners, led by their beloved firebrand Arthur Scargill, downed tools and went on strike in protest. The industrial action polarized the country, becoming a year-long showdown between the left and the right, the old and the new, and very much between the two central figures of the era: prime minister Margaret Thatcher and the NUM leader Arthur Scargill.

At first things went well for the miners. Much of the country rallied behind them, responding to the message of livelihoods lost and communities destroyed. But Thatcher's Conservatives had prepared for this battle. They were not going to fold in the face of industrial action as previous governments had. Before the strike had even started, the authorities began stockpiling coal, converting power stations to oil, and chartering hauliers. The picketers failed to bring the country to a standstill, and after the infamous 'battle of Orgreave', at which thousands of miners and police brutally clashed in South Yorkshire, events began to go against the miners.

As the year dragged on, conditions began to bite. Soup kitchens and clothes drives became a fixture of life in the North as the union struggled to keep the fight going.

So, as Christmas approached, Scargill decided to put on a big benefit show to raise money for the families, particularly the children, of his striking miners. The Clash, true as ever to their political commitments, agreed to do three consecutive nights in support of the cause.

The established venues such as the Albert Hall and the Hammersmith Odeon wouldn't touch this gig with a ten-metre pick handle. The last thing they wanted was several thousand angry, hyped-up miners led by, horror of horrors, a *punk band*. They were afraid their dainty seats might get broken.

The Academy, on the other hand, was made for this kind of thing. We had already had The Clash down once before, and Brixton was just the area for people to rise to the message of the event. And I personally wanted to help. I felt a lot of sympathy for the miners in their struggle. These were the guys I played rugby with as a kid. I came from a wealthy family, but I knew those communities they were trying to save.

When the call came in I offered the venue for free. We booked Arthur Scargill's Christmas Party, with three nights of The Clash headlining.

To be honest, we were also desperate for the bookings. Though we were still struggling on with the reggae gigs and the production rehearsals, which kept us ticking over, the rock gigs we really needed to make the venue grow were still few and far between.

One of the few we had actually managed to get, in October that year, was a left-field Irish band with a decent cult following. I had never heard of them, but I remember thinking they had hands-down the worst band name in the history of pop. But when U2 took the stage, my god did they blow me away. Bono hadn't yet mutated into the odd creature that he would become, and gave a stunningly honest and passionate performance. After the concert I followed open-jawed as thousands of euphoric fans poured out onto the Brixton streets, all singing 'Pride in the Name of Love' in unison all the way up to Brixton station.

U2 were a strange case. Over the following years I would see countless bands play their 'first big gig' at the Academy. It became the place where artists came to prove themselves in a higher league. For U2, it wasn't their first big gig; it was their last 'small' one. This was the *Unforgettable Fire* tour. From that moment they leapfrogged the 10,000–15,000 seat auditoriums and went straight to the stadiums. It was amazing to watch as they exploded across the USA with *The Joshua Tree*, sweeping all before them like a conquering army. It's rare for bands to make the jump to megastardom that quickly, but it was obvious to me from that show at the Academy that there were the seeds of something special in this band.

At the time, we got U2 because they were Irish and, like me, didn't carry any prejudices about which areas of London were acceptable for gigs. The British rock bands, and the English agents who controlled the American bands, always the real prize, still didn't want to know about Brixton.

Then The Clash stormed back to the Academy for Scargill's Christmas bash. For three nights the venue was full of tough, rowdy Northern miners, venting all the pent-up anger and frustration of the past year. Things got wild. Pat and his security team had their hands full holding the place together. No wonder those wimpy, established venues had chickened out of these shows. Once again, though, the gigs were amazing. There is something uniquely special about leading a beautiful woman up onto the proscenium arch of the Brixton Academy, high over the crowd just as they're going crazy for one of the greatest bands of all time, and knowing that no one can see what you get up to because of the glare of the stage lights. As Christmas parties go, I highly recommend it.

We finished that three-night run with a sense that, not only had we pulled off an amazing series of gigs, but that we were a part of something bigger happening around us. I began to feel that the ice might be breaking, that something in the national mood needed expression, and it seemed we were the only ones who could provide the space for it. We ended 1984 with a fantastic, attitude-heavy concert by Lou Reed. I took this as a further good omen. It's another one of those cast-iron laws of rock 'n' roll that whatever Lou Reed does, everyone else will probably be doing within two years, and usually on a more commercial scale. As I watched the great rock pioneer sleaze his way through classics like 'Sweet Jane' and 'Walk On The Wild Side', I thought to myself, If we've had The Clash *and* Lou Reed here, surely the others have to come.

And come they did. It took a little time, but people were about to get the message.

There is a common myth that rock 'n' roll is full to the gills with free spirits and independent thinkers, each blazing their own brilliant, nonconformist trail through the drudge of everyday convention. Don't you believe it. The music scene, both the bands themselves and the industry guys in particular, operates on the same trend-based, herd mentality as every other business. They see someone doing something cool; they want a piece of the action too.

All of which worked out fantastically for us in the mid 80s.

The Clash gigs with Arthur Scargill made a huge splash, generating a wave of publicity. It seemed that as soon as The Clash had graced our stage for the miners, not only every other punk band suddenly wanted to play down in Brixton, but every right-on cause and charity in Britain was queuing up to do fundraisers at the Academy.

It started with another miners' benefit show, this time organized by Roddy Frame and Aztec Camera. Fellow Glaswegians Orange Juice were also playing for free, along with English pop sophisticates Everything but the Girl, and a fun local skiffle-punk fusion band called The Wooden Tops.

The evening started off well. I was amazed at how popular the event seemed to be. These bands were all doing well, but none of them were massive on anywhere near the level of The Clash. Yet the venue was filling up fast, the queues outside stretched around the block, and people still kept on coming.

Our guys on the door were clicking people through and keeping a tab on the numbers. Their counters passed 3,000; then 3,500; then 4,000. As we approached our capacity of 5,000, there were still hundreds of people all clutching tickets, waiting to get in. What was going on?

Pat took me aside. 'Boss, I reckon some mug's gone and done a load of counterfeit tickets. It's the only explanation.'

What kind of bastard floods the market with counterfeit tickets to a benefit concert?

But as Pat said, it was the only explanation.

So I was faced with a dilemma. Do I start turning people away, though many of them must have bought legitimate tickets? Even the guys with fakes would have purchased them in good faith. It was a big risk. If anything nasty happened that evening, if someone got injured and I was found to be over capacity, I would be in a lot of trouble. Should I stick to the rules, or take the chance for a great gig?

I thought of how I had watched Roddy Frame and his crew running around frantically all day; all the work they had done to put this together. It also crossed my mind that the last thing the Academy needed, just as it was beginning to get a reputation as a hip, anti-authoritarian venue, was to send a thousand music fans back off into the night, though they had actually bought tickets and travelled all the way down to Brixton. I thought of how I would feel had I turned up to a show and queued for forty-five minutes, only to be turned away because of health and safety rules. It also flashed through my mind that this was exactly the type of thing Rank would do at the Odeon. That sealed it for me. I gave Pat the nod to keep letting people in. It certainly got crowded in the Academy that night, but it made for a great atmosphere.

Then, as I walked around backstage, I saw the four bands all gathered around, engaged in what sounded like a blazing row. I moved closer to investigate.

There were all these booming Scottish voices shouting, 'Well we're no' goin' on first, we've organized the whole blinking thing.'

Only to be countered by a south London drawl: 'Well you can fucking fuck off, coz we're not fuckin' doin' it.'

This was hilarious. For a bunch of supposedly rebellious, anti-establishment rockers, they all seemed incredibly preoccupied with hierarchy and pecking order. No one was willing to go on first!

I motioned Johnny over; we stood back silently, watching the sparks fly and trying not to wet ourselves.

Eventually Edwyn Collins of Orange Juice, who I thought were probably the most exciting band performing that night, stepped up and broke the deadlock. His lot would take the opening slot. This seemed to soothe the other egos in the room sufficiently.

Orange Juice took the stage to rapturous applause from the greatly swollen audience. They performed a fantastic set, then, just as they were coming to a close, Edwyn stepped up to the microphone and announced that this would be the band's last ever show.

It came out of nowhere, and hit the audience like a thunderbolt. Without giving the news time to sink in properly, Edwyn launched into a beautiful version of Kevin Johnson's 'Rock 'n' Roll, I Gave You the Best Years of My Life'. I was standing in the wings of the stage watching as big no-nonsense Scottish post-punk fans, all dressed in the uniform Doc Martens boots and plaid shirts, openly blubbered in floods of tears.

That wouldn't be the last time an iconic band would announce their split from the Academy stage, but I remembered the special atmosphere of that night years later, when I heard the news that Edwyn Collins had suffered a massive stroke and was having to learn how to speak, sing, and play guitar all over again. The generosity with which he stepped into that petty, diva-ish argument over running order had made a big impression on me. He seemed like a genuinely decent guy, and you don't meet a lot of those in the music business.

It was great when Edwyn recovered enough to release another record, and in 2010 I heard he even came back onstage at the Academy with The Maccabees to do a version of Orange Juice's big hit 'Rip It Up' – returning to the stage where his band had last performed that song twenty-five years earlier.

The punk and post-punk bands kept on coming. We were becoming the favoured venue for groups that wanted to prove to the world, and perhaps to themselves, that they were a bit edgy and out of the

Paul Weller with
Style Council, playing
for Nicaragua

mainstream. At the same time, we had every major leftist movement and radical cause knocking on our door, further cementing
our anti-establishment image.

As a venue operator, the problem with doing benefit concerts is
that everyone wants your place for free, and I am not so stonehearted
as to take money out of the pockets of striking miners, or African
orphans. But thankfully for us, righting the wrongs of the world
and protesting against free-market reforms are thirsty work. Our
bar take on these nights was usually very healthy, making them
just about financially viable for us.

Over the years we had everyone through the Academy for one
charity or another. I was thrilled when Paul Weller brought Style

Council down and did an absolutely stunning show as part of a benefit for Nicaragua. I had always loved The Jam, but that night Style Council had such a playful confidence in their songwriting and their performance that they totally won me over. I was even more blown away when Pete Townsend of The Who came down for a charity show, and invited David Gilmour of Pink Floyd onstage for a jam.

Perhaps inevitably, the growing buzz about the Academy led to my first real disappointment in one of our gigs. I had been so excited when we booked The Smiths. I always thought of them as one of the truly original voices in British music. But when they actually came to play, the band was so riven with internal tensions that its members were barely speaking to each other. It was impossible to hide this animosity and emotional distance onstage, and the performance seemed to lack any real joy or defiance.

Johny Marr and the boys more than made up for it a few months later, though. The Smiths came back for a second Academy show,

'Morrissey at his best, as a mercurial, prancing dandy'

this time with Artists against Apartheid. We were heavily involved with AAA, who had already done a storming gig with Madness a few months earlier, and this performance could not have been more different from the last. Morrissey was at his best as a mercurial, prancing dandy, spitting razor-sharp banter with the crowd. The band also seemed in high spirits, as if they were all in on some kind of joke that the rest of us didn't get. During the encores there was the obligatory stage invasion, and, as fifty or so people danced onstage for the last song, the band tore through a version of their first ever single, 'Hand in Glove'. That song ends with the line 'I'll probably never see you again'. No one listening that night in 1986 could have known just how apt a show-closer that would be. It was the last gig The Smiths ever played.

MEN OF THE PEOPLE

It wasn't just the benefit concerts that kept the Academy full of activists and fellow travellers in this era. We began to host regular meetings and conferences for many of the trade unions and political movements involved in the key disputes of the day.

The printworkers' union SOGAT, in particular, became a regular fixture at the venue. They would bus in thousands of workers and union reps from all over the country for massive rallies and ballots. It was a very different vibe to hear the Academy filled with the sound of rabble-rousing political speeches rather than AC/DC rehearsing, or Desmond Dekker jamming with his band.

I watched over time as the SOGAT crowd grew progressively more militant in the lead-up to their showdown with Rupert Murdoch in the winter of 1985–86. From one assembly to the next, their gatherings came to feel more and more like wartime strategy sessions, or morale-boosting rallies for troops about to go to the front. An atmosphere of paranoia and suspicion became pervasive, as the hardcore union stalwarts grew convinced that they were being infiltrated by shadowy agents of the Murdoch Empire. Our security guys would regularly have to face off with burly union reps over who would control the flow of people around the building. Even I started getting trouble: 'Oi mate, you're not allowed in there. A closed meeting's still in progress.'

'Sorry *mate*, it's my venue, and I'll go where I damn well please.'

During one particularly impassioned harangue on the evils of the capitalist system, a shout went up from a section of the crowd, 'Journo, journo!'

It seems a very young Mark Mardell had snuck into the meeting undercover to report on the dispute for Independent Radio News. His tape recorder had been spotted, and he now found himself surrounded by an increasingly furious mob baying for blood.

My team and I were genuinely worried that some of the more 'direct action' SOGAT types were going to take him around the back of the building and make an example of him. It was only when Brenda Dean, the steely but softly spoken head of the union, intervened, giving assurances that he was a 'friendly journalist', that the bloodlust abated. Mardell was ejected from the building, obviously relieved to be still in one piece, and went on to become the BBC's chief political correspondent.

Though these celebrated causes kept the Academy growing over this period, and definitely helped enhance our underground street cred, my personal exposure to many in their leadership made me increasingly wary of both their motives and their methods.

I got a real shock when I was taken to lunch at Scott's Fish Restaurant in Mayfair by an old schoolfriend. As we approached I noticed a line of very fancy cars lined up by the entrance: Jaguar, Mercedes-Benz, all the high-end brands. Being Mayfair, I assumed there was some foreign potentate, or financial 'master of the universe', out for a meal with their cohorts. Imagine my shock when I saw Arthur Scargill himself, with a load of other guys I recognized from our charity events at the Academy, all at some union AGM or banquet, chomping cigars and swigging down glasses of brandy. All those grand cars outside belonged to these self-professed 'men of the people'.

It was one thing to be taken out to lunch at a place like this by a mate who had made a pile of money in the City, but I was absolutely horrified to see these guys blowing at least £300 each for a meal on the union dime. Only months before we had been giving them the Academy for free to raise money for hungry miners and their families up in Yorkshire.

I witnessed the same kind of hypocrisy at some of our big union rallies.

1985–6 witnessed fierce conflicts between British central government and local councils, as Whitehall forced through savage cuts in public spending. As an act of protest, several of the more radical councils refused to submit workable annual budgets. These extreme elements were spearheaded by Derek Hatton up in Liverpool, and Brixton's own Lambeth Council, run by 'Red Ted' Knight and Linda Bellos.

Naturally, this lot found common cause with SOGAT in its fight with Rupert Murdoch. They would frequently come down to address the union brothers in solidarity. 'Red Ted' in particular, being just up the road from us, became a regular face at the Academy.

I sat up at the back of the balcony and listened to these guys speak very openly about how they planned to target the cuts specifically at youth centres, employment agencies, and other services for young people. Their idea was to create such disaffection amongst the already angry youth of the country's most deprived areas that the ensuing riots would, in their words, 'bring down this Tory regime'.

I was amazed at how crude and plainspoken they were about their intentions. I also couldn't help thinking, what a bunch of bastards. I was shocked that people like this, who claimed to care so much for the working classes, could be so intent on creating trouble for Thatcher that they would enforce deliberate misery on the poor themselves.

I had got to know a lot of young guys off the estates around Brixton. They were the faces at our reggae gigs; they worked for us as runners and box office staff. I didn't want them put under any extra pressure, and I certainly didn't want them turned into cannon fodder to achieve some self-styled leaders' political agenda. But these councillors' only concern was sticking one in the eye of Thatcher, and they were willing to sacrifice the wellbeing of the very people that trusted them in order to do so.

I felt this was a deeply shabby display. Especially when I witnessed the fruits of their efforts a few months later.

On 28 September 1985 I was attending the wedding of another old Gordonstoun friend. The reception was at the Belfry Club in Belgravia: the lacquered mahogany, officious waiting staff, and starched white tablecloths, another world from the grit and hustle of Brixton High Street.

In the midst of the usual wedding small talk, one guest's girlfriend, who worked as a nurse, came rushing in, breathlessly excusing herself for being late. Apparently her A&E ward was overrun with casualties from major riots going on in Brixton.

Those were the words I'd been dreading since I first started the Academy.

The 1981 riots in Brixton had scarred the area for years: both physically, with burned buildings and ruined businesses, and also by further enhancing Brixton's reputation as a lawless, menacing netherworld.

Obviously, I was terrified that someone would attack the Academy. But I was also thinking that the last thing we needed, just as the venue seemed to be taking off, was another round of sensationalist reports in the media that would scare off white concert audiences for another five years.

I made my excuses, slipped out the back, and hightailed it back to Brixton.

I was greeted with a scene of devastation. The corner of Stockwell Road where the Academy sits was right at the centre of the action. Glass from shattered windows covered the pavements; overturned and burning cars blocked the roads. Gangs of Brixton youths were darting from doorway to doorway, as lines of police advanced and then retreated under barrages of bricks and bottles.

Coming from that posh wedding in Belgravia, I was picking my way through this mayhem still wearing my coat and tails, with a top hat. The 'stylish kid in the riot', indeed! I must have cut a pretty surreal figure as I pushed my way through the broken glass and angry mobs and slipped in through the back door of the Academy.

Pat was already waiting for me. We went straight into action, reinforcing the doors with heavy chains, and moving up all our extra fire extinguishers to the foyer.

Right outside our door the situation was developing into a full-scale street war. Directly across the street from the Academy sits a building called Blue Star House. Nowadays it houses a fast-food chicken outlet and a sports clothing store. Back in the 80s, though, it was the Blue Star Petrol Station. This spot became the central battleground of the riots. Gangs of kids would fill up bottles at the petrol pumps, light them up, and hurl them at the police, who were arranged in a line further up the road. The cops would then charge forwards, and the kids would race around the two sides of the Academy and down Astoria Walk, to disappear into the Stockwell Park Estate.

This went on for hours. We stood guard in the foyer, surrounded by the sounds of smashing glass, screams, and police sirens, along with the acrid smell of burning petrol. At times the battle seemed to calm down, only to flare up again a few hours later. It was impossible for us to know exactly what was going on. Pat and I just stood in the foyer, with a couple of our guys holding baseball bats, ready to defend the building, or put out any fire started by an errant Molotov cocktail.

During one lull in the fighting I went outside to survey the damage. It was pretty horrific to witness what one day of violence can do to an area. Only the evening before, Brixton High Street had been its usual bustling self. Now it looked like downtown Beirut.

I spotted a lone policeman standing on the corner, separated from the rest of his group, looking lost and bewildered. I took pity on the guy, walked over, and asked if I could help. He responded by stabbing me hard in the chest with his truncheon and shouting at me to 'Step away'.

I staggered back to the Academy, completely winded and a bit pissed off. I know that cop must have been stressed and under pressure, but was a one-armed guy wearing a penguin suit and top hat really such a threat? It seemed indicative of the generally heavy-handed, overpowering approach that the police took in Brixton at the time. And if that's what I got, how much worse must it have been for the local kids? What did the authorities think created the explosions of anger we were witnessing? The results of these police tactics were equally clear the following week when Broadwater in Tottenham, in north London, erupted in similar violence.

On the other hand, as I looked over the wreckage the following day, when things had died down, I couldn't help but think of the speeches I had heard from Red Ted and his crowd. They wanted, and to my mind deliberately engineered, a riot to cause problems for the government. What they got was misery and destruction for the local community. Rumours were rife around the area that many of the rioters had been directed by outsiders carrying fancy Motorola radios. I never saw anything like that, but it added to the sense of confusion and resentment around Brixton. People on the street felt they were being used and ignored by leaders on both sides of the political divide.

As it happened though, the 1985 riots did not tarnish Brixton the way the 1981 riots had. Music fans had started to enjoy the edgy atmosphere of the Academy, and they kept on coming. If anything, a bit of civil conflict only added to our growing rebel chic. Or perhaps we were just starting to book better gigs.

MAGGIE MAY

Another irony of this period was that, just as I was keeping the Academy going with Arthur Scargill, SOGAT, and The Clash, I ended up having lunch with Margaret Thatcher.

Since we had opened, I had been trying to position the Academy as a force for the regeneration of the area. I had always hoped that the local council would see the obvious potential and give me some support. I had had some success with projects like bringing over Fela Kuti from Lagos, but what I really needed was help with repairs on the building itself. I could only keep patching it up for so long, and there was a Schedule of Works that I would have to fulfil over the next couple of years to keep the venue operating with a licence.

In my search for grant money and support, I had become part of a scheme aimed at young London entrepreneurs called LENTA. Through them, an event was arranged where a group of us would get a sit-down meeting with Mrs Thatcher.

I thought this could be my ticket to finally leverage some real financial support for the Academy. Surely after all the unrest, a Conservative government would want to be seen to be doing something good for Brixton? At the time we really were the best thing going in terms of community cohesion and regeneration. Thus far, I had received a pretty lacklustre response from the council and all the various agencies I had approached. I thought that if I could get the prime minister onside, I'd finally be in with a shot. Why not go in with some friends right at the top?

Now, I've met some impressive characters in my life. I've done tequila shots with Keith Richards and passed joints with Dr Dre. Through family and school, I've met the entire British royal family several times over. But no one I've met, no rock star or heavy Brixton mobster, has ever come close to Margaret Thatcher in terms of sheer command of a room. She had an aura of absolute power and assurance.

We were ushered into a small, plain meeting room and sat around a pile of sandwiches on a plastic table. Rather more modest than Arthur Scargill's lunch with his cronies at Scott's of Mayfair, I couldn't help wryly noting to myself.

Then the Iron Lady herself swept in, flanked by two aides. She sat down and looked over the lunch spread on the table. Without a word to the young entrepreneurs all gazing at her expectantly, she turned to the organizer of the event and snapped, 'What's this?'

'It's lunch, ma'am,' the guy stammered. 'It's sandwiches, as we discussed with your staff.'

'I know what sandwiches are, thank you. What's this?' she asked again, pointing at the bottle of Perrier sparkling water which was standing on the table next to a stack of plastic cups.

'This is French water,' she continued, in a tone of implacable disdain. 'I'll have British water please.'

You should have seen the poor guy turn pale as the blood drained from his face. It was like a cartoon.

'Yes ma'am, I'm so sorry ma'am.' He almost tripped over himself as he forgot his carefully planned introductory speech and rushed to remove the offending Gallic water from the room, sprinting breathlessly back a few minutes later with a bottle of Highland Spring.

In the meantime the prime minister turned to survey our group. 'You must be Mr Parkes from Brixton,' she said, staring straight at me.

I have no idea how she knew who I was. I suppose someone must have told her to look out for the guy with one arm.

'Yes ma'am,' I replied, 'I run the Brixton Academy, the concert venue.'

I had the whole pitch perfectly arranged in my mind. I would keep things general, not get too bogged down in details, and concentrate on the Academy's employment and community-building potential for south London.

'Indeed. You have thirty-six load bars there, don't you?' asked Mrs Thatcher.

This took me completely by surprise. How the hell did she know about theatre load bars, let alone how many we had at the Academy?

'Yes ma'am, that's right, thirty-six,' I stuttered.

'Hmm, they must be very difficult to maintain? And such a large stage, one of the biggest in the country. Very impressive.'

'Yes ma'am. Thank you. We manage.' I grinned weakly.

'Well, jolly good for you. Keep up the good work,' smiled Mrs Thatcher, and promptly turned to the next member of our little group.

And that was that. I was stunned. My whole meticulously plotted pitch had gone up in smoke.

She proceeded to do exactly the same thing to each of the hopeful young businesspeople in the room. She would fire some question at them about the minute details of their project, and by the time they were finished answering, she was on to the next person. Everyone got their five seconds, but no one had the chance actually to ask her for anything. Pure politics. She made completely sure that everything was done unquestionably on her terms. I was in awe, watching a true operator at work.

I've never seen anyone walk into a meeting so well briefed. And our little group could hardly have been a key item on her agenda.

No wonder she ran rings around well-meaning but self-involved loudmouths like Scargill and 'Red Ted' Knight.

After a few minutes, Thatcher finished her spitfire round of questioning, and swept back out of the room. I assumed that it was all over, and that I had blown my big chance. Over the following weeks, however, a lovely guy named Alex Oldham from LENTA got in touch. He intimated that, in fact, the people that needed to be impressed had been impressed. A grant to help with works on the building might be possible.

The possibility was hugely exciting. We were surviving as a venue, but only just. There was no way, in our current situation, that I could even think about starting to repair the crumbling fabric of the building.

Over the next few weeks the discussions developed, and it started to look more and more likely that I would be able to access some community development funding.

Then my past caught up with me.

I walked into a meeting with some of the agency people we were in discussions with, to find another guy I'd never met before, waiting for me with a suit and a briefcase. He was very straight with me.

'I'm sorry, Mr Parkes, we won't be able to give you any financial assistance. If the press ever got hold of the fact that we were handing out funding to the grandson of Sir Basil Parkes of Boston Deep Sea Fisheries it would look very bad for us.'

I pleaded and remonstrated. Since my parents' divorce, I had barely even been on speaking terms with my father. The family certainly wasn't giving me any money, let alone helping with the Academy in any way. It made no odds. They wouldn't budge. The risk of some newspaper editor getting hold of this non-story was just too great. It was the birth of 'the age of spin' happening right in front of me.

I left that meeting bitterly disappointed. The double-edged sword of my family background was to become a constant hassle while running the Academy. I watched as far less worthy ventures got buckets of support from every government agency going, while we were left out in the cold. All because of my surname and the petty fears of local politicians.

Looking back, though, perhaps that's what gave our little team its energy and hustle. We needed to make things work on our own terms. People with no support have to get creative, think on their feet, and invent more unorthodox methods of getting by.

I hadn't even begun to discover just how unorthodox we could go.

PART TWO

THE GUNS
OF BRIXTON

WAR IN A BABYLON

Johnny Lawes had plans for us.

Since his trip to Birmingham to book UB40, he had been working to forge connections between the Academy and the underground players on the Brixton scene. His first move was to bring in the 12 Tribes of Israel Rastafari Collective.

There are three major sects, or Mansions, in the global Rastafari movement: the Niyabinghi, the Bobo Ashanti, and the 12 Tribes of Israel. Though the 12 Tribes have always been considered more liberal and inclusive than the others, back then it was still an uphill struggle to convince them to do business with a white guy.

Johnny set up a meeting between myself and a couple of 12 Tribes elders, including their local leader, Winston Crawley. It was immediately obvious that these weren't just some dudes with dreadlocks and a Bob Marley poster on the wall. These characters spoke more like priests or prophets: serious, deep Rastas who took their religion deadly seriously. They spoke to each other in a mixture of Bible quotations and Jamaican patois so thick I could barely understand it.

I held out my hand for Winston Crawley to shake. He left it hanging in the air, as he looked me up and down.

'Johnny, 'im say your name be Simon,' he said in a deep, gravelly voice.

Not a bad little double act: Johnny Lawes
and I cutting loose after a gig

'Yeah, I'm Simon Parkes, good to meet you.'

'Simon is from Simeon, second son of Jacob. You are of da Tribe of Simeon: *he who has heard God*. Do you understan' dis ting?'

'Umm, yeah ... for sure.' I'd been expecting music biz deal making, not a theology lecture, but this was pretty intriguing.

'All right Simeon, mebbe we want to make a gathering in disya Academy of yours.'

OK, this was more familiar ground. 'Great man, sounds like a cool party. Let's make it happen.'

Over the next few months I hung out with Winston and the 12 Tribes crew quite a bit. I grew to really like listening in on their intense biblical discussions, and the awesome dub records they constantly played. They were cool guys with some deep thoughts about the nature of freedom, materialism, and 'chanting down Babylon', which they would rehearse extensively after a few joints.

Even so, when the 12 Tribes eventually did their 'gathering' at the Academy it totally surpassed all my expectations. Rastafarians came from all over Europe. We had groups of guys in dreadlocks and flowing robes speaking in Dutch, French, and German, as well as the obligatory West Indian slang. The music was the hardest, heaviest dub I'd ever heard, with bass so deep you seemed to listen to it as much through the vibrations in the soles of your feet as through your ears. Needless to say, the ganja smoke was so thick it made the entire ceiling of the auditorium seem obscured by one huge internal cloud.

They were so happy with how the night went that we got invited to the after-party. So, once the venue was locked down, Johnny, his Rasta friend Naftali who had started working for us, and I all piled into a car and drove down to what appeared to be a deserted garage on a council estate somewhere in deepest south London.

The second we stepped through the door the conversation in the room suddenly stopped. Every eye in the place turned towards us.

This was a period of tense race relations in Britain. Amongst the 12 Tribes crowd any white guy was immediately under suspicion of being an undercover cop, or at least a spiritual agent of Babylon.

Mine was the only white face in the room. I could feel the tension rising with every second we stood there. I got very nervous and started preparing to back slowly out the door. It was only when Winston Crawley sauntered up and gave the three of us a warm greeting that everyone else visibly relaxed, and the party continued.

Gradually the evening seemed to become less of a relaxed after-party and to develop more into a Rastafari ritual. They brought out drums and started chanting while beating out loud, intricate polyrhythms. The ganja smoking switched from spliffs to the big traditional Jamaican pipes, or chalices.

If I thought the smoke had been intense earlier at the Academy, this was another level completely. I could barely see through the dense haze. It seemed to envelop everything so that the room became a blur of hands beating drums, swinging dreadlocks, and eyes made red from the weed. With every breath I took my lungs would fill with this hot, almost viscous smoke. I was getting absurdly high. But even as my mind was spinning, I felt privileged to be there: these rituals were something very few outsiders ever got to be part of.

Eventually someone packed a chalice for me and I took several long hits from the ceremonial pipe. I don't remember much after that. Johnny and Naftali must have pulled me down from the clouds and loaded me into the back of the car; my only recollection is lying on the back seat and watching the street lights flicker by as we sped through the south London night.

I got a sharper lesson in the fraught racial disharmonies of 1980s Britain when the return-to-Brixton comeback gig that Johnny had booked with UB40 finally rolled around. We were expecting a good party as the show fell on 31 October 1985: Halloween night in Brixton. UB40 were at the absolute peak of their popularity, and the support band, Simply Red, had just had their breakthrough hit with 'Money's Too Tight (To Mention)'. The ticket price for these two huge acts was £5: very different from the squeeze-all-the-money-you-can-out-of-the-punters mentality you get from the live music business these days.

The gig sold out very quickly, and the night itself was a fantastic, good-vibes knees-up. I was being extra solicitous towards UB40, trying to erase any bitterness from their previous experience of getting ripped off in Brixton. In the end they couldn't have been nicer guys about it, laughing it all off with Brummie stoicism and the world-weary gallows humour of music industry veterans.

The real learning experience was to come the next day.

Johnny and I had to get the bar take from the night's gig up to the bank before it shut at 3 p.m. You didn't want to leave £40,000 cash lying around the venue for too long. At the time some of my accounts were with the ultra-exclusive Coutts Bank, a hangover from my privileged schooldays.

Johnny and I were well used to making the run up to the bank in Pall Mall. We had a system. The bags of cash were loaded into the little green Metro van we used for flyposting; in the front, we each sat with baseball bats cradled between our legs. There was no way anyone would drive through Brixton carrying forty grand without some kind of protection. We knew the Academy was still being watched by the local hoods, and we had to be constantly on guard, in case anyone tried a heist while we moved our money around. It's just how business ran in south London in those days.

Our usual route was to go over Vauxhall Bridge and up the Mall towards the bank. On this morning there was a nasty-looking traffic jam up that way, so I turned the car around thinking we could avoid the snarl-up by heading through Lambeth and over Horseferry Road.

We took a shortcut down a little side street when I saw a white van starting to back out of a building. I beeped my horn and saw their brake lights flash red, so I began manoeuvring to try and get around them. Then, with no warning, the van backed out extremely quickly, pinning us against a parked car so that I couldn't open my door. I started hitting my horn like mad, angrily wondering where these crazy bastards learned to drive.

Then two men jumped out of the van and started running very

aggressively towards us, reaching into their back pockets. 'Oh fuck, it's a fucking robbery,' shouted Johnny. He grabbed his baseball bat and leaped out onto the road. My door was pinned shut, so with my pulse racing in panic, I had to scramble awkwardly over the passenger seat to join him.

What we didn't know was that this side street ran down the back of a police station. These two guys were plainclothes cops, but they produced no badges or warrant cards. All we saw were a couple of blokes sprinting towards us with obvious aggressive intent. And all they saw was a Rasta with a baseball bat and a wild-eyed guy with one arm yelling, 'Come and have a fucking go, then.' They shouted for help and within seconds there were about twenty more gung-ho officers in the alley, all hyped up for a fight.

Johnny and I were very quickly disarmed and slammed down on the bonnet of our car. My face was pressed hard onto the cold metal, my arm jammed violently behind my back. The police were ludicrously rough, giving us each a totally unnecessary kicking. We were both enraged and coursing with adrenalin, raging at them to fuck off and leave us alone. We had had no idea those first two guys from the van were cops; we were just trying to get to the bank.

The police shouted back at us to 'shut up and fucking stay still'. The word 'darky' started getting thrown around in Johnny's direction.

There was one funny moment when a cop tried to put cuffs on me, but couldn't quite figure out how to make it work with my one arm. 'Having a little trouble there, officer?' I giggled as he squirmed around, trying to figure out what to do. Then he killed any humour I saw in the situation by leaning in close and hissing in my ear, 'You shut your mouth, you fucking niggerlover.'

That snapped me out of my wild rage and into a very cold, hard form of anger. He had just turned this into something serious.

I went absolutely still, and put on my best public school accent. 'Excuse me sir, I regard that language as extremely offensive, and would like to speak to no one less than your Chief Inspector.'

I felt the guy tense up behind me. Maybe he had got this wrong?

Pulling this kind of posh boy act with cops is always a risk; they either soften up immediately or they'll give you an extra going-over just for being a toffee-nosed git. I felt the cop back away from me, but made an effort to turn and get a look at his face.

The police, of course, assumed we were drug dealers. They brought the dogs down and within seconds had discovered £40,000 cash in the back of our van. 'Well, well, going somewhere with all this money are you?' my anti-niggerloving cop asked, obviously fancying himself as some tough guy off *The Sweeney*.

'Yes, to the bank,' I replied coolly. 'Coutts of the Strand, actually. You'll find all the account books in the van. I'm the proprietor of

Good times with the gang: Johnny, Mark Oliver, Claire Hogan, Myself holding the champagne, and Naphtali

the Brixton Academy Theatre, this is our bar revenue from last night's performance.'

Dope dealers aren't known for volunteering their bankbooks, particularly not for accounts held at the branch where the Queen of England arranges her finances. I watched the guy's face fall as he felt his big bust disappearing before him.

Eventually we were approached by another cop with three stars on his epaulette. I knew from my dealings with Brixton police that this signified a ranking officer, exactly what I was looking for.

I managed to maintain my outraged public schoolboy act while trying to calm the situation down, explaining how 'there had been misunderstandings on both sides'. I made a point of how horrified I was by the blatantly racist language his officers had used.

Eventually the Chief came to understand what had occurred, and seemed genuinely embarrassed by his men's crudeness. He sent us on our way, and I'm sure was relieved to see the back of us.

We didn't have time to make much of a scene at that point: it was already 2:45p.m. If we missed the bank, I didn't relish the idea of having to drive £40,000 back into Brixton. But we weren't going to take this kind of nonsense lying down. What those cops didn't know was that Johnny Lawes's uncle happened to be the highest-ranking black civil servant in the Home Office. About three weeks later we received a grovelling letter of apology from the head of the police station for the 'offensive and unacceptable' behaviour of his officers during the incident.

That confrontation with the police was an eye-opener, but hanging out with Johnny became my real education in just how deep the racial divide in Britain was during this era.

I first came to Brixton with no knowledge or expectations about these issues. It sounds a bit naive, considering how aware people are nowadays, but up till that point I genuinely don't think I knew what racism was. Up in Lincolnshire when I was growing up there weren't any black people to be racist about. I think there was one Indian family in town that ran a takeaway, but that was about it, so racism was never even an issue. And, again, I was raised not to judge people on appearances, so that whole way of thinking was completely alien to me.

So when I got down to the rough and tumble south of the river, I found so many little incidents with Johnny completely shocking. Cabs wouldn't stop for us on the street; I would book a table at a restaurant for a meeting, but when Johnny walked in before me suddenly there would be no space. I remember one morning we came out of an appointment at a major government department in Millbank, trying to access some funding scheme or other. We were both suited and carrying briefcases, Johnny had his dreads tied back and looked dapper as can be. Every single cab in the line outside refused point blank to take him back to Brixton. I took down all their numbers and complained.

That mindset seemed ridiculous to me, but all my black friends would usually laugh at how angry I would get. They had grown so used to this kind of treatment, especially from the police. For them it was just a fact of life, and getting enraged about it was like complaining about the weather. During the 80s the cops had been given extraordinary stop-and-search powers in response to IRA terrorism. They tried to turn London into a ring of steel. Unsurprisingly, the police soon began pushing these powers way beyond their intended remit. When my black mates would try to drive over to north London at night, usually to get to some club in King's Cross or something, they would automatically allow extra time for the inevitable search, with all its attendant hassle and indignity. As a white guy, I never even had to think about things like this, and the injustice really pissed me off.

Even the music business at this time was riven with racial prejudice, though showbiz folk were usually more adept at hiding it than cab drivers on Brixton High Street. Eventually Johnny and I found a way to turn other people's prejudices to our advantage, and to have a good laugh doing so.

Though the record labels were more than happy to sell product by black artists all day long, the executives themselves were uniformly white and male. Even when so-called *urban* music took off, the big labels would usually have one black guy involved in their Urban Division, leaving the rest of the power structure lily white.

So Johnny and I learned to play with people a bit. I would book a meeting, and then he would walk in. Of course no one would ever actually say anything, but there was a lot of stuttering, 'Oh ... ummm ... uhh ... hello, are *you* Mr Parkes?' These little stunts immediately threw people off their stride at the start of a meeting, leaving them vulnerable, and enabling us to cut better deals. It was also very funny. Johnny and I used to walk out of meetings and break into hysterical laughter at other people's awkwardness.

It was considerably less amusing when I ended up on a neo-Nazi hit list.

I suppose hosting regular gigs for Artists Against Apartheid was never going to endear me to the lunatic fringes of Britain's far right. The trouble really kicked off a few years later when John Curd and I put on a punk all-dayer on the last Saturday of August, charmingly entitled Fuck Reading – a bit of underground competition to the increasingly commercialized Reading Festival.

On the bill for this day-long cider-fuelled melee was a band of south London punk stalwarts called The Business. These guys were veterans of the Oi! punk scene that emerged during the late 70s and 80s. They were very politically engaged, and had become extremely vocal in their opposition to the appropriation of punk music by the racist, National Front sub-sect of the skinhead movement.

This had earned them some nasty enemies. A few months before our mini-festival they had played a gig at a small venue in King's Cross called the Water Rats. The concert had been stormed by a crowd of hardcore white-power skinhead thugs who smashed up the venue and put several audience members in hospital.

In the weeks leading up to our all-day gig we began getting a suspicious amount of calls asking at what exact time The Business were due to play. So we put out some feelers and started picking up gossip from the street that various right-wing skinhead gangs were planning to infiltrate the show, and start a riot when The Business came on.

What to do? There was no question of The Business not playing; we would be damned if we were going to let a bunch of thick NF louts intimidate us. John and I came up with a very simple solution. We just started replying to the callers that The Business would be playing at 9p.m, while quietly switching their actual stage time to 4p.m.

So, when the day of the gig rolled around a load of these National Front guys turned up towards the evening, only to find they had missed the band they had come to sabotage. Without a cue as to when to start their riot they suddenly became less an organized militia and more just a couple of hundred racist idiots surrounded by five thousand equally hard ultra-left-wing skinheads, in the middle of the biggest West Indian community in Britain. They slunk back out into the night, only to be ambushed by a group of militant hard-arses from the Anti-Nazi League who gave them a savage kicking all the way up the Stockwell Road.

We thought it was done and dusted, and I felt quite pleased with the simple way we had outsmarted those creepy white-power tosspots. But a few weeks later I received a typewritten letter sent to my house from Combat 18 telling me I would be punished for 'sticking up for the niggers' and that I was a 'marked man'.

The '18' in Combat 18 stands for A and H, the first and eighth letters of the alphabet, and the initials of Adolph Hitler. Back in the day, this gang really were some of the nastiest pieces of work that one could come across. By this time at the Academy I was used to dealing with threats from some heavy characters, but the fact that this note arrived at my home address was genuinely concerning.

So the flak jacket went back on, and I drove home a bit more cautiously for a while, but those guys turned out to be as cowardly as all bullies really are, and they never made a move.

ANGER IS AN ENERGY

Iggy Pop gets into the crowd

Over 1986 and 1987 our gigs were getting cooler and cooler. From Iggy Pop to James Brown, the guys who I used to pay touts on the street to see were starting to come and play my venue. It was an amazing feeling.

And just as I had always known they would be, the gigs were incredible. There was something about this place, some strange magic that seemed to bring out the best in both performers and audience. I think it has a lot to do with the construction of the building itself. The sloping floor of the auditorium makes the hall seem much smaller than it really is. When you stand on that huge stage looking out, the optical illusion of that inclined floor makes the back wall of the Academy seem only about 20 metres away. This gives performers a very different vibe from that of other venues of this size. They get the feeling of intimacy that they might expect from a 1,500-capacity venue, but with the intensity of the collective energy of 5,000 people being focused back at them onstage. It's an explosive combination, and totally unique to the Academy.

The alchemy of any great gig comes from that special communication between the performer and the audience. The band transmits a vibe to the crowd, and it sends it straight back, pushing the artist to even greater heights. At its best this becomes a self-reinforcing spiral of energy that produces *once-in-a-lifetime* performances for the artist, and *nights-they'll-never-forget* for the audience. That's the whole trick. At the Academy we seemed to be able to create this energy in a special way. From the attitude-heavy drone rock of The Jesus and Mary Chain to the thumping electro of New Order and the relentless assault of Motörhead, so many bands did extraordinary shows with us in this era. I was particularly pleased with bagging Motörhead; *No Sleep 'til Hammersmith*, my arse – now even legends like Lemmy were ditching the Odeon and choosing to play in Brixton.

Occasionally though, this explosive energy feedback loop could become so intense that it span out of control.

I had really congratulated myself when Johnny and I managed to book Public Image Ltd. We'd done The Clash and their successor band Big Audio Dynamite, so the last big name in punk was the man himself, John Lydon. PiL were riding high at this point, they'd just released *Album* and had scored a genuine chart hit with the single 'Rise'. The main hook of that song is Lydon's brilliant chanted refrain 'anger is an energy'. That energy was certainly palpable the night PiL came to Brixton.

With their big hit, PiL had reached a whole new generation of fans, and the gig had sold out very fast. But right down at the front were a crowd of about three to four hundred hardcore, old-school punks who had come creeping out of the squats of Camden and Shepherd's Bush to greet their hero. To these guys the winter of 1977 had never ended. They still wore their original studded leathers, and came down with all the aggressive bad manners of punk's heyday. And that meant spitting.

As the gig progressed these guys down at the front kept on gobbing all over the stage, and all over the band. Lydon, who had had ten years of this nonsense, was covered in spit, and was getting pissed off. He responded in his own uniquely diplomatic way, by repeatedly calling the audience 'a bunch of cunts'. This only worsened the spitting, which soon expanded into people hurling any available missile at the man on stage with the oversize suit and the orange hair.

John Lydon is a very smart guy, and has never been shy about expressing himself when annoyed. He went on the attack, dancing around the stage and baiting the crowd with sharp, witty insults. The gang of punks at the front burst into full ruckus-mode and surged forward, thinking that if they couldn't get to Lydon, they could at least have a crack at our security guys.

Pat's team of bouncers were hardly shrinking violets themselves, and gave as good as they got; but there were 15 of them, facing about 400 juiced-up punks looking for a fight. It exploded into a full-scale riot, a disordered amphetamine tumult of fists, head-butts, and smashed bottles. As security reinforcements rushed down from elsewhere in the building, even I got dragged into the scrap. I saw some punk smack one of our guys, so I grabbed him from behind. He twisted to try and shake me loose, which brought us both crashing to the floor. I landed with the full weight of my body on top of him. It must have been pretty uncomfortable for the poor guy: his clothes were full of metal studs and safety pins.

As more of our security team arrived, the violence only got worse. Lydon was living up to his Sex Pistols 'I am an anarchist' boast, and goading the punks on, seeming to thrive on the explosive violence of the situation: 'Anger is an energy' indeed. I saw some crazy bastard climb to the top of the shaky tower of PA speakers and drop his trousers to his ankles. Looking up at that guy on his precarious perch, waving his equipment around, I decided that enough was enough. I gave Pat the signal, and we dropped the fire curtain.

As far as I remember, it was the only occasion during my life at the Academy that we actually had to cut a show. Lydon came offstage like a furious ranting maniac, swearing that he would never play in London again. I was a bit pissed off too, but somewhere deep down there was a little part of me that said, 'Well, you wouldn't get that kind of excitement at the Hammersmith Odeon.' People may have been rioting, but at least they weren't sitting down.

For all Lydon's bluster, when Public Image Ltd. did their thirtieth anniversary reunion tour in 2009, they not only played London, they came back to the Brixton Academy.

In those days, riots could sometimes spontaneously break out at concerts when the crowd got too hyped up. Music fans back then considered themselves far more than just passive consumers of 'product'. Occasionally though, the riots became the carefully managed main event, with the music only thrown in as a soundtrack.

I was approached by a guy called Colin from Rough Trade, looking to put on a show for some of his upcoming punk bands. He seemed legit, if a little inexperienced and highly strung. I thought it was a bit weird that he always wore a suit, when most of the indie-label guys I knew usually turned up in jeans and T-shirts. But I was always happy to lend a hand to newcomers to the music business. I was still an outsider attempting to break into the industry myself. So I helped walk him through the bureaucratic rigmarole of putting on a large gig.

As the day of the concert grew closer, I was called in by Brixton police. They presented me with a leaflet they said was circulating around the area. It was a classic modernist design, modelled on those early Soviet posters by Alexander Rodchenko. It depicted a sniper with a rifle sitting on the roof of a building that looked suspiciously like the Brixton Academy, next to some snappy slogan along the lines of 'Excellent. Just shot another cop!'

Needless to say, the police were none too impressed. They claimed to have received intelligence that our concert was being used as a cover for getting five thousand angry, militant punks together to attack Brixton police station after the gig.

It wasn't beyond the realm of possibility. The anarcho-punk movement of the mid 80s was very vocal in its visceral hatred of the police. But there was no way I was going to call off the concert on the basis of some hearsay from the cops and a few photocopied flyers doing the rounds in Lambeth. I talked to Colin, who denied knowledge of any ulterior motives for the gig, so we pushed on.

When the day of the show rolled around, though, it became clear just how amateurish Colin and his team were. They missed the most basic things that anyone who had put on a major gig would know. Essential stuff, like if you want to hang huge cloth backdrops for your stage show, you have to get them fireproofed. Or if you require large, impressive stacks of television sets to show film clips while you play, you need to have insurance. All these details that should have been easily taken care of became fractious disputes between his crew and my own team. Suddenly, they were talking to us as if *we* were the establishment trying to keep them down for the sake of it. I understood that they were idealist punks standing against 'the system', but as they spent their precious prep time before the show putting up stalls in the foyer, promoting every cause from nuclear disarmament to radical vegetarianism, I began to wonder if they knew anything at all about what it actually takes to put on a rock 'n' roll show.

Their real priorities became clear once the concert began. The gig kicked off with an excellent spoken-word performance by the poet Benjamin Zephaniah. He was on fine fiery form, and got the militant crowd whipped up into an anti-authoritarian fervour. As he finished, the TV monitors stacked onstage flickered to life, and a fifteen-minute film clip began playing a montage of various scenes of police brutality against protesters. The crowd roared in collective rage.

The film ended and the main act of the evening, the band Conflict, slouched sullenly onto the stage. I got a sudden shock to see Colin, the guy from Rough Trade I had been liaising with all this time, walk onstage and take up a position in front of the centre mic. The suit was gone, replaced with a ripped T-shirt. His hair, which had been carefully slicked back, was now styled straight up like an electrocuted porcupine. He wasn't from Rough Trade at all; he was the lead singer of the bloody band! That's when things clicked into place, and I knew I'd been conned. There was no record label involved here, just a disorganized anarcho-punk collective looking to advance their agenda.

I was a little pissed off at the deception, but also a bit confused as to why they went to the effort. I probably would have given them the gig anyway without the subterfuge. I knew the irritation of getting blocked by music industry insiders too well to inflict it on anyone else.

Then, just before they started playing, the band enacted a weird little piece of performance art. A couple of guys dressed as policemen marched on stage and proceeded to simulate a savage beating on Colin himself. This sent the audience into an absolute frenzy of anti-cop hatred. As Conflict launched into their set, the crowd picked on the nearest representatives of authority they could find to vent their revolutionary frustration on. Unfortunately, this happened to be the Academy security staff. Once again Pat's stage team had their hands full with flailing anarcho-punks looking for a fight.

This time, I didn't want to drop the fire curtain and cut the gig short. Despite being lied to, I knew Colin's gang had poured a lot of effort into putting this show on, and I didn't want to let them down. I also thought that if I gave this crowd that kind of trigger, it might well escalate into a full-scale riot.

In the end, aside from having a crack at our security guys, the wankers in the crowd caused several thousand pounds' worth of damage to the building, smashing up toilets, kicking in doors, and spraying graffiti all over the corridors. I did take that a little personally. In those days I was still coming in every morning to muck in with the mopping up.

At this gig the action in the crowd was also distinctly more diverting than the music. It seemed the band had put more time into ensuring that the burger vans outside their venues only served vegetarian food than into getting their licks down on their instruments. Even when Steve Ignorant of the anarchist 'stars' Crass joined them on stage, it failed to lift the music above a derivative punk dirge.

Eventually the band came offstage, and our team started ushering people towards the exits. We just wanted to see the back of these joyless poseurs whose idea of a good night out seemed to be a lecture on Trotsky and a scrap with a bouncer. But, when all these hyped-up punk kids streamed out into the Brixton night, they were confronted with 1,500 fully kitted, tooled-up riot police.

I have no idea if the Conflict guys and their militant allies had indeed planned to use the gig, or the 'Gathering of the 5,000' as they called it, as a cover to organize an attack on Brixton police station. But the cops certainly weren't taking any chances. They came out in force, with a point to make.

As I had already experienced, Brixton police in this era weren't known for handling situations like these with a particularly sensitive touch; on the other side, the punk kids had just been whipped up by an anti-cop hate-fest. Who knows which side threw the first punch, but it escalated fast.

Within minutes we really did have a full riot in progress. Shop windows were getting smashed, and there were scenes of mayhem as punks and police clashed violently on our doorstep.

As furiously as the kids threw themselves into the fight, they were no match for a fully equipped, highly organized, and extremely aggressive police onslaught. I started seeing young kids getting truncheoned across the face, and receiving vicious beatings when they fell. I immediately told Pat to reopen the Academy doors, and a few thousand punks streamed right back in to take cover in the venue that only shortly before they had been vandalizing. We let them hide out for a few hours while things died down outside, then helped them escape in small groups of five or ten out the side exits of the building.

About forty or so people were arrested in the street clashes that night, clashes that caused about £30,000 of damage to the local community and businesses. I was left with a bitter taste from the whole affair. The Conflict crew had messed me around completely unnecessarily. We were the only venue who would give guys like that a shot. The Hammersmith Odeon wouldn't have even had a conversation them. I had been totally willing to help out with their show, and then they turned around and treated my team and me as if we were *the man*? And how dare they damage my beloved Academy; talk about biting the hand that feeds.

Still, as a relative newcomer myself it was another harsh lesson about the nature of the music business. In this industry when you do someone a good turn, the response is usually not 'thanks', but 'more'.

On the other hand, it turns out that five thousand juiced-up punks looking for a fight can actually be less viscerally irritating than one self-righteous local councillor with a bee in her bonnet.

I believe it was a Gil Scott-Heron gig. I was really enjoying the show when I got a buzz on our new radio system. Apparently there was a complaint to be dealt with down in the foyer.

When I arrived I was confronted with the sight of an enraged woman facing off with one of our security guards. They were standing smack in the middle of our entrance hall, an area where punters were not even meant to be. She must have been in her early thirties, wearing Doc Martens boots and a wide-brimmed Peruvian hat, and carrying a woven hemp bag: pretty much fulfilling every cliché you'd expect from a white woman at a Gil Scott-Heron concert in the mid 80s. Our poor security guy looked completely bewildered as she jabbed her finger aggressively in his face. He was more used to dealing with rioting punks and Brixton wide boys than outraged *Guardian* readers.

It took a little time to work out what was going on, but from what I managed to piece together, she had gone up to this security guard to inform him that the women's toilet was running low on paper. As she approached him he had committed the cardinal sin of asking, 'What's up, love?'

This woman, who lost no time in telling me at length that she was the Head of Gay and Lesbian Issues for Hammersmith and Fulham Council, was scandalized by the inherent sexism in his use of the word 'love'.

This guy was a working-class south Londoner. Of course he hadn't meant any insult, it's just how people talk in that part of the world. There was even something a bit distasteful in the spectacle of a middle-class woman telling a working-class man how he was allowed to speak in his own neighbourhood. But more important, I had a gig to run.

I tried to be diplomatic with the lady, but she had decided to take offence, and nothing was going to stand in the way of her righteous indignation. She began haranguing me about how our security team wasn't fit for purpose. To illustrate her point she started firing questions at the utterly baffled security guy.

'What's this for?' she spat, pointing to a nearby fire extinguisher.

Now, I knew this was a W9 category extinguisher: water-powered, meant for burning wood or plastics, but not for use on electrical or chemical fires. It was my job to know this. I was the owner of the venue. But there was no reason at all why our security guy would be aware of these kinds of details; it just wasn't in his job description. He looked at her blankly.

'Uhhh ... it's for putting out fires, love,' he offered.

He must have said it without thinking, running on autopilot in an unfamiliar situation. But this second use of the word 'love' made the woman explode. She flew into full self-righteous, politically correct outrage mode.

Eventually I just thought, Bloody hell, this woman has missed half the gig she came to see. I offered her a choice. 'Look, you can either go and see the rest of the gig, or here's your money back with our apologies.'

But she wasn't having it. She preferred giving us lectures to enjoying Gil Scott-Heron and his excellent band. Some people are just like that, I suppose.

'Look,' I explained, 'either go see the show or take your refund and leave, but you can't stand here. It's a fire hazard, and in a few minutes five thousand people are going to exit through those doors and trample straight over you.'

'Well, I'm not moving, and don't you dare touch me,' the woman snarled, looking daggers at the small crowd of perplexed bouncers that had gathered round to see what was going on.

Pat was very keen to 'sling the cow out', as he gently put it. But I decided to handle this more diplomatically. The last thing we needed now was a man laying hands on this woman and giving her an excuse to get even more wound up.

I left the building and wandered around outside until I found a policewoman, who I drafted in to help encourage the petulant gender-warrior to leave the venue. Even when asked by a female cop to move on, the lady refused, stamping on the floor like an angry kid. Eventually, the policewoman had to forcibly remove her from the premises.

Two days later an angry letter about the 'sexist' Brixton Academy appeared in *Time Out* magazine. This was the 80s: misusing buzzwords like that was still new and exciting for people. I wasn't going to let this stand, so I wrote a reply and sent it to the editor. Over the next few months this woman and I had a lengthy exchange of letters at the back of the magazine. I tried to keep it funny and light, as for me the whole affair was totally ridiculous, but I wasn't going to let anyone besmirch the Academy's reputation. Once again, you can try to be as right-on as possible, but someone somewhere will always find an issue to enrage them.

'RESPECT'

Seeing off humourless local councillors was an irritating distraction, dealing with raging anarcho-punks a hazard of the job. Going into business with Yardie gangsters, however, was something else entirely.

Our star was rising. As we became the centre of the more underground side of the British music scene, people both inside the industry and out were beginning to take us more seriously. Guys like Harvey Goldsmith, the really big fish of UK music, who wouldn't even take my phone calls two years earlier, were starting to sniff around. While these early successes were encouraging, they also brought their own complications. Once again, our growing profile was bringing us to the attention of the local heavies.

Since Pat's manoeuvre with his private army at the Gregory Isaacs shows, the villains around Brixton had known they couldn't try anything too audacious at the Academy. But we were all too aware that we were still being constantly watched and our defences continually probed for weaknesses.

There were always new street players coming up who might try and make a name for themselves by having a crack at the Academy. There was one emergent crew, in particular, that I knew we had to watch out for. The Railton Road boys were a loose Jamaican-British family firm, headed by the three brothers, Freddie, Darren, and John, but involving any number of cousins and associates. I don't know what these guys were fed as children, but they each stood around six feet five inches tall and weighed about twenty stone. They were absolute monsters. They had a nasty, violent reputation, and I knew that, as their street profile rose, so would their interest in us.

There was no way we could ignore guys like these. Brixton operates on Brixton's rules. We couldn't pretend that we were somewhere else, or that the heavies magically didn't exist. We had proved that they couldn't just take us over, but one way or another, our relations with the local power players would have to be negotiated.

So Johnny Lawes and I came up with a radical solution. Instead of having to be constantly on guard against these characters, why not employ them?

Back then the music industry was a very different beast to the slick corporate operation it is today. From Allan Freed and the Payola Scandal in 1959, through to the gang wars that have blighted hip-hop, there has always been a porous line between the criminal underworld and the entertainment business. That's not to say there aren't still criminals involved in music today, only now most of them wear suits and call themselves *executives*. As Woody Guthrie sang, 'some will rob you with a six-gun, and some with a fountain pen'. Back in the day, it was just a little more in your face.

Nowhere was this more true than in the Jamaican music business, and consequently in Brixton. All the serious mobsters in Brixton had dealings in the entertainment industry, and all the great stars of reggae music were mixed up in some way with the chaotic gang politics that have disfigured life in Jamaica for decades. Music mythology has it that Lee 'Scratch' Perry burnt down his seminal Black Arc Studio in Kingston to rid it of evil 'Duppy' spirits. Anyone in the biz will tell you it was because he was coming under so much pressure from rival criminal firms to pay protection money that he finally snapped and brought the issue to a close himself.

The same tensions and pressures ran deep in Brixton at the time. I wasn't interested in any of this criminal nonsense; I just wanted to put on great gigs. But there was no way to pretend the problem wasn't there. We had to find our place within the scene in which we operated.

My thought was that certain local mobsters would jump at the chance to co-promote shows with us at the Academy. It was non-negotiable that we would keep our hands absolutely clean of any criminality, but the Academy would be bigger than anything else these guys had been involved in, so it could be done more on our terms. They would make money, and doing big shows with us would vastly boost their reps in the area. In return, we thought if we brought a few of these guys onside, they could help ward off interest from the really nasty characters like the Railton Road boys, or even old Rondall and Wilson, who we knew were still circling like sharks, waiting for us to slip up.

Through his street connections Johnny made the initial contacts. It began, naturally, with reggae gigs; I think it was a Desmond Dekker show. Johnny and I cut a deal with a local player named 'Bones' Cooper. We would front the money for the deposit and take care of ticket sales through the box office; his crew would handle promotion and sales through local record stores. Most important, they would use their underworld clout to ensure there was no nonsense from other local gangs on the night itself. It was a risky strategy, but one way or another these perilous waters had to be crossed. And despite my initial nerves, the show was brilliant and went off without a hitch.

Over time, these 'arrangements' with local Brixton characters became a regular feature of how we operated at the Academy. We ended up doing business with just about every street kingpin around, up to and including the Railton Road boys and their gang. It began with the reggae gigs, but quickly expanded to promoting the new musical genre that was just beginning to make an impression in the UK: hip-hop.

Rap was born in the mean streets and block parties of New York City in the mid to late 70s. It had taken a while to make it over to Britain, but through genre-busting pioneers like The Clash, and the obvious parallels with the stripped-back beats and chanted 'toasting' vocal styles of Jamaican music, this new sound was starting to generate interest in the UK.

In hip-hop there will always be an 'America versus everywhere else' divide. That's just how the culture operates. But when rap did come to Britain, there was only ever one place it was going to get its start: Brixton.

Our first hip-hop show was sometime towards the end of 1986; a guy named Schoolly D, widely credited as the first gangsta rapper. I thought he was awesome – though I was a little taken aback when he came out with the lines 'rock 'n' roll living's a thing of the past, so all you longhaired faggots can kiss my ass. Say it loud, I love rap and I'm proud'. Personally, I happened to think rock 'n' roll had a lot of life left in it yet, and some of my best friends happened to be long-haired faggots. But there was something irresistibly fresh and exciting about this new music. Obviously there was the aggression and energy in it that got your blood racing, but most of all it just sounded so *new*. It was different from anything anyone on these shores had heard before.

We put on more and more of these shows, bringing over the first wave of rap superstars: LL Cool J, Public Enemy supported by Eric B and Rakim, and an amazing double headline bill of Run DMC and The Beastie Boys, featuring a stage show with go-go dancers in cages.

At the start of Public Enemy's seminal 1987 album *It Takes A Nation of Millions to Hold Us Back,* Chuck D and Flava Flav are heard addressing the crowd at the Hammersmith Odeon. That show took place during the band's first UK tour. After that gig there had been a bit of trouble outside the venue, and the British

It's Tricky: Run DMC, the go-go dancers just out of shot

The Beastie Boys fighting for their right to party. And party they did

tabloids had gone into a typically sensationalist frenzy about this new music inciting violence in 'the youth'. I don't remember if any of them came right out and called attention to hip-hop as *black* music, but the implication hung heavy in the air.

True to form, the Odeon had panicked and banned *all* hip-hop concerts. They just weren't rugged enough to handle the trouble associated with rap music, and they knew it. But we were the Brixton Academy. We defined rugged. Their loss was our gain, and we became rap's natural home in the UK. When the US stars came over, they came straight to us. Not only was their fan base on our doorstep; we were the only ones who would book the gigs.

It wasn't just the venues that found hip-hop too much trouble to deal with. Most of the established agents and promoters wouldn't touch it either. Which left the field wide open for the gangsters. The bad guys moved straight in to fill the gap in the market. So, for lack of any other option, we found ourselves co-promoting more and more hip-hop shows with the local Brixton street players, along with our steady flow of reggae gigs.

The more we dealt with these characters, the better I got to know them. These weren't distant, mysterious criminal masterminds; they were well-known faces around the area. Guys like the Railton Road boys made themselves big personalities in the bars, fast food joints, and barbershops of the neighbourhood. Anyone even slightly connected in Brixton knew exactly who they were, and what they were up to. Half the time, when they weren't co-promoting gigs at the Academy, they would show up as audience members and try to blag their way in.

What I quickly learned was that aside from hard cash, what really mattered to these dudes was 'respect'. It was a word you heard a lot. Their clout on the street was based on the reputation, the *respect,* they commanded. It was always 'nah trouble, respect bruv', or 'nuff respect Simon, here's the money from Red Records'. On the flipside, you were always hearing stories about some guy you knew getting stabbed, shot, or beaten up because he had shown the wrong guy *disrespect.*

What complicated things was that it was near impossible to tell what might be construed as disrespect at any given time. You never knew when some minor perceived slight could blow up into serious violence. This was a chaotic and violent world to navigate.

There were a couple of reasons why I think, by and large, I did all right in managing this tightrope walk. The first is simply that I wasn't a criminal. I played absolutely straight with every- one, and never got involved in any violence or illegal dealing. So I never became a threat to any of these guys' business interests. Looking back, I probably could have made a lot more money if I had dipped my beak in the shady business that went on. But I knew that the second I got my hands even a little bit dirty, I would get sucked into that world. It's like virginity: you can't be a little bit of a gangster.

Likewise, whenever an issue of 'respect' came up, the fact that I was a complete outsider, and a white guy to boot, was actually immensely helpful. If I had been some street-savvy south London operator with my ear to the ground, then people would have expected me to prove what kind of respect I commanded myself. But I had learned from that first confrontation when I asked Rondall and Wilson for their CVs. My best bet was to stay so far out of the game that I wouldn't even be perceived as a rival. Characters like these knew how to deal with violence and confrontation, but friendliness and simple professionalism completely confused them. So I was usually able to play my naive, public-schoolboy outsider role, and bumble my way through without stepping on anyone's toes. It was a hard act to maintain, and it often took discipline not to rise to provocations.

Similarly, their perception of me was that, as a white guy, they could never be sure that I wouldn't go to the police. Within the West Indian community it was completely anathema to involve the cops against one of your own. So, within their own milieu, the gangsters were kings. They could do whatever they wanted. But to them, a guy like me was an unknown quantity. And that's just how I liked to keep it.

For their own part, the Brixton police grew to absolutely love me. It's not surprising really. I was the only player in the area who wasn't neck-deep in the rackets. I got to be quite good mates with a lot of the local coppers. They would often stop by the Academy for a late-night beer after their shift, seeming much more interested in the pretty girls walking by than in the ganja being lit up all around them. I even let the CID use the roof of the Academy for surveillance on Stockwell Park Estate behind us. While, of course, also letting the kids from the estate hide in the building if they needed to lay low for a while. My job was always to strike the balance and keep both sides happy.

So I learned how to play it. If I saw one of the big street characters show up on our door with their entourage, I'd always make sure that they and a girlfriend got ushered straight in on the guest list. Their mates would have to line up and pay like everyone else. The mobsters loved that one; it allowed them to play out their Scorcese-movie gangster fantasies in front of their associates.

On the flipside, though, I couldn't let myself be perceived as soft. In the Brixton jungle, the old and the weak get picked off fast. No matter how nice you try to be, people need to understand that, if pushed, you've got the brass to back yourself up. You can't always just play the guy who *might go to the cops*.

Most of the time I managed to walk the line. I could usually take some troublemaker aside and say, 'Look, I've let you in for free, but now you're taking the piss. Clear off and we'll talk next week.' Most of the time they would take it in their stride, grumble 'All right Simon,' and tone things down. It was in their interests to keep me on side. They knew if they pissed me off too much, there would always be some other local mobster ready to put on shows at the Academy.

Occasionally, though, someone would cross the line and an example would have to be made.

It was another rap show. We'd brought a big act over from the States, which meant a bunch of heavy Brixton characters hanging around our upstairs bar, each trying to play the Don. There were always problems when several local gangsters ended up together at the same gig. It would descend into a macho pissing contest with depressing predictability, as they all tried to out-front each other to impress their entourages. And that meant trouble for me.

At this particular show, it got to the point where I decided enough was enough. The main troublemaker was a young guy, surrounded by his mates. He was new on the scene, and obviously trying to prove his hard-man credentials. I quietly asked him to leave. He ignored me and carried on drinking the rum that I had given him and his crew on the house. I asked him again. This time he jumped off his bar stool, pushed his chest into mine, and spread his arms in a classic confrontational street pose. 'Fuck off ya bloodclart,' he screamed in my face.

'Look,' I said softly, 'it's not a big deal. Let's just call it a night, and I'll stick you on the list for next week.'

'Raasclart, I'm tellin' you to fuck off. I don't care whose fuckin' club dis is; I'll fuckin' do you.' He was leaning right into my face now, getting intensely threatening, so close I could smell the rum on his breath.

The guy was obviously showing off to all the other local players there. He glanced over to his mates and grinned. 'This white boy don't know who the fuck he's talking to.'

Turning back to me, he jabbed his finger into my chest and smirked. 'Look bruv, you're fuckin' lucky. I'm not going to hit you, because you've only got one arm.'

The other guys in the room, who had been watching the proceedings, started to laugh. I could see the two Railton Road boys, Darren and John, keeping a careful eye on how I responded. The situation was getting out of hand. This guy was making me look weak in front of the other mobsters, and, as ever, in the back of my mind there was old Mac's lesson from my childhood: 'never let yourself be threatened'.

'You're right,' I replied evenly, 'that is lucky', and head-butted him in the face.

Very much to my surprise, the big guy went down with one shot, collapsing in a heap at my feet. He may have dropped as much from the booze as from the head-butt, but the place went completely silent. Every gangster in there watched to see how the others would react. Some of the guys' entourages started to make a move towards me, but thankfully at that moment Pat charged through the doors with Big John, and they thought better of it. Eventually we scraped the dazed gang leader off the floor and put him into a taxi outside.

This was a very high-risk manoeuvre, but it did the trick. The heavy guys around the area had grown too used to seeing me as Simon the naive outsider. I wanted to make sure Darren and John knew that I could get tough, if pushed. Occasionally, it's good to keep guys like that guessing about who you are, and how you will react.

Pat was as surprised as anyone else. He knew exactly how dangerous the guy I put down really was. 'Bloody hell, Simon, you must really be off your fucking head,' he laughed. It seemed that was becoming my mantra.

STICK-UPS AND STEAKS

Most of the time, though, it was Pat who was on the front line. I was only able to play the nice guy because I always knew I had him and his team backing me up. They were the ones who had to deal with the worst that Brixton had to offer, confronting the crooks when they tried some petty scam, and throwing the rude boys out of the venue when they got too wild.

This earned Pat a lot of enemies around the area. Because of how he had 'come back from the dead' at those Gregory Isaacs shows, Pat had become a local legend. Trading on his 'indestructible' reputation with the local hoods was quite handy for us. Occasionally, though, it meant the bad guys would try and go through me to get to him, instead of the other way around, as it was meant to be. Like the time I found myself with a gun to my head.

It was 3 a.m. or so, and the venue was eerily quiet after the noise of the gig. We had co-promoted one of our bread-and-butter reggae acts with a set of up-and-coming street hoodlums, closely associated with the Railton Road boys. They had tried to mess us around every step of the way, from how the tickets were sold to the old scam about who would do the front-door security. Eventually, after yet another round of petty, aggressive bullshit from these guys, Pat had slung them out of the venue in his typically unceremonious way. This wasn't unusual, and wouldn't ordinarily have led to anything other than a laugh amongst our own crew. Tonight, though, Pat had lost his temper and thrown these guys out in front of their mates. They had been shown disrespect, and now they would have to make some kind of comeback or they would lose face on the street.

I was completing a final check of the backstage area before locking the venue down for the night. As I passed the stage door, I noticed it had been left on its latch. Cursing my backstage crew for their slackness, I walked over to lock it properly.

Just as I reached out to push it shut, there was a violent crash. The door flew open, and I staggered back in shock. Five huge guys in balaclavas burst in, and I was instantly surrounded. Three of these characters were brandishing baseball bats; two were holding handguns. I found myself pinned against the wall, a pistol barrel pressing into my cheek.

'Where the fuck is Pat?' one of them shouted, leaning right into me.

When you have a gun pointed at your face everything starts to move very slowly. I've heard people describe being involved in car crashes in the same way. I became weirdly, preternaturally, calm.

'I don't know,' I replied in a dead monotone.

'Shut the fuck up. Where is he?' they yelled back, shaking me and pushing the gun hard into the side of my face.

Half of my brain was going crazy with terror; the other half seemed to be floating above, as if watching all this happening to someone else.

I heard myself saying, 'I don't know, I don't know.'

The guys holding the bats were shouting, 'Do him, fucking do him,' and for a moment I did think, Fuck, he's actually going to pull the trigger. I was about to die.

Then the dead calm returned, and the thought ran through my mind, if he was going to shoot me, he would have done it by now.

My eyes flicked up to the cameras that were dotted around the room capturing all this. I knew that at that moment there would be sixty very hard security guards moving through the building towards us.

'Get out.'

I said it very clearly and quietly, but with enough authority to make my point.

'Shut the fuck up,' one of them screamed. They might have had their faces covered, but I knew exactly who these guys were. Their gang was a nasty lot, hard enough to run with the Railton Road boys, but something deep down told me that they weren't about to shoot me. It just didn't make sense.

'Just fuck off,' I said.

It's not easy to tell someone holding a gun to your head to fuck off, but I needed to take control of the situation. 'Seriously, just get out. Get out now.'

There was a moment of silence in which I locked eyes with the guy holding the gun. We held each other's gaze for a few interminable seconds. I knew precisely the same mental calculations were clicking through his mind. He would know that at any second my security team were going to burst through the doors.

I felt the cold metal of the gun barrel come away from my face. The big guys gave me a shove, and as I staggered back, they sprinted out the door.

I leaned against a wall and sank down to the floor, gasping for breath. Pat and his team came charging in, and helped me up. They locked down the premises, and led me over to the bar for a very stiff drink.

When I went to the cops about the incident they said their intelligence confirmed that my name was floating around as a potential gangland target. They placed me under official police protection.

For months I had to check in with them when I arrived home every night to confirm that I was OK.

For his part, Pat was convinced that the fact the stage door had been left on the latch meant that this was, at least in part, an inside job. He promised to undertake a thorough purge of his team. 'You probably don't want to know too much about that, boss,' he assured me. I was happy to let him get on with it, without asking too many questions. God help the guy who sold Pat down the river.

There wasn't even really enough time to get scared or worried about incidents like these. This kind of thing was all in the game in south London. And I was about to learn a bit more about the guys I had fighting on my own side.

Perhaps I had impressed him by keeping my cool during the stick-up, but for whatever reason, Pat decided to give me a glimpse of the world he belonged to.

I had been getting to know Pat and his main crew much better. Big John, Pete the Mercenary, Black Nigel, all those scary guys who I was first introduced to by Mad Mick Murphy had gradually become my close friends. When I carried any serious amount of cash through the Academy we would go as a convoy, with two big guys ahead of me, two on the side, and two guarding my back. It made me feel like the ruler of some Middle Eastern country with his security detail. I started calling this core group my A-Team. Fending off Yardie gangsters, fighting rioting punks, and dealing with stick-ups certainly instils a sense of camaraderie within a group. It's definitely more effective than playing paintball on some corporate 'team-building' exercise, or whatever it is companies do these days.

We had just finished locking down the building after yet another very stressful gig. The crowd had been fractious and jumpy, and we'd had our hands full with one incident after another. Weirdly, after a night like that you don't actually feel tired at all, you're keyed up and full of adrenalin. I used to get home from the Academy and lie in bed for hours unable to sleep. But tonight, as we locked up, Pat tapped me on the arm and said, 'Hey Boss, you fancy coming for some grub with me and the boys?'

Well, why not? I wasn't going to sleep anyway. We all piled into Black Nigel's van and drove off into the night. Eventually we pulled up in front of an unassuming brick building somewhere in deepest, darkest Peckham, and clambered out into the cold London air.

Pat walked up to the door. He knocked loudly three times, paused a second, then knocked twice more. He obviously had the code right, as the door swung open and we trooped inside, passing a couple of very burly doorkeepers on the way.

I was confronted with a scene from some classic British gangster film. This spot was an after-hours gambling den exclusively for the use of high-level villains and their cronies. The room was full of very hard-looking guys with cropped hair, expensive suits, and big gold rings, sitting around small tables drinking and playing cards. Some of them had much younger, overly made-up women sitting next to them, their eyes fixed on the poker chips piled high on the green felt tables. A few huge bodyguards stood a few feet back, scanning the room for potential threats. Clouds of cigarette smoke hung heavy in the air, and there was an atmosphere of suppressed tension amidst the clinking glasses and convivial chatter.

Pat seemed to know everyone there. As we walked through the place, all these hard guys would nod our way: 'All right Pat', 'All right Jim.' 'All right Pat', 'All right Frank.'

Our group was led into a back room and seated around a large wooden table. A woman with a giant blonde 80s perm, a cigarette dangling from her lips and an astonishing amount of gold jewellery, came sashaying up to us coquettishly. ''Ello Pat my love,' she cried. ''Ello Jenny, darlin',' Pat replied with a wink.

'You having the usual then, Pat?' she asked.

'I think so love, the usual all round please,' Pat replied, giving her an affectionate slap on the bum on her way out.

'Oi, none of your cheek,' she snapped. One got the sense that not everyone could have got away with that kind of familiarity with Jenny, who exuded an air of steely ruthlessness beneath the girlish flirting. Pat very obviously enjoyed some status in this place.

After a few minutes Jenny returned, and we were presented with pints of lager, followed by huge T-bone steaks. I hadn't realized how ravenous I was, and tucked in immediately.

But my fork froze halfway to my mouth, as Pat and all the other guys removed their flak jackets before eating. As they peeled off their vests, they also unburdened themselves of the tools of their trade, pulling out knives, coshes, and brass knuckles, and laying them down next to their plates, as if this were the most normal pre-dinner ritual in the world. Pete the Mercenary reached over his shoulder and produced a full machete that he had strapped to his back.

I was shocked. On reflection, though, I shouldn't have been that surprised. I knew these guys were hard, and a bit rough around the edges, but the last thing I needed was my own team chopping people up at the Academy. That's not what I had set the whole place up for.

Sensing my unease and seeing my fork still frozen in mid-air, Pat winked at me. 'Oh don't worry, boss, this stuff's not for the Academy. This is all for the lads' *other* interests.'

I tried to play it as cool as I could. 'Yeah, all right Pat.' I didn't want my team wielding machetes in the building, but I knew these guys well by now. I had to trust that they would use discretion. Besides, I reasoned, they might be barbarians, but they were *my* barbarians. If you're going to need protection from the Brixton underworld, you might as well make it as tough as possible.

After that night, going out for steaks with Pat and the boys became part of our routine at the Academy. It was a great way to unwind after a stressful gig. I also got to meet some pretty colour-ful characters, and hear the hilarious stories of the capers they had pulled.

For his part, I think Pat quite liked introducing his token posh mate to his underworld connections. I could sense that I was a bit of exotica on display for these guys. Which was fine by me; we were all in show business, after all.

One evening a few years later Pat invited me to a private party at some pub on the Old Kent Road. Before we left the Academy, he specifically asked that I wear a tweed jacket. I think someone had heard that I had gone to school with Prince Andrew, and through the Chinese whispers of the London criminal networks the rumour had spread that I was somehow distantly related to the Royal Family. There has always been a strange connection between high-level British gangsters and the Royals; it's an odd sort of patriotism where these crime bosses will break all the laws of the British state, while holding the head of that state in absolute veneration. They'll call the police 'the filth', but God help you if you insult the Queen.

So I obliged Pat by wearing a tweed jacket, which I guess was somehow supposed to be the uniform of the landed aristocracy, and went along to this party. It was a good laugh, full of proper villains and their very attractive, but definitely out of bounds, molls, all coming up to me throughout the night to clink glasses and toast the health of 'young William and 'arry, God bless 'em'. I was happy to go along with Pat and not disabuse everyone about my nonexistent royal connections. After all, you never knew when you might need a favour, and guys like these might come in handy.

By now I was spending most of my time with Johnny, Pat, and the crew down in Brixton; they were fast becoming my close friends. At the same time, though, I still had all my old posh mates, who inhabited a completely different world. I ended up leading a very strange double life. It was very much a matter of ducking out of elite weddings in Belgravia to go and clean up the wreckage of riots in Brixton.

This weird yo-yoing between different worlds gave me a strange perspective on life. I suppose it was only natural that I gradually began to feel more affinity with the guys I was working with in some pretty extreme circumstances at the Academy than with the posh boys swanning around their polo clubs.

I began to get really annoyed with the snobbish class prejudice rife in the toff crowd. I'd be sitting at a table and some guy would ask me what I did, but as soon as they heard the word *Brixton*, their eyes would either glaze over or they'd come out with some awful bullshit like, 'Oh, where the riots were. It's all a bit bloody much down there, if you ask me. Lock them all up, I say.'

Interestingly though, as the Academy's reputation grew, I began to get a very different reaction from the women in that crowd than from the blokes. The posh boys might have been dismissive, but their girlfriends, as soon as they heard me say 'Brixton Academy', would suddenly get very interested. I'd quickly have three or four of them all gathered around, hanging off my every word. Maybe it was just that I did something a bit different from their husbands and their friends, but those posh girls seemed to become extremely curious about the ins and outs of the Brixton music business. Which, needless to say, had certain pleasant knock-on effects for me.

Indeed, I was only just beginning to figure out exactly how pleasant running the coolest music venue in London could be. If you're chatting to a girl at some after-party and she asks you, 'So who do you know here?' it can have quite an effect when you nonchalantly reply, 'Actually, this is my gaff.' But as *pleasant* as things were now, the real fun was only just beginning.

NIGHTCLUBBING

Our gigs kept getting cooler, but it was another innovation that really established the Academy as *the* venue for the hip end of the London scene. We began running our own very special, bespoke, club nights.

I wish I could claim that this key step in the Academy's rise was purely my own flash of inspired genius, but in reality it all began with a bunch of transvestites dressed as mermaids.

In early 1985 I was approached by the legendary artist and impresario Andrew Logan about hosting his next Alternative Miss World extravaganza. The AMW parties were a series of madcap performance art happenings that Logan had been running on and off since the early 70s: essentially beauty pageants for drag queens, freaks, fops, and dandies. Each Alternative Miss World was a high-concept party with a unifying theme, and Logan's latest plan was to do a quartet of shows around the four elements: earth, water, air, and fire. Our night at the Academy was to kick the series off with the Water theme.

The Alternative Miss World events had a reputation for getting very wild. Back in 1980s Britain, out-and-proud gay clubs, as we know them today, were few and far between. Folks were still only just getting used to the idea that gay people might not want to hide themselves away in shame. There was Heaven in Charing Cross, but precious little besides. So when the gay crowd, who really can party better than anyone else, did finally get a space like the Alternative Miss Worlds to do things on their own terms, they went seriously Bacchic and let it all hang out, often literally.

I wasn't sure how my macho south London security guys might react to very explicit gay action. I thought it best to call everyone together, draw a line in the sand, and say that anyone who had a problem with 'that sort of thing' should probably take the next Saturday off. It's a sign of those times that about a third of the guys chose not to work that night.

It was their loss. The show was absolutely incredible. Following the Water concept, the AMW crew transformed the entire Academy, building a full-scale working waterfall in the middle of the auditorium, and creating a spectacular little world-unto-itself in the middle of Brixton. Andrew Logan and Janet Street-Porter hosted the pageant, with Zandra Rhodes swanning around as one of the judges. The night was also the UK launch of Swatch Watches, adding an extra glitzy frisson, and the drag acts themselves were brilliant, responding to the water idea with real wit and panache. I remember Miss Tuna Turner and Miss Jacuzzi Floozi being two particularly standout efforts.

The sheer imagination, ambition, and attention to detail with which these guys approached their show took my breath away. They stopped at nothing to get every feature exactly right in giving their party its own unique atmosphere. The way they totally reimagined the Academy space fired up my own ambition. If the drag queens could do wildly inventive, crazy parties here, why couldn't we do our own unique club nights on the same scale?

The following year Logan was planning the Earth instalment of his four elements series. With his usual vision, he had booked the ancient Chislehurst Caves in Kent, a typically inspired choice of venue. Then, just days before the event, the local council cancelled his licence without warning. In the mid 80s, ignorant panic about AIDS had spread through Britain like wildfire. On learning that the Alternative Miss World was a gay event, the council had gone into a crazed tailspin, fearing the spread of HIV through the Portaloo toilets. They revoked the licence on public hygiene grounds.

I got an anguished call from Logan, frantically begging for help. Of course we welcomed the AMW crew back to the Academy, where they put on another amazing night. How could I say no? To me, Andrew was one of the true visionaries of the party scene. He was light years ahead of his time, and a real inspiration to me as I put our own first few club nights together.

The other debt of thanks I owe to Andrew Logan is that it was his glamorous showbiz crowd who introduced another key player into the Academy mix: the powerhouse that is Lynne Franks. Lynne was a sharp, hugely influential PR woman, and minor deity of the London high life. Hard-working, and even harder-partying, she was famously the inspiration for Jennifer Saunders's character, Edina, in the TV series *Absolutely Fabulous*. Lynne was smart, experienced, and more connected than a BT switchboard. She immediately saw the potential of what we could do at the Academy, and came aboard as a central member of the team.

At first I was worried that I wouldn't be able to bring together a crew creative enough to pull off parties as wild as I envisioned for a straight crowd. In the end, I found them right on my own doorstep. The upstairs of the Academy is a labyrinth of offices and spare rooms. So I used to give up-and-coming artists free studio space, setting their rent at one painting per year. We had a stage lighting company headquartered in the building, and I gave free office space to a cool young guy named Jaimie D'Cruz to start *Touch*, the UK's first hip-hop magazine. I even found the Academy its own in-house photographer – a glorious eccentric named Justin Thomas, or, as we called him, Just-in Case – to record all this madness. My thought was that if I had the room, why not help out other young creative mavericks? It was also fantastic to have a crowd of very cool, slightly mad people always around to bounce ideas off.

Out of this creative cauldron I discovered Joel Coleman and Graham Ball, two guys who I thought might just be crazy enough to join me in putting on Academy club nights. We sat up together night after night, fuelled by rum and hash, pushing each other on to ever-wilder ideas. The product of all these late-night sessions was the glorious monster we called West World.

The concept of the party was based on the Yul Brynner movie of the same name. We turned the entire Academy into a futuristic, western-style theme park. I took a huge financial risk and put £60,000 into getting everything just right, from the décor to the costume design for our bartenders. As it was a western-themed party, Lynne Franks struck a deal with Jose Cuervo and we set up a huge Cinco de Mayo-style tequila bar in the auditorium, and had a huge, mechanical Bucking Bronco amusement park ride installed in the foyer. Our crowning achievement, however, was extending the stage, and turning the whole thing into a giant circuit of fully working dodgem cars.

It was never just about the set design, though. Any club is only ever as cool as the people in it. We wanted to attract the hottest people in London, not in the sense of celebrities or any of that crap, but the most adventurous spirits and the wildest partiers. So we took a monumental risk and decided that there would be no conventional advertising or flyering for the night. We went for something much more daring.

Joel and I got in our van, drove up to Nine Elms fruit market, and bought ourselves 15,000 lemons. The guy at the fruit stand must have thought his ship had come in. We spent the next few days individually wrapping each one in coloured paper, with a message saying that if you brought this lemon to the West World tequila bar at the Brixton Academy, you would get a free shot. Joel then went out and personally delivered all these lemons to the hippest record stores, bars, restaurants, and hairdressers he had connections with. The idea was that they would get passed around hand to hand, and the people who were intrigued enough by getting a lemon invite would be the exact people just crazy enough to make a great party.

It was a huge gamble. On the night itself we were beside ourselves with nerves as we looked over our dodgem cars and Bucking Bronco machines. I was particularly worried. I had fronted all the money to put this thing on. If no one responded to our lemons, it would be me facing some quite serious financial trouble.

Then people started trickling in. The trickle became a flood. Before we knew it the place was full, people were dancing, and there was a line of punters stretching around the block to get in. The lemons had worked! We had created a word-of-mouth intrigue around this night that seemed to have attracted all the wildest, coolest people in London. The party was epic. People weren't used to walking into a club night and finding fairground rides. I think they really appreciated all the little touches we had put together to make the night special. This attention to detail, and concern with creating a total, immersive experience were something very wild and new in the clubbing scene. Everyone got into the madcap, creative spirit of the event, and we had a truly fantastic night.

Based on the success of that first party, Joel, Graham, and I put on more West Worlds, each with its own special theme. We never did any advertising: no tacky posters, no photocopied flyers, no ads in the back of the *NME*. We did things our way, and reached the people we wanted through a genuine underground buzz. Letters actually started appearing in *Time Out*, with people assuming that there was some sort of secret society involved, and asking how they could become a 'member of West World'. Rumours would fly around the hip London scene about when the next West World was, and what the theme might be. There was a palpable sense that this was something genuinely innovative, cool, and underground; that people really had to be in the know to keep up with what we were doing.

Our initial success pushed us to become ever more ambitious. One of my proudest moments was when we installed a full fairground twister ride on our stage. This was a huge monster of a

Dodgem cars in a nightclub.
No one had seen anything like that before

machine with long mechanical arms that spun around extremely fast, with terrified and exhilarated clubbers strapped to the ends. The beast weighed 38 tons and we had to do major reinforcement work on the stage to hold it up. As the machine spun, it cleared the back wall of the Academy by just two inches. This Health and Safety Inspector's nightmare must have been completely mind-blowing for clubbers full of booze and Lord knows what else. It certainly sounded like it from the screams that cut through the pumping music of the DJ mix. Most of all, the whole contraption looked just phenomenal spinning through the air amidst the flashing lights and smoke of the club.

Another hat-tip I have to give to Andrew Logan in all this, is that he was the one who taught me one of the most effective methods of avoiding trouble in a late-night club: simply find the most outrageous drag queen around, and make her your door girl. The type of south London wide boys most likely to cause problems at a cool night are usually so pathetically homophobic that they'll see a transvestite on the door, and think, Ughh, poofs, I'm not going there. These idiots were generally more scared of a glammed-up queen than of a team of hardbitten security guys. Little did they know that, just inside, the most beautiful people in London were all going crazy.

Eventually the buzz around our club nights went international. I got a panicked call from Harvey Goldsmith, probably the most important music promoter in Britain. Harvey was frantic. He begged me to tell him who these 'West World people' were.

It gave me quite a bit of satisfaction to reply coolly, 'Well, Harvey, that's me actually.'

As the conversation unfolded, the story became clear. MTV were launching their European division, and they had called Harvey from Los Angeles saying they'd 'heard about this West World thing' and could he do them a 'party like that' for their big launch event in Amsterdam. Sensing a big opportunity, Harvey had immediately agreed, thinking he would figure out further down the road what a West World actually was. It was a classic showbiz bluff, and nothing that I wouldn't have done myself in the same circumstances.

As it happened though, West World was a little too underground for Harvey. Now the launch date was approaching, and he was getting desperate. So, sensing an opportunity myself, I stepped up and offered, for a very reasonable fee, to arrange the perfect West World party in Amsterdam on Harvey's behalf.

He flew Joel and Graham out to Amsterdam that very afternoon. I had some Academy business to take care of, so I joined them two days later. We needed to work fast; everything about this party had to be perfect.

MTV had things organized so that there were two afterparties for the event: one black-tie schmooze-fest for the executives, and one more relaxed hang-out for the artists on an Amsterdam barge. My plan was to check in with the businesspeople and do a bit of Academy networking before everyone got too wasted. But when I rocked up in my tux, I found someone had taken my name off the guest list.

I explained to the doorman, somewhat forcefully, that I had set the 'whole fucking party up, and hadn't been paid yet', so I could just as easily call my crew and start dismantling the whole set right now. He quickly relented and I got through, but I was a little shocked that even after I had saved their collective arse, the British music players would still try to keep me away from the

The Twister Ride, West World's crowning glory.
You cleared the back wall by two inches: utterly terrifying, very fun

MTV bigwigs and claim the credit for the night themselves. It was yet another lesson in just how dirty showbiz politics can operate.

As it happened, I found partying with the executives as dull as daytime TV, and soon wandered down to the artists' barge looking for a better time. And my god did I find it. There, the party was in full swing. Everyone from Elton John to Mick Jones of Big Audio Dynamite was on that boat. We were making a fantastic, very debauched night of it, when all of a sudden we felt the barge engines kick into life beneath our feet. The whole boat gave a sickening lurch forward. People staggered into each other; trays of glasses were sent crashing to the floor, along with a fair few small mirrors and rolled-up bank notes. We all rushed out front to find out what was going on, only to see Boy George, up to his eyeballs on everything Amsterdam has to offer, trying to take the boat for a spin. It was a good job he was quickly led away from the wheel before he could crash and send a good portion of the late 80s music scene to the bottom of a Dutch canal.

I was very proud of that party. It was hard work, with very little time, but our crew pulled off an incredible night that became somewhat legendary in showbiz circles. I remember meeting people years later, still talking about how great it was.

Back in London, West World eventually became such a success that we expanded the concept, taking over Fulham swimming baths to create a series of nights called Wet World. It was West World in bikinis, with rubber dinghies for dodgem cars. These nights were great fun, and extraordinarily licentious.

The Academy's art deco foyer can hold 1,300 people without even opening up the main auditorium. We put on some truly magical nights, just using that space, that we called the Mad Hatter's Ball. People went all out with their Alice in Wonderland costumes, and I loved the crazy, fantastical vibe these parties created. I would wander out into the midst of these nights, look out over this outrageously dressed crowd going mad in our beautiful marble foyer, and it was like being in some fairytale movie, albeit with a lot more sex and drugs.

Johnny Lawes hooked up with a young agent named David Levy to set up another awesome club night, called Metamorphoses. Unbelievable as it sounds now, they had Soul II Soul as their house band, creating a really cool little scene around the night. Hip American record companies would compete to send their breaking funk and R&B acts over to play one-off, semi-secret sets at Metamorphoses, to warm up the UK audiences before booking proper European tours. Bands like Ten City, Troublefunk, and my favourites De La Soul all launched their UK careers through Johnny on the Academy stage.

The best house band in the world? The fabulous Soul II Soul

Soul II Soul at Metamorphoses

One of the most groundbreaking things about these club nights was that they bridged the racial divide in a way that gigs sometimes couldn't. In the 80s it was still rare to see many white faces in the crowd at a dub reggae show, or a lot of black dudes turning up for a band like The Cult. Nights like West World and Metamorphoses seemed to provide a space for a much more mixed crowd, which was fantastic, and pioneering for its time.

In many ways our club nights were just as important in building the Academy's reputation as the rock gigs. These parties allowed us to do things completely our own way; to stamp our brand on the Academy, and the Academy brand on the London scene. We were able to let our creativity loose, and make something really new.

I was also about to figure out how, in the music industry, I could be just as creative in business as I was in putting on great shows.

THE BOX OFFICE ARRANGEMENT

As we booked more and bigger gigs, and the club nights took off, I found the Academy entering an unfamiliar new phase: we were actually turning a profit. I discovered that I was often sitting on quite serious amounts of money in advance ticket sales for upcoming nights. Seeing all this cash just lying in my box office account gave me another one of my key ideas that was to push the Academy ahead of its rivals.

In this era, promoting large concerts in Britain was tightly controlled by a small clique of major players. Insiders like Harvey Goldsmith kept an iron grip on the industry, making even legends like John Curd operate as leftfield mavericks, let alone young guys trying to get their break. The main factor that allowed this elite group to maintain their power over the scene was that only they could afford the huge deposits needed to book major acts. This situation made it almost impossible for up-and-coming promoters to make the leap to larger venues. The music scene was very much a closed guild; you were either in the clique, or you weren't.

My brainwave was that I could use my box office money to advance young, hungry promoters that crucial deposit. This would allow them to book higher-profile bands and start playing in the big leagues. It made a lot of sense: I was also an upstart trying to batter my way into the industry, and if the established players wouldn't do business with me, then why shouldn't I act as a bank to help the up-and-coming guys who recognized the Academy's potential? If my deal was good enough for Brixton heavies like the Railton Road boys to put on hip-hop shows, then why not for cool young rock promoters?

I knew there was so much untapped talent out there on the London scene, so many sharp young promoters being held back by the way the system operated. Guys like Simon Moran and Bob Angus were making do with putting on 700-person gigs at places like the Garage on the Holloway Road, when I knew they were ready and able to do so much more.

They didn't need to be asked twice. The chance to run shows at a 5,000-capacity venue was a dream come true for ambitious guys like these. And between us having had bands like The Clash and PiL, and West World being the coolest club in town, they loved the idea of making Brixton their base. We swung straight into action, putting on the best gigs the underground had to offer.

This system was revolutionary in the mid 80s. It was also another example of how I was forced to figure out how to use our maverick, outsider status to our advantage. My 'Box Office arrangement' would have been completely impossible at one of the big dinosaur companies like Rank. No planning committee or department vice president would have ever approved it. Those big companies may have been the established players with the financial muscle, but I had the edge on them in that I completely controlled my own cash flow. I was independent, and I could move faster when opportunities came up. At a moment's notice I could get out there and take risks that would make any board of directors shudder in horror.

Many of the relationships I formed through this deal really lasted. My 'arrangement' not only enticed all the up-and-coming talent to the Academy, it formed strong bonds of loyalty with those I helped find their foothold. A lot of the characters involved went on to do great things. Simon Moran founded SJM Promotions, and Bob Angus started Metropolis Music, two of the companies that continue to dominate live music in Britain. Both these guys, and many more, made their first big moves at the Academy. It worked for me too; these were the dudes with their ear to the ground, who could spot the next cool band before they had sold millions of records to attract the attention of the big sharks.

My team and I also set ourselves apart from the big, faceless institutions simply by taking care of people. If we knew that Bob Angus liked to drink white wine, we made sure that there were a couple of fine vintages in the cooler. When John Jackson from Helter Skelter Promotions got nervous about parking his Ferrari in Brixton, I immediately volunteered to have an extra security guard with a Rottweiller assigned to it all night at my own expense. It seems so simple, but just being all right with people, and knowing how to have a good time, makes a huge difference.

And not just with the industry guys.

I was always on at my barmen to be polite, have fun with their job, and maybe even give people a smile now and then. Everyone was there to enjoy themselves, after all. That was the whole point, wasn't it? And if you're nice to punters, they're going to come back.

When we ran our own box office, we had a system to spot when the same details were popping up again and again. So once in a while, when one of these regulars would call, we'd just say, 'no worries, this one's on the house'. You should have heard the astounded thanks we'd get. It really meant something to people that we remembered them. It doesn't take much to let your customers know they're appreciated.

Likewise, if I was walking around at the end of a night and saw some sixteen-year-old crying because the last tube had gone and she was stranded in Brixton, it was never a big deal to just whip £20 out of a till and hand it to her so she could get a minicab. These were music fans like me; they were the ones that kept the Academy running. In the end, they were the ones the whole thing was all about. I wasn't going to abandon them to Brixton at 2 a.m.

As the Academy's status grew so did my visions and ambitions for what we could achieve. It was great to be the kings of the underground, putting on awesome punk shows; but now we had achieved that. I wanted more. Always looking for the next challenge, now I wanted to make the big rock acts, the really huge stars, come to Brixton.

The big British agents had come to accept punk and hip-hop shows in Brixton, but they were still unwilling to send their best acts south of the river. They were especially protective of their big cash cows, the American bands coming over for major tours.

So I figured if the London power players weren't going to give me what I wanted, I'd have to go over their heads, straight to the source. I whipped together a little proposal and flew to Los Angeles with nothing more than some names scribbled on a piece of paper.

It was so crazy that it just about worked. The American music bigwigs were obviously intrigued enough by this Englishman claiming he'd just travelled five thousand miles without an appointment that they actually gave me meetings.

These slick LA guys weren't aware of any stigma attached to Brixton. When they asked where the Academy was, knowing what

Americans want to hear about England I blithely claimed, 'Oh, it's fifteen minutes from Buckingham Palace,' which, once you're on the Victoria Line from Brixton station, is technically true. I gradually started to warm up a few contacts in LA, and began to put together some ideas for gigs.

Bucking the established system in London by going straight to America was a pretty bold move. I seriously annoyed the powers that be on the UK music scene. But they were also forced to start taking me seriously. They saw that I wasn't going to back down and let myself be pigeonholed as a punk promoter; and I wouldn't necessarily play by the established rules.

Over the following years I flew out to the States at least once every couple of months for meetings, and just to see gigs and keep my finger on the pulse of what was going on out there. These trips were a revelatory wake-up call on how differently the entertainment industry operates on either side of the Atlantic. For starters, I had never realized how little the American entertainment industry guys thought of their British counterparts.

Look at it like this: your average London music biz character will roll into work at about 11 a.m., in a leather jacket stinking of booze and fags, having been at some dingy club in Camden or Hackney till 3 a.m. He'll hang around the office for a few hours to put in a few phone calls, before buggering off again to make the scene down at the pub.

The Americans are suited and booted for breakfast meetings at 7 a.m. They're not in it to make the scene; they're in it to make money. Dealing with the slacker, too-cool-to-actually-do-any-work Brits drove them far crazier than the seven-hour time difference. It didn't take me long to clock what the Yanks were after, and I made sure I gave it to them. They were delighted to have an actual venue operator to talk to, rather than going through the same old agents and promoters. From my side, I appreciated how direct and open they were about what they wanted. It was a totally different mentality from the London scene. The Americans didn't care if you were part of the established clique. If you could make things happen, they wanted to talk to you. It was refreshing, and I ended up making good friends with a lot of guys over there, as well as organizing some great shows.

WHAM, BAM, THANK YOU MA'AM

One slightly random gig we put on during this era was very English, but about as non-punk as you could get.

In the summer of 1986, Wham were gearing up for their farewell concerts at Wembley Stadium. They had rented the Academy for production rehearsals to get their razzle-dazzle stage show together for these huge gigs. Lynne Franks hit on a smart PR move. Since all their gear was set up anyway, they should use the Academy to do an impromptu charity gig for Help a London Child. Wham, performing on the same stage that The Ramones and The Damned had shared only weeks before? Well, why the hell not? We were used to reggae acts, rappers, and punks, but a pop band playing Brixton in those years was completely unheard of. Why not shake things up a bit?

They announced the gig on the radio at lunchtime. By three in the afternoon thousands of kids across London had simply walked out of school and turned up at our door to queue for tickets. Part of the fun of this gig was that everyone was supposed to wear white or fluorescent colours (it was Wham, after all). So Brixton High Street became a river of very shiny middle-class teenagers, all giggling and flirting with each other. Lord knows what the locals thought.

It was a very hot June day. All these excitable young fans had run off from school to make sure they got a ticket; of course they weren't going to leave the queue to get a drink of water or eat any food. So by the time we opened the doors, it was a crowd of very dehydrated, overheated teenagers that packed themselves into our hall.

I was watching from the wings of the stage as the curtain went up. Wham played their first two drumbeats, Boom Boom, and about thirty-five kids in the front row fainted on the spot. A whole line of them dropped like a scene from a First World War movie.

I raced down and helped the security guys haul the kids to our medical area backstage. We always had four or five paramedics on duty. At any gig you could guarantee at least half a dozen injuries, usually from stage diving accidents or other random madness, and of course the odd fight or drug casualty. But we now had thirty-five kids needing attention all at once.

We frantically cleared our catering tables, which can seat a fifty-person crew, and laid all these kids out like a field hospital. But those thirty-five initial fainters were just the first wave. As Wham played, teenagers kept passing out from dehydration, and perhaps proximity to a young George Michael. Backstage was complete chaos. My poor paramedics didn't know what had hit them.

Eventually we got the situation under control as best we could, and I went back up to check everything was OK onstage. It was there I got a reminder of how crafty teenagers can be. Of course, some of these kids had noticed that if someone passed out, they were immediately carried into the backstage area. So suddenly all these young girls began throwing up their hands and collapsing. If they didn't get noticed fast enough, then they'd simply get up and do it again even more dramatically. It's one way to get a backstage pass.

The biggest problem, though, didn't come from the kids but from their parents. All these youngsters had raced out of school that day and come straight down to us. So when little Suzy or young Tommy hadn't turned up at home that evening, their parents had panicked. Then, when they heard through the parental grapevine that their little angels were in *Brixton* of all places, they completely flipped their lids.

By 10 p.m. the Stockwell Road was jammed with Volvo estate cars as irate suburban parents raced down, demanding entry to the venue to rescue and/or discipline their children. I was stuck with the job of holding them off. I explained as gently as I could that they couldn't come in without a ticket, and that the gig was sold out.

They didn't like that very much at all. If you think Yardie gangsters can get aggressive, you should see an enraged Surrey housewife on the warpath. I had mothers screaming in my face, swearing that they would shut us down. 'I just bloody well hope you're not selling my daughter alcohol,' they'd shout. And all I would think was, Not half as much as I bloody hope we're not.

These little hitches aside, the gig was actually a lot of fun. I had high hopes that it would be a great PR exercise for us. So it was extremely disappointing to see an article in the *Daily Mail* the next day about how '35' handbags had been stolen at the Wham concert in Brixton last night. I walked straight over to Brixton police station and asked if they had had reports of any stolen handbags at the Brixton Academy. They hadn't the faintest idea what I was talking about.

When I called the *Daily Mail* to see what this was all about, they admitted straight out that they had invented the entire 'story' off the top of their heads. I was enraged and demanded they print a retraction, which of course they had to. In typical tabloid style, they ran a perfunctory little paragraph about the size of a postage stamp, on page 46 of the paper, the following week.

Pushing things beyond the perceived limitations of what a rock venue could achieve was always exhilarating. It wasn't just booking camp pop bands. We had a magical few weeks in which the Kirov Ballet from St Petersburg, or Leningrad as it was still then known, rented the entire Academy to rehearse for a special show they were putting on at the Royal Opera House. It was strange and inspiring to see graceful, swanlike ballerinas gliding across a stage usually filled with greasy rockers. They seemed almost to levitate around the venue. As this was still the era of the Cold War, for every two ballet dancers there was one surly KGB agent hanging around, chain-smoking Western cigarettes and keeping a watchful eye lest any of their dance stars tried to defect.

That wasn't the only time we had secret service agents at the Academy. Culture Club came in for a few weeks of production rehearsals before a major world tour. This tour happened to kick off in Israel, which meant that every single piece of equipment – every instrument, flight case, and bit of lighting gear – had to be meticulously checked by scary-looking Mossad guys with tans and dark sunglasses. They actually turned out to be quite nice dudes, taking it very much in their stride when some of the more flamboyant members of Boy George's entourage took a shine to their olive-skinned, tough-guy image and started flirting with them outrageously.

I dreamed up all sorts of crazy schemes with the gang of assorted artists, dopeheads, and loonies who used the Academy as their base. At one point, I got in touch with the Royal Academy to try to organize a huge exhibition of major British artists in our own, very different, Academy. I thought we could do something truly amazing with our space. But after much discussion, the lords and ladies of the RA chickened out of leaving the genteel safety of Piccadilly to bring great art to the badlands of Brixton.

Channel 4 were a bit braver. They approached me about filming a series of high-end TV shows at the Academy based around live performances by the biggest acts in the genre only just coming to be known as World Music. So *Big World Café* was born. The show ran for two seasons, with a total of 26 episodes featuring Mariella Frostrup's debut as a television presenter, along with Jazzy B and Eagle Eye Cherry. Hosting these shoots was great fun. I learned a lot about television production, and got to see some outstanding acts from all over the world. Artists like Salif Keita, Diamanda Galás, and Nusrat Fateh Ali Khan would probably never have performed at a place like the Academy in a purely commercial context. Now they all came, and gave some unforgettable performances. One of the most joyous shows I ever saw at the Academy was a Cuban band called Los Van Van who electrified the place with their *Big World Café* show.

All these off-the-wall gigs were really exciting. I loved how the venue could overturn people's expectations. You think a rock band won't come and play in Brixton? Well, we've just had The Clash. You think we're just a rock venue? Well, we installed a massive fairground ride inside for our club night. It's always good to keep people on their toes.

Occasionally though, I got caught by surprise myself, when other people totally confounded the stereotypes I had of them.

When we booked Ozzy Osbourne I was expecting a night of extreme debauchery. Pat and I decided it would probably be wise to put extra security backstage for that show, and I got the dressing room fridges well stocked with every kind of booze the self-styled Prince of Darkness could possibly desire.

Then, only a couple of weeks before the gig, I got called into an urgent meeting with Ozzy's manager, and wife, Sharon. She informed me that Ozzy had recently come out of rehab, and their team wanted the entire gig to be completely dry. They demanded that no alcohol be sold anywhere in the venue, as Ozzy might find it just too tempting, and take another tumble off of the wagon.

It was well known how much work Sharon Osbourne had put into rebuilding her husband's career after his split from Black Sabbath: a career that so easily could have ended years before in a drug-addled mess on the floor of some LA motel room. I respected that commitment, and admired how obviously protective she was of her husband. I had also heard enough of the music biz chatter to never doubt for one second her infamous business acumen. Sharon Osbourne wasn't someone you wanted to try to pull a fast one on. On the other hand, I made most of my money on any rock gig from the bar take. Even if they were willing to cover the £50,000 or so I stood to lose by putting on a dry gig, which I seriously doubted, no amount of money was worth me having to go out and tell five thousand Sabbath fans they weren't allowed to buy beer at a gig they'd paid to get into.

In the end we reached a compromise. Backstage would be completely dry, with no booze at all, which was fine with me as it meant I saved money on the band's rider. The punters themselves would be able to buy drinks, but we agreed to turn off all the brightly lit displays with beer company logos that lined our bars. I guess Sharon was convinced that just seeing those glowing icons from the stage would be too much temptation for Ozzy in his fragile psychological state. I was happy to make that small concession for a rock legend like Ozzy Osbourne. And to his credit he pulled off a great, raucous rock 'n' roll gig without any chemical stimulation whatsoever. Just when you think you've got someone all figured out, they can still surprise you.

TEN POUNDS SHORT

Some aspects of life, however, never seem to change. One of them is the Jamaican music business. No matter how big a star we were dealing with, putting on reggae gigs was always a fraught affair, with an ever-present undertone of double dealing and vicious street politics.

Bunny Wailer, the last surviving member of Bob Marley's original Wailers, was probably the biggest name in the roots reggae world. He was also a battle-scarred veteran of Jamaica's cut-throat music industry, which had claimed the lives and careers of so many of his contemporaries. When we booked him for a three-night run, we were still forced to operate as if we were running some Kingston sound system clash. The Wailers might have sung a lot of songs about 'one love' and everything being all right, but don't ever let anyone fool you – those guys were as tough, wily, and ruthless as they come. They couldn't be any other way. They came from a place where nobody could survive, let alone achieve success, without developing a highly evolved killer instinct.

I had made a fairly standard deal with the band's management team, paying them half the deposit for the gigs in advance, the rest to be paid with a cheque after each show.

However on the Sunday night, just before the final concert, with no warning at all, the band suddenly decided that they wanted

£10,000 in cash. If this had been a weekday it wouldn't have been a problem, I would have simply driven over to the bank and had their money in crisp new notes. But this was a Sunday night, the banks were shut and, with good reason, I didn't keep that kind of money lying around the venue.

I don't know if the band were trying to pull a fast one with the taxman, or even with their own management team. Perhaps they were just so used to being ripped off by promoters in Jamaica, that they decided not to take the chance. Whatever it was, they were dead set on getting their fee in cash. I pleaded with them to accept the cheque as agreed, but they were adamant, refusing to go onstage until they had the full amount in hand.

They started getting quite aggressive about their demands, shouting about 'bloodclarts' and 'chi chi mans' in loud patois. Trying to calm the situation down, I struck a compromise. I agreed

Bunny Wailer: One Love, but you better have the right money

to find the cash, but explained that since I didn't have it to hand, what I would have to do was wait for £10,000 to be spent at the venue bars. At which point, I could take it out of the tills, run it up to them, and write a big IOU in the account books to explain the ten grand missing from the bar take. The guys in the band seemed to accept this, but made it very clear that if they didn't get the money in their hands, then I would be left with a full venue and no band onstage.

I spent an anxious couple of hours watching every bit of cash that passed through the tills, then whipping it straight upstairs to be counted. We didn't do much business on the bars at reggae shows; they were always more about smoking than drinking. It was a race against time to hit our ten grand target before Bunny Wailer's scheduled stage time.

Eventually, the word came from the office. I stuffed the piles of crumpled five- and ten-pound notes into a bag and headed backstage to where the band were hanging out with their entourage in a thick sinsemilla haze. I was still naive enough to expect a smile and a thank you. Instead, the bag was snatched roughly out of my hands, and two heavies moved in front of the door, blocking my exit. The cash was poured onto the table and a couple of the guys started counting it out. It was very clear I wasn't leaving until they were satisfied they had every penny. This was the entertainment business, Trenchtown style.

This was a bit irritating, as I had a lot of stuff to be getting on with. But I was fairly relaxed, as I knew I had gone out of my way to accommodate the band's request, and that they would probably do a great show knowing that they'd been taken care of.

So it was a great shock when one of the guys at the table sprang up and shouted, 'What da fuck is dis? Dis money is short.'

I froze. This was impossible, I had been emphatic with my team to count exactly the right amount.

Within seconds I was slammed up against the wall and surrounded by four big, dreadlocked guys all shouting at me at once. Whenever I tried to get a word in edgewise it just seemed to make them angrier and I'd get shaken violently. It was all 'raasclart' this and 'babylon' that and 'what de fuck you tink you're doin' ripping off superstar artists?' I really thought I might be in for quite a serious beating.

Just at this precarious moment the door swung open, and in walked a duskily beautiful young woman. I recognized her immediately. She worked for a PR company that specialized in promoting black artists and sports stars. I'd had a few conversations with her boss in the run-up to this gig, but they'd been fairly pointless, as I had always been completely distracted by this girl. She was not only one of the most beautiful women I'd ever seen, but smart and funny with it.

My back was still against the wall, and I'd been lifted off my feet by one of these enormous geezers. She paused at the door taking in the scene before her. My eyes locked with hers, and I tried to maintain some sort of cool, while also communicating a fairly urgent sense of 'some help would be useful'.

She didn't miss a beat, walking coolly up to the massive guy holding me by the throat, and saying in a gentle, but reassuringly firm voice, 'It's all right Gus, I know him. He's OK.'

There was a pause. Gus and I locked eyes. Finally he seemed to accept her assurance, and I felt his grip loosen on my neck as I was lowered to the floor. It's astounding what a relief that sensation that can be. My whole body relaxed as the immediate danger seemed to have passed, but I also knew I had to regain control of the situation. 'So is there something the matter with the money?'

I asked, hoping a bit of charming British understatement might help defuse the tension.

'Your count be ten poun' short,' Gus snapped testily. 'Dere only be nine thousan', nine 'undred, an' ninety poun' 'ere.'

Ten pounds? All this aggravation over £10?

'Oh, I'm dreadfully sorry about that. It's a bit difficult when you're counting the money straight from the bar tills.'

Gus looked unimpressed.

'I think I may actually have ten pounds on me,' I hurried on.

I reached slowly into my pocket, pulled out a crumpled tenner, and offered it to Gus. He snatched it quickly, and I backed slowly out towards the door.

'Well, have a good gig then guys. Enjoy it,' I managed as I slipped out of the room, followed by the beautiful woman who had just rescued me.

The moment I was outside the door I leaned against a wall and exhaled deeply.

She smiled. 'They're actually really nice guys once you get to know them.'

'Well, they're certainly precise with their numbers,' I replied, doing my best to come across as cool and nonchalant. As the panic of the situation receded I was able to refocus on the woman in front of me. She really was captivating. Flashing, bright eyes, and the body of an Amazon princess. I couldn't stop myself. 'And what's your name?' I asked.

'Pippa,' she replied. 'You're Simon, right? You run this place?'

'That's right, it's my gaff,' I said, taking her arm and walking her back down the corridor. 'Well Pippa, I think seeing as you just saved my life, the least I can do is to take you out to dinner.'

'I'm not sure my boyfriend would like that too much.' She

giggled coyly. My heart fell. 'But you could put me on the guest list for Metamorphoses next week.'

'I'm sure that can be arranged for you, Pippa,' I said, and gave her arm a cheeky squeeze. There was hope at least. Boyfriend or no, I was going to see her again.

I didn't know it as I watched this extraordinary woman walk off towards the bar, but a few years later we would get married and have three children together.

But that was all still a long way off. There were plenty of other adventures to come in the meantime. Things were about to get explosive.

'AND THEN I WENT AND GOT MORE PISSED THAN SHANE MACGOWAN'

Looking back over my years at the Academy, I must have seen it all in terms of debauched partying: from the bands that took the most obscene amounts of drugs to the ones who got the most obscene girls. But I can say with absolute certainty that when it came to a pure riotous, drunken melee, there was nothing more visceral and hardcore than The Pogues.

They were one of the first bands to truly embrace the Academy and make it their natural home. The band had blown me away when I first saw them years before up at the old Town & Country Club in Kentish Town, but from the late 80s on, it was the Brixton Academy to which they returned each year to throw their annual London shindig.

There was no band quite like The Pogues. The exuberant Irish stomp of their rhythm section, the raging punk spirit of their delivery, and of course Shane MacGowan's swaggering gimlet-eyed poeticism up front. I loved their ferocious energy and always looked forward to their Academy shows, though I knew my liver would ache for days afterwards.

In 1989 the band were at their absolute peak. It was that golden era when they'd just had a massive hit with Kirsty MacColl in 'Fairytale of New York', and put an album in the Top 10, but before MacGowan went completely off the rails and pulled the whole thing apart. That year we had them booked with The Chieftains as their opening act. As expected, the show sold out almost immediately, and the whole team at the Academy was geared up with excited, slightly nervous energy to welcome them back. You could always count on some trouble with Shane and the boys, that's what made them great. But you didn't always count on the Troubles ...

The day of the gig went smoothly enough, soundchecks and warm-ups passing off with nothing more than the usual chaos of putting on a Pogues show in Brixton. Though I made it a personal rule never to touch a drop until a gig was over, needless to say the same did not apply to the band, or their crew. It was a bit messy, but we got The Chieftains on fine, and about halfway through their 45-minute set, I went on my usual rounds, checking everything was running properly, and catching up with the band backstage as they got fuelled up for the show. Then my radio crackled to life. I heard Pat's voice saying, 'Simon, you'd better get down to the doors, we've got a little situation here.'

In Pat's and my code, the smaller he made the problem sound, the bigger I knew it was. A 'little situation' always meant some serious shit was going down and I'd better make it over fast. I raced through to the foyer, sprinting down the side passages of the building to avoid the crowds. Pat motioned me over to the side, where he was standing with a policewoman from Brixton police station. I knew this woman from my regular contact with the Brixton

Shane MacGowan of
The Pogues: always explosive

cops. She had just been promoted to Inspector, and I was about to smile and say congratulations, but she interrupted me with clear, desperate urgency. I don't think I'll ever forget what she said next. 'Simon, we've received a coded bomb threat from the Provisional IRA, and we have reason to believe there is an incendiary bomb somewhere in, or around, the premises. We have forty minutes till the device is meant to go off.'

I froze. I had a sold-out venue, with 5,000 people all going crazy to The Chieftains. And there might be a bomb in here?

Trying to clear this place out would be no joke. I knew that to evacuate the Academy with any degree of safety you need twenty minutes at the very least. If you just ran into that crowd and shouted 'Bomb,' people were going to get trampled. This required organization and discipline.

Still, even as my heart was racing in panic, something felt wrong about this. Why on earth would the IRA want to bomb The Pogues? I mean, talk about alienating your own demographic. Yet with that band, and their entourage, you never quite knew what kind of trouble they might have got themselves involved with. My head was spinning as the policewoman continued, 'We can't confirm the threat, but we have received it, and we are obliged to inform you.'

When you run a circus like the Academy, what other people call 'crisis management' you learn to call 'standard operating procedure'. Pat scrambled his ten best security guys, and I went over the details in my mind. I knew that no bomb could have come through the front doors with the crowd: security would have spotted it in a second. If there were some sort of device in the building, it would have had to come through the stage door with the gear at the load-in that afternoon. I sent Pat and his team to search under the stage, while I went to talk to the band and their manager.

It's a difficult question to have to ask guys who have become your friends over the years, especially hardbitten Irish toughs like The Pogues and their crew. I gathered the band and the management, stared them down, and said, as calmly as I could, 'Look, I'm only going to ask you this once, and I need a straight answer: is there *any* reason, *at all*, why the IRA would want to bomb you guys?'

There was a brief moment of incredulous silence before Frank Murray, The Pogues' legendary manager, snorted, 'You've got to be fucking kidding, right?' He handed me a clipboard and continued, 'Look at our fucking guest list.' I followed his finger down the page and saw exactly what he was pointing at: the names Paul Hill, Gerry Conlon, Paddy Armstrong, and Carol Richardson. The bloody Guildford Four: fresh out of prison, on the guest list, and in the building. There was no way the IRA was going to target this show. But on other hand, there *had* been a threat, and I had 5,000 people's lives on the line. Whoever had called in the message certainly knew something about rock 'n' roll shows; the bomb was supposedly timed exactly for when The Pogues were due onstage, just when the crowd would be surging forwards. Maximum damage, maximum impact.

I took the Inspector, now visibly regretting her promotion, back to my little security room, a protected backstage office with a bank of thirty-two monitors on which I could survey every corner of the Academy. Time was running out. The Chieftains had finished their set and were coming offstage. We now had ten minutes left to decide whether or not to evacuate the whole building, before our window of safety expired.

I radioed Pat. 'Ain't found nothing, boss,' came the reply. Pat's team knew the building inside and out. If there was a bomb near the stage there was no doubt they would have found it. Then another thought flashed through my mind. We couldn't find any explosives inside the Academy, but there could just as easily be a car bomb sitting outside the venue. If I did evacuate the crowd, I could just be herding them straight into the path of the explosion. Now time was ticking, and I was starting to sweat. I turned to the policewoman and asked straight out, 'Look, who has the final call on this?'

She looked right back at me and said, 'Simon, it's your venue. It's your call.'

My heart was thumping harder now. I looked at the bank of security monitors. I could see The Pogues in the backstage corridors, getting ready for the show. I could see the crowd milling around the stage, or heading to the bar. My eyes glanced at the large red emergency button that I would have to use to override the PA system, should I decide to evacuate the building. I now had three minutes to decide. The wrong choice now could mean a lot of people were going to get hurt; and I could be going to prison for a long time. I could feel the blood pounding in my temples as I ran the possibilities through my mind.

Then it all seemed to slow down, the decision seemed very clear, coming more from my gut than my head. I remember saying very slowly and deliberately, 'No, we're not going to evacuate, we're going to go on with the show.'

The decision was made; the die was cast. I looked at my watch as the seconds slipped by, past the crucial point where we could no longer evacuate the building. We were committed. I felt every second as it ticked away. Those were the longest minutes of my life. It was now half an hour since we had received the threat, so we had exactly ten minutes until the bomb was supposed to blow. Nine minutes, eight minutes. I compulsively glanced at my watch, but then had to look away again: back and forth, back and forth. Seven minutes, six minutes. My legs were twitching uncontrollably. I kept looking at the security monitors, at the crowd in the auditorium. They were all enjoying themselves, totally oblivious to the fact that their lives were in my hand. Three minutes, two minutes. I was beginning to feel physically sick. My breathing was becoming shallow, just on the edge of hyperventilating.

I looked at my watch again. One minute, thirty seconds. I was biting my lip so hard I almost drew blood. Twenty seconds, ten seconds. Breathless. Zero.

Nothing happened.

I felt relief wash over me. The Pogues bounded onstage.

But here's the kicker. What no one had told me was that The Pogues' show began with a giant pyrotechnic display. So just as they ran onto the stage, just as I was going limp with relief in the backstage security room, there was this huge explosion.

My heart jumped in my chest, and my head snapped up to the monitors. The three screens covering the stage had gone completely white in the blast. I don't think I have ever, before or since, felt such abject terror. Having Yardies put a gun to your head doesn't even come close. I couldn't breathe from a panicked combination of dry heaving and hyperventilation. All I could see in my mind were mangled bodies at the front of my stage.

And then, suddenly, as if from another world, I heard this unmistakable chugga-chug, kick-drum, snare, and rhythm guitar pattern kicking off. I looked back up at the screens to see the smoke clearing, The Pogues going for it full-pelt, and the audience intact, and going mad for them. I burst out laughing hysterically, some would say maniacally. I don't think I stopped until the end of the song. Never in my life have I been so glad to hear a bunch of Irish loonies making an almighty racket. I sank into my chair, my body weightless with relief. Lord knows what the police inspector must have thought of me.

As it went, there was no IRA bomb in Brixton that night. The Pogues played a blinder of a show, and the audience were absolutely mental. It was a hell of a gig, one of the best. And afterwards I made damn sure that I went backstage and got more pissed than Shane MacGowan, which really does take some doing.

BLAGS
AND SCAMS

I've always thought it was strangely funny that after seeing off threats from the IRA and the Brixton Yardie gangs, and after putting on the most hardcore rap acts like Public Enemy, NWA, and Schooly D, that I actually ended up getting stabbed at a Salt-N-Pepa gig.

The pop-rap trio had just had a massive hit with 'Shake That Thang', and we were doing very brisk business on the night of the show, as kids clamoured for tickets at the box office.

By now, we had streamlined our system at the door. Our first set of guards would check people's tickets as they came through the doors. Then the punter would cross a small space to where the second line of guards would search them, before tearing their tickets and letting them through. The space between the two lines allowed Pat and I to scope out any prospective troublemakers before they even made it to the bag check.

The kid must have been no older than fifteen: wiry frame, tracksuit, and surly south London street attitude. I watched as he passed through the first set of guards. Then, with no warning, he suddenly tried to duck past me and sprint through, avoiding the second, more important, security cordon. I didn't know if he was trying to avoid being searched or just wanted to get through without his ticket being torn, so he could pass it out of a toilet window to friends waiting outside.

Either way, I was having none of it. I caught him by the scruff of the neck and pulled him back towards where the guards were waiting. He immediately whipped around and started fronting off with me, sticking his chest into mine and giving it all the usual Brixton 'bloodclart' and 'I'll mash you up' routine. By now I'd heard that stuff so many times it was just noise. Besides, this kid was so skinny I could have put him over my knee without worrying; I could see Pat standing behind him grinning at the scene being played out.

The kid may have been skinny, but he was fast. And strong. Before I knew what was happening, he made an abrupt move. His arm flashed out, and he jammed a knife hard into my side. I was wearing a Kevlar vest, but the impact seriously hurt. When I took the vest off later, there was a dark bruise spidering out across my lower ribcage. To bruise someone through Kevlar you have to strike with real force. It was a bit shocking to realize that kid meant to do me serious damage. Had I not been wearing the vest I would very likely have been killed, all over some petty dispute about tearing a ticket.

Needless to say, Pat was all over this brat in under a second. The kid was led away, his arms pinned behind his back, to experience some of Pat's own brand of justice before the police arrived. He was arrested of course, but I never found out what happened. Maybe he was let off with a caution because of his age; maybe he got caught in the trap of being a young black male in the 1980s British justice system? Either way, it was a lesson for me in how random violence can be in that part of the world.

Stabbings aside, the other memorable moment of that Salt-N-Pepa gig was that it was the scene of one of the more amusing blags I experienced at the Academy. People were always trying it on at gigs, claiming to be a friend of the band, or the management, but this scam was definitely one of my favourites.

That afternoon the phone had rung, Johnny had picked it up and said hello, then turned to me a bit nervously. 'Umm Simon, it's Grandmaster Flash. He wants to talk to you.' It wasn't like Johnny to get star-struck, but this *was* Grandmaster Flash. He passed me the receiver.

'Uhh, hello.'

'Yo, this is Flash. I hear you got Salt-N-Pepa up in your place tonight. I'd like to come check that out while I'm in town.'

I could hear the sounds of a bustling crowd and PA announcements in the background. Of course, he was on tour and calling from the airport. It made perfect sense.

This was fantastic. I'd been thinking for a while about putting on a series of mini-festivals at the Academy, each exploring a particular genre, curated by some grand name of the field: a bit like what the Southbank does now with the Meltdown festival. Grandmaster Flash masterminding a hip-hop spectacular at the Academy could be pretty damn cool.

'Of course,' I replied quickly, 'that sounds great. I'll put you on the guest list with an Access All Areas pass.'

So that evening, as I steadied myself after the knife incident, I told the girl doing the guest list that when Grandmaster Flash came in she should call me over so I could personally show him around.

Eventually the call came, and I strode over to the doors. Then I saw the guy and laughed my head off. He may have been a black American guy in a tracksuit, but this was definitely not Grandmaster Flash. He was about twenty years too young, fifty pounds too heavy, and a foot too short, just for starters. He looked at me sheepishly, knowing immediately he'd been caught out. Still, I admired the sheer chutzpah of the guy's play.

'Look,' I said, 'you've got balls, I'll give you that. And this is the funniest scam I've seen in a while. You can go in and watch the show, but there's no way you're having an Access All Areas pass.'

The guy couldn't believe his luck and raced into the venue. Pat raised his eyebrows at me. I shrugged; I'd just been stabbed, I suppose that can make you prone to random acts of kindness and magnanimity.

That Grandmaster Flash blag showed a lot of brass, but for sheer inventiveness and ambition, the prize has to go to what Pat and I came to call the 'sound-desk/stage-door scam'.

I can't remember exactly what gig it was, but definitely something dance-oriented and bass-heavy. Midway through the show a hue and cry went up backstage that several thousand pounds in cash had gone missing from the promoter's office. There was a safe in there, but very often there would be significant amounts of cash just sitting in a desk drawer. Promoters always needed ready money to settle up with runners, provide bizarre rider requests for bands, and deal with all the other last-minute hassles of putting on a big gig.

Unfortunately, that corridor was one of the few places in the Academy that we didn't have cameras set up. But it was obvious that whoever took the money had to be someone carrying an Access All Areas pass. That limited it to backstage crew, catering, or a friend of the band's, which seemed a fairly unlikely scenario. So Pat and I sealed up backstage, with no one allowed in or out, and started triangulating the footage from the areas around the promoter's office. We narrowed things down to a fifteen-minute window in which the theft must have taken place, and were fairly confident we would catch the culprit.

As we went through the footage we started seeing these three guys popping up again and again hanging around near the stage. They were young dudes, all wearing long white coats; they all had passes around their necks, but no one knew who they were. By now we had been going as a venue long enough that all the stage crews knew each other very well. These three guys were definitely outsiders. Bingo, I thought. We've got 'em.

Pat took Black Nigel and Pete the Mercenary, and within minutes had collared the interlopers and frogmarched them into my office. Pat and his guys could be extremely scary characters when they wanted to be. By the time I walked in, the three dudes were visibly bricking it.

It was strange: they had 'guilty' written all over them, but they didn't look or talk like criminals. It took only minutes for them to break down and confess what they were up to. But their confession caught me completely by surprise. These guys hadn't stolen the money from the promoter's office; their scam was so much bigger, and so much cooler.

It worked like this: when the three of them saw an exciting upcoming concert, they would scour the live-sound industry magazines for details about which band used what equipment. The companies that manufactured sound desks were always keen to brag when they had scored a major tour, and would take out ads like 'Soundcraft are proud to work with The Prodigy.' Anyway, these three characters really did their research about their chosen gig. They would find out who the promoter and agents were, who was handling the PA installation, and all the other useful little details of the production.

They would then print themselves passes with the name of the sound desk company. After that, all they had to do was stroll up during the band's afternoon load-in and flash their passes at the security guys, saying they worked for the sound desk company and were coming in to monitor how the system performed. Not only would they get to see the gig, but they would get Access All Areas passes and be able to watch everything right from the side of the stage.

At first Pat didn't believe them. He was so used to dealing with serious, hardened crooks that he couldn't grasp why anyone would go to such trouble for no financial gain. But I was a rock 'n' roll head. I understood immediately, and actually admired these guys' ingenuity. We checked them out and they weren't street villains at all. They turned out to be a lawyer, an accountant, and an estate agent: entirely more genteel forms of criminality. They were terrified of Pat, but also scared we were going to call the police and wreck their careers.

We were led out of the venue to where their car was parked a few streets away. They opened up the boot, and sure enough there was their professional-grade laminating machine, along with hundreds of backstage passes from various gigs, which they had kept as trophies. Looking through their collection, I was blown away. These guys had pulled their scam at some of the biggest shows in the country. Huge concerts by Bruce Springsteen and Pink Floyd, and their crowning glory: Access All Areas passes to Live Aid at Wembley Stadium.

I was so impressed with what they'd pulled off that I completely forgot to be angry. The sheer audacity of their blag and the fantastic attention to detail with which they'd carried it out were seriously impressive. If it hadn't been for that missing cash from the promoter's office, we would never have caught them. I let them go with a wink and a smile, but also a stern warning not to try anything like that at the Brixton Academy again.

In the end we never did prove who nicked the money from the promoter that night. Pat had his suspicions though, and once again I thought it best to let him undertake his own form of justice without enquiring too deeply.

Sorting out the backstage passes was consistently the most tedious hassle of putting on a gig. There was always an ever-changing rainbow of coloured wristbands, each denoting who was allowed where. Then, just when we thought we had it all figured out, some record company would phone up with two hours to go, and say they wanted to have their own after-after-party for their executives who had flown in from overseas. So I would have to go and brief my team yet again, this time about what this new pink wristband meant, so that they didn't manhandle some confused Japanese record company boss.

Club nights were the worst. At least with a gig, you knew you had the band, their crew, and some catering staff. Everyone had a role. With the clubs, only the DJ and the promoter really had a defined part to play, but there were invariably hordes of hangers-on. For these people, their wristband determined their status. They would all desperately try to make out like they were more important than each other, angling for better passes. There was always a more elite inner circle to be part of. It was pathetic, and it created constant difficulties for my security staff.

Some of the seedy old rock 'n' roll clichés also proved disturbingly true. One of the lower points I had at the Academy was overhearing a mother offering a bouncer a blow job so that her daughter, who turned out to be fifteen years old, could get backstage and hang out with the Beastie Boys. It was lucky for the security guy in question that he turned her down. Had he gone for it, losing his job would have been the least of his worries when Pat got hold of him.

Then there was the old classic of hearing some loudmouth yelling at one of my guys on the door that they had better let him in because he was a 'close personal friend of Simon Parkes'. Of course I had never met the guy before, but I really enjoyed the look on his face when I let the bomb drop: 'No, you're not a close personal friend of Simon Parkes, because I'm Simon Parkes, and you have exactly zero chance of getting in here tonight.'

The one person who could get away with this trick, though, was Pippa, the beauty who had saved my neck from Bunny Wailer's crew. I got called backstage at a Neville Brothers gig, only to find her in a heated dispute with our backstage security, having blagged her way in by dropping my name. It turned out she'd been pulling this stunt for months, getting backstage whenever she wanted. Some women just have the charm to pull it off; and I suppose I did owe her a favour.

I, of course, tried to parlay this fortuitous meeting into a date. But just as I was about to ask her out, this absolutely enormous bloke, built like a rugby player, ambled over and slung an arm around her shoulders. I knew when to pick my battles and backed off, but I told myself that I wasn't going to let this one go.

We even found guys working for us on the take.

It was a West World club night. I started to notice that every time I walked past the stage door I would hear this strange clicking noise. After about the twentieth time, I got suspicious. I figured this sound must be a kind of signal or warning to protect some shady goings-on of one sort or other.

I called Pat and we came up with a plan. None of our inner circle would have tried anything, but we also supplemented our in-house crew with security guys hired from the big five London firms, to run various bits of the venue on any given night. We were pretty sure that one of these guys was up to something. We just had to catch him at it.

These outsiders didn't know the building like we did. They had no idea that there was a trapdoor leading to a passage under the main auditorium, meaning that I could go right under the building and avoid their little click-click warning system.

Pat and I descended, and made our way under the floor of the Academy, with 5,000 clubbers in full swing pounding on top of our heads. We popped up just next to the stage door. Bang. Right in front of us was one of our outside security staff in the act of selling entrance to the backstage area to a random punter.

Pat had the guy up against the wall in seconds. We searched him and found about £700 in cash tucked away. He quickly came up with the story that he was holding the petty cash for the company to pay their people at the end of the night. This was obvious nonsense. Firms like that cashed out their staff with crisp twenties straight from the bank, not with the crumpled fivers and tenners that this guy had stuffed into his pockets.

It could have gone very badly for the fella if Pat had had his way. But I recognized him as the son of the head of one of the big security firms. That was hassle I didn't need. We let him go with a warning, but I kept the money, just to send a message.

That guy never worked the Academy again, but there was also no comeback from the firm about the money, so I knew we had read the situation correctly. All those security companies tried hard to keep me sweet. It was massive kudos for them to work the Academy. They built their reputations in the industry on it. If you could work a 5,000-capacity venue in Brixton, you could work anywhere.

After a while even I developed my own little guest list scam.

As exotic as it sounds in the desiccated music industry of today, back in the 80s and 90s, record companies would still give their bands a level of tour support. This often involved them buying up 400 to 500 tickets to a gig as soon as it was announced. They would hand these tickets out to their own people, but the purchase also served as an incentive to promoters to book their acts. The industry formula in those days was that for every person who went to a gig, you could expect to sell 10 records via word of mouth. So, for a 5,000-capacity venue like the Academy, the labels could expect to sell 50,000 records. Not a bad return. Certainly worth shelling out for a few hundred tickets as a little bribe to ensure that promoters wanted to book your act over your rivals'.

Looking back on the way they operated it's not all that surprising that the record companies have taken a fall. They were stupendously wasteful. Let's say you had someone like Lenny Kravitz, on Virgin, coming to play a gig. They'd buy up a few hundred tickets. Then, if the support band were also on Virgin, one department would invariably fail to talk to another, and they'd buy up another couple of hundred to give out to exactly the same people. On top of that, there would also be a press department sending out another couple of hundred to journalists who were never going to come to the gig, but still needed to be buttered up. It all would amount to quite a large block booking.

The Academy was one of the first venues in Britain to start barcoding tickets. I got the idea from Ollie Smith who ran the Town & Country Club in Kentish Town. It was fantastic to be able to start keeping track of trends, and know who was buying which tickets. I began to notice a very consistent pattern emerging. At

Lenny Kravitz at his prime

almost every gig, exactly half the record company sales wouldn't turn up, and those tickets would go in the bin. It was amazing how constant the numbers were: it was always exactly half. If the label bought 500 tickets, 250 would show up; if they bought 300, it would be 150.

I thought it was silly to have all these tickets going to waste, so I struck a deal with promoters. They would show me how many tickets the label had bought in advance; then we would reprint exactly half that number and sell them on to actual music fans. All off the books and on the QT: it worked like a charm.

I never actually made any money from this set-up. I just used it to give promoters I liked an extra bump. I always tried to keep good promoters loyal to the Academy, and I knew the young newcomers to the industry appreciated it.

I also thought that promoters were often the unsung heroes of the music business. Those guys operated on such razor-thin margins that they were constantly in danger of going under on one off night. The guys I worked with would take a massive risk on every gig: an extra 200 to 300 tickets could mean the difference between success and insolvency.

It was the exact opposite of the agents who, once the deal was signed, knew they were getting their 10 or 15 per cent and could just sit back and collect the money. Don't get me wrong, some of the agents were great guys, but many did gain reputations as insufferably rude, arrogant arseholes with little interest in talent or the creative impulse. The promoters had to hustle constantly, and I always respected that.

ROCK THE CASBAH

It seems hard to believe now, but up till this point at the Academy I had been managing to bluff and improvise my way through with Lambeth Council, using an ever-expanding series of occasional licences to put on our shows. Now, however, things were picking up at such a pace that, just in order to keep up, we had to become a more legitimate enterprise. To receive a real, permanent venue licence, the council demanded that we fulfil a comprehensive Schedule of Works, completely overhauling the building in line with new regulations. Which meant serious money.

I was just starting to get worried about where all this cash was going to come from when help came from an unexpected quarter.

Watney's brewery, from whom I had originally bought the building for £1, were extremely happy with their exclusive beer sales. Your average pub would go through two or three brewer's barrels a week; we could do twenty a night. I had cultivated my relationship with Jim Millar and Bob Scaddon at Watney's, and we had developed quite a mutual respect. I had grown to admire their wealth of business experience, and they were impressed with what I had pulled off so far in getting the Academy off the ground.

So Jim and Bob stepped up. Watney's agreed to lend me the £750,000 needed for the Schedule of Works, and we got our licence from the council.

Then, just a few weeks after the deal went through, I had an encounter that made me see the old boys in an entirely new light.

It all started when an old mate of mine from school, Charles Dolby, got in touch. Charles's family was very involved in stalking deer, mucking about with horses, and all the other country pursuits the British aristocracy find so fascinating. Charles himself had actually wound up in Dubai, training horses and setting clay pigeon traps for the crown princes.

This was when Dubai was just beginning to open up and transform itself from a desert settlement into the schizoid, hedonistic metropolis it is today. As part of these efforts to 'modernize', the princes wanted to start putting on shows by big Western music acts. The only hitch in their plan was that they refused to deal with any Jewish people. And in the entertainment industry, that can be a serious problem.

Charles's angle was that I was properly 'British' enough to be their man in the UK. The fact that my father's entire side of the family was actually Jewish was to be kept very quiet. We figured that with blond hair and a surname like Parkes, I could bluff my way through.

So Charles made the connection and I soon started getting messages about how keen the Emirati royals were for a gig by Bananarama. Well, there's no accounting for taste.

The princes insisted on meeting face to face before we began any kind of business, and flew over to London to talk over their ideas.

What I was to discover was that when Arab royals come to London, they don't just want to chat about gig logistics, they want to party. I walked into the bar at the Hilton to see these guys in their elegant, flowing robes, surrounded by leggy blondes, with six open bottles of Dom Perignon on the table.

I greeted everyone warmly before pulling Charles aside in a panic. 'I hope to hell I'm not meant to be hosting these guys and buying the fucking champagne here, Charlie.'

Charles just smiled, 'Simon, you don't pay for anything. Don't dare even offer; it'll be considered an insult. Whatever happens, just go with it. It may get a little wild.'

Well then, that was a very different story. If these guys were buying the rounds, I might as well have a good time. It would be rude not to.

Charles was right. It did get wild. We all piled into their Bentleys and were dropped off at some high-end casino. None of the princes would ever carry cash. They just waved their lackeys up to a little window and received large trays of chips. I watched in horror and fascination as one of them promptly bet, and lost, a quarter of a million pounds on roulette without so much as blinking.

Eventually the casino closed, but everyone was still in full party mode, and keen for the night to continue. I suggested a little after-hours club called Fidenza, where I was a member. It was a place that stayed open all night specifically for people who worked in the entertainment business and needed somewhere to unwind after their shows. Cool little showbiz industry joints like these exist in all big cities. You always know the drinks will be good as these are the spots where the promoters and barmen go to get loaded. It caused quite a stir when I burst in with these Arab princes and their entourage, who proceeded to buy pretty much the entire bar.

Then, in the midst of this madness, who should I see but Jim Millar from Watney's brewery, in the company of two very attractive young women, one on each arm. He was obviously planning on a very pleasant end to his evening, but froze like a deer in headlights when I strolled up and said, 'Hello there, Jim.' I just smiled and gave him a wink, but in the back of my mind I couldn't help thinking that maybe the terms of that £750,000 loan I had taken from Watney's might have just got a little bit easier.

I woke up the following afternoon with a vicious hangover. I was barely able to pick up the call from Charles informing me that

I had been deemed worthy. The princes wanted to meet to discuss plans for putting on gigs in the desert. Based on the evidence of the previous night, I thought this venture might be both lucrative and fun, so I was excited.

The plans were ambitious. The princes wanted to test the water by bringing over Bananarama to play at the Al Nasr Ice Rink. The thought of an ice rink in the desert was almost as strange to me as the thought of anyone getting *that* excited about putting on a Banarama show, but the princes were also dropping some very heavy names. They were talking seriously about performers like Michael Jackson and Elton John, pretty much the biggest acts in the world. And it wasn't like these guys had any trouble backing up their talk with hard cash.

The plans started to come together over the following months. I sent a couple of my people over there at my own expense to recce the place and see what kind of logistical support would be necessary to pull something like this off. Gradually things fell into place, and it got to the stage where I actually felt confident enough to start booking some bands. Then everything fell apart.

The deposit needed to book Banarama was $10,000. It really wasn't all that much for a big-selling band, and nothing the Emirati Princes wouldn't drop on a couple of rounds of drinks. But when I spoke to them, I was met with a stony 'We don't give deposits.'

These people were royalty. It was considered beneath their dignity to put a down payment on anything. It was as if you were casting doubt on their word that they would, or could, pay.

I sweated blood trying to explain to them how the Western music industry worked. No deposit meant no band. To no avail. For the princes it was a question of honour. Fair enough: that's how they did business. But try explaining that to a hard-nosed London music agent. For agents, a sense of 'honour' meant only stealing *half* your closest friend's savings the moment his back was turned. And here I was with the proposition, 'Fly your band out to a country you probably hadn't even heard of before you picked up the phone to me ... and, oh yeah, we're not going to pay a deposit.' It was a classic mismatch of two very different manners of conducting business: the Arab *adab* and the London barrow boy. It was just never going to happen.

It could have been such a good deal for me that I seriously considered trying to raise the cash for the bands myself. But in the end the risk was just too great. It was one thing to put up ten grand for Bananarama, but quite another when one started talking to Michael Jackson's people and suddenly you were talking figures of a million pounds and up. I could have raised the money if I needed to; and I would have gone into it being 99.9 per cent sure that the Emirati royals would come through. But these people were erratic; they acted on whims as only the cartoonishly wealthy can afford to. There was always the possibility, no matter how miniscule, that something in one of the performances might anger or embarrass them and they would call the whole thing off in a fit of pique. Artists like Michael Jackson and Elton John were hardly what you would call 'conventional characters'. If one of the emirs suddenly cottoned on that maybe these guys weren't exactly *straight*, as they understood it, or if they just thought Bananarama showed too much leg for their tastes, they could just walk away from the deal, leaving me completely exposed.

In the end, the risk was too great. I decided there were enough uncontrollable variables I had to navigate without even leaving SW9, before I started putting myself in line for possible financial ruin on the whim of spoiled, unpredictable aristocrats half the world away.

THE KING
OF GIGS

I was very proud as I watched the repairs being carried out on the Academy building and we got a proper licence at last. It felt like we were growing up as a venue, that we were moving beyond the phase of having to patch over the cracks just to get a show on.

But even I didn't realize exactly how far we'd come. The reality kicked in when I got a call from Robert Sandall at the *Sunday Times* asking if he could interview me about how we had replaced the Hammersmith Odeon as the London's premier music venue. My first reaction was a shocked, 'Have we?'

In my mind we were still the young upstarts, and Hammersmith was the established institution. But combing through the trade journals I saw that the Odeon's bookings for 1989 were all way down. They were standing empty more weekends than they were putting on shows. I did some hunting around on the industry gossip circuits, and discovered that Rank were completely restructuring their entire strategy. Their flagship plans for the following year revolved around a flashy production of *Joseph and the Amazing Technicolor Dreamcoat*. Holy shit. We hadn't just grown up, we had won the fight. All those rock 'n' roll bookings that would have been going to the Odeon two years before were now coming straight to us. Of course I couldn't help think back with a wry smile to old Penfold back at the Rank offices, with his patronizing little 'Yeah, good luck, son' all those years ago.

The *Sunday Times* did eventually run their piece on the Academy and me. A big picture of my grinning mug ended up splayed across their pages under the headline 'The King of Gigs'. Well, I thought that title could do me quite nicely. Then, in typical fashion, when Sandall asked me about why I thought the Academy had such an appeal to music fans, I blurted out, 'Well, we dominate the indie-rock scene because this is a great venue for people who like to go mad.' It probably wasn't the most poetic way to put it, but from the raucous gigs we were putting on, it certainly felt like the truth.

Truth be told, I've never paid all that much attention to the press, and I wasn't sure the *Sunday Times* was exactly the place to go to learn about the hottest new underground sensation. Not long after that article appeared, however, the Academy's place at the apex of London's music pantheon was confirmed by true pop royalty.

Aside from her invaluable help at the Academy, Lynne Franks had a roster of megastar clients who included the undisputed Queen of Pop, Diana Ross. Ross's new record was going for a zeitgeisty 'club feel', so Franks came up with a brilliant PR move. They would launch the album in Europe with a secret show at Johnny's Metamorphoses night at the Academy. It was a classic stroke of Lynne Franks genius: the perfect crowd to generate a word-of-mouth buzz for the album; a way to show that Ross still had her finger on the pulse of what was hip and underground; and a juicy talking point for the press.

We obviously found the idea incredibly exciting. It was Diana Ross for heaven's sake, the biggest-selling female artist of all time.

This was no scrappy punk band or thuggish rapper. If we could get a star like her to play Brixton, we could get anyone. Apparently the only person who needed to be convinced was Ross herself, who wanted personally to check the venue out before greenlighting the idea.

The record company did their best to put the fear of God in us. Diana Ross was flying in from Switzerland, where she lived as a superstar tax exile, specifically to give us the once-over. At the label's insistence we scrubbed the whole place down, bought in a load of flowers, and stood in a group waiting in our newly sparkling foyer. Meanwhile, all these record company stooges ran around, fretting over every detail like overwrought wedding planners to ensure it was *just so* for when 'Diana' arrived. They even demanded I wore a suit. And I never wear a suit for anyone.

One hour passed. Then another. We stood there in our goofy welcoming committee waiting for Diana Ross to pull up in her limousine. Obviously, anyone in this industry was used to big stars turning up late. But Ross was nowhere to be seen, and she was completely uncontactable. Somehow, these label press department guys, with all their assistants, and their assistants' assistants, had managed to lose her somewhere in London. This sent the PR clowns into a real tizzy: running around like extremely camp headless chickens, squawking frantically into their huge 1980s brick mobile phones.

Then, just as all these guys were about to really flip their lids in panic, up walks Diana Ross herself, coming out from behind us all with a casual 'Oh, hi everyone,' wearing a pair of jeans and a faded T-shirt. It turned out she had driven up to the back of the building herself, in a beaten-up Volkswagen Golf borrowed from a friend, and had spent the last hour being shown around the venue by a sixteen-year old kid named Jason from the Stockwell Park Estate, whom we had taken on as a runner.

Queen of Pop:
Diana Ross comes
to Brixton

You should have seen the flap the PR queens flew into: 'Oh my god, we didn't know if you were all right, Mrs Ross,' the whole silly routine. Ross herself sailed gracefully above it all and simply said, 'I love it. It's fantastic. Let's do the show here.'

I stood back, watching this whole scene, feeling like a bit of a chump in my suit, and thinking, wow, you absolute star. To me it was obvious she had pulled the whole stunt on purpose just to wrong-foot her own team and keep them on their toes. It was a pleasure watching a true operator like that at work. She was perfect: absolutely gracious and charming, and an angel to young Jason, but with a steely sense of what she wanted, and how she wanted it done. Diana Ross was always a step ahead.

She also knew exactly when to turn on the star power. On the night of the show itself there was no question of denim jeans and an old Golf trundling up Brixton High Street. Then it was all limousines and entourages: the full, explosive glamour of American stardom in action.

At 1 a.m., the height of the club night, the Metamorphoses DJ turned down the mix and, as Soul II Soul trouped onstage picking up their instruments, he announced a *very* special guest. The audience hushed, turning expectantly towards the stage. Impromptu, secret performances were part of the game at Metamorphoses, and everyone was expecting to see the latest hot underground funk or hip-hop group bound onto the stage.

When the DJ actually said 'Diana Ross' and she strode into the spotlight, the whole place went ballistic. People couldn't believe it. They had paid six quid to get in, and were getting to see one of the biggest stars in the world. Ross herself was fabulous, mixing new material with her old hits, and holding the stage with the effortless grace that only those who have been performing most of their adult lives can achieve.

Then, the second her set was finished, she flashed everyone that famous smile, and was gone. Back in the limo, away from the hurly-burly, every inch a true star. Ross was one of the rare genuine, dyed-in-the-wool class acts that I encountered during my time in the trenches of the music biz.

Once again though, I had the shine taken off my buzz by the good old British media. Diana Ross was interviewed on Terry Wogan's show the following evening to promote her record. His first question was, 'So, I heard you performed in Brixton last night?'

Perfect, I thought, a good bit of PR for us! But just as a big smile appeared on Ross's face and she began trying to say how great the whole night was, Wogan cut in with, 'Weren't you scared?'

'What a fucking idiot,' I fumed at the TV. These pathetic stereotypes about Brixton just never seemed to stop.

Ross herself just looked confused. She didn't know what Wogan was talking about. She didn't have any prejudices about Brixton. All she knew about the area was there was a great venue there called the Academy. Besides, Diana Ross grew up in the badlands of Detroit. I don't think London was going to throw up anything to faze her.

Ever the star, Ross batted the silly questions away and managed to give a charming, generous interview nonetheless.

A few months later we got a very different insight into what fame and stardom can do to the human personality. After all the grace and elegance of how Diana Ross had conducted herself, it was a disappointing comedown to then experience another, very different kind of grace: Grace Jones.

You can usually expect a little bit of ego from bands on the way up. In their first flush of success some musicians get carried away with the trappings of stardom. If they have any savvy, they soon realize just how vapid the whole charade is, particularly once they find out that all those expensive lunches and flashy cocktails are actually coming out of their own pocket. Teeny pop groups are the absolute worst – acts thrown together by some manager, instead of spending hours in a garage honing their craft. They often start to believe the hype, poring over the recycled drivel churned out in the tacky pop magazines. Established artists, the ones who really

Keeping up with the Jones.
Grace in action

got into it for the music and have been around for a while, are usually pretty cool about the whole showbiz circus. They see it for what it is, and don't take themselves too seriously.

Grace Jones was something else.

First off, she turned up extremely late for soundcheck. This might not sound like a huge deal, but big gigs are planned with minute precision. They need to be. When you've got tech crews, security staff, safety inspectors, and the rest of your team all lined up to do their specific jobs, you need to run on a very tight schedule. Everybody relies on everyone else to do their part, professionally and on time. An artist turning up late can set everybody back several hours, and throw the whole machine into chaos.

This show was part of a club night, which meant a slightly later performance time than usual. Jones was due on at 11 p.m., to be followed by DJs till 2 a.m. as part of a special extended licence.

It was ten years since she had released a hit album, which meant that by now most of her fans were new parents with young families. The idea was to get her on at 11 p.m. so all these early-thirties types could get the last train home to relieve the babysitter, leaving those who wanted to party to stay and dance with the DJs till 2 a.m.

In theory, it was a great plan. But everything fell apart when, after the soundcheck, Grace Jones disappeared back to her hotel and was completely unreachable. She eventually flounced back into the venue at midnight, with her entourage in tow.

In the meantime, I was left to deal with hordes of punters furious at being forced to leave to get the last train, without having seen the artist for whom they had paid an unusually high ticket price. I could see their point. If I had just paid to spend three hours looking at an empty stage and listen to a load of DJs on playback, I would have been pissed off too. Almost as pissed off as I actually was now, at having to spend the evening handing refunds back to angry customers, in between frantic trips backstage to see if anyone had managed to track down our star.

When Jones did eventually grace us with her presence, pun very much intended, things only went from bad to worse.

She had requested a certain type of Cristal champagne for her rider. When she arrived there was a different type of Cristal waiting in her dressing room. It was still Cristal, equally expensive, in the same gold bottles. But that wasn't good enough for this diva. She went into a thermonuclear strop, screaming blue murder at my crew and me, and refusing to go onstage until she had the exact champers she had originally demanded.

By this point I was sorely tempted to set Pat on her and sling her out on the street. But there were still a couple of thousand fans who had waited patiently for a show, and for their sake I decided it would be easiest just to give her what she wanted.

But where to find eight bottles of Cristal at midnight on a Friday in south London?

As luck would have it, I happened to know the bartender at one of the fancy Park Lane hotels. I also knew that this meant paying £250 a bottle instead of the usual £80 or so. Still, in the situation we found ourselves in, there was little to be done. So, with a venue still half full of dedicated fans waiting for their star, I sent a runner on a motorbike up to Park Lane to pick up the booze.

When we did eventually get Grace Jones onto the stage, her performance continued in the same erratic tone. She did all her usual impressive costume changes and salacious dancing, but there seemed to be something missing. Perhaps it was that she had chosen to sing with backing tracks instead of a live band? This probably saved her a lot of money, but it left her looking a bit lonely and weird up on that huge stage with no one but a few backing dancers to interact with. It was one of the very, very rare moments when I found a show at the Academy disappointing.

Having finished the gig she promptly disappeared into her dressing room with five very fit dancers, all kitted out in bondage gear. They didn't emerge for four hours. We always respected our artists, and didn't interfere with whatever Roman orgy was going on in there; but I did feel bad for the security guys, who had to stick around till 5 a.m. waiting for it all to finish.

RADIO BRIXTON

Grace Jones and her nonsense aside, this was a euphoric time for me. We did a special anti-apartheid night to celebrate Nelson Mandela's release from prison, with great music from Afrika Bambaataa and Jungle Brothers, and both Winnie Mandela and Jesse Jackson addressing the crowd. I remember Jackson in particular as one of the most inspiring figures I have ever met. Winnie Mandela, on the other hand, enlisted a load of gangsters as her 'security detail', surrounding herself with some of the nastiest elements Brixton had to offer. Where Jackson seemed genuinely to reach out to the crowd, Winnie seemed more interested in maintaining her own position as empress.

I think it was only as I looked out over the Academy that night, as these global heavyweights crossed our stage, that I was able finally to accept the idea that I had won. The Academy had taken the Odeon's crown. I had shown Rank that I could beat them at their own game, and we were on top.

As ever, this only prompted one question for me: what's next? I was always looking for the next challenge. I had fulfilled my silent promise to Penfold in the Rank offices, now I needed a new giant to conquer.

We started cooking up some serious plans.

In my mind, the Academy could be so much more than 'just' a great music venue. I began envisioning a kind of Motown set-up, not necessarily in terms of a record label, but simply

Public Enemies: Jesse Jackson and Flavor Flav
celebrate Nelson Mandela's release from prison

bringing much more of the production in-house. With all the
mad, talented people we had hanging around the Academy, I
was sure I could find the right team of bright sparks to make
anything happen.

My first project was to try to set up our own radio station. A
tender had just been put out for an independent London-based
radio station, specializing in black, or, as it was just coming to be
known, 'urban' music. Amazingly, nothing of the kind existed in
the UK at the time. My thought was, where better to house such
a station than the flagship venue for black music in Britain, the
Brixton Academy?

So ABC, the Academy Broadcasting Company, was born. I hired in architects and engineers to draw up plans for converting a few of our spare offices into a state-of-the-art studio, and began pulling together a team to run the station.

The plans were exciting. I got the legendary reggae DJ David Rodigan to agree to come over to us from Capital Radio, and signed up the comedian Julian Clary as our phone-in agony aunt, to be joined by Cynthia Payne, the famous Streatham brothel madam. We put everything together into a very strong proposal.

We didn't get the licence. Instead, it was awarded to the new station Choice FM, despite the fact that they didn't even have developed plans for a studio. Amidst my disappointment, I did crack a wry smile when only a week later I got a cheeky call from Patrick Berry and Yvonne Thompson at Choice asking if they could use *our* studio for their broadcasts!

Within months their lack of infrastructure forced Choice to sell to Chiltern Radio, which then became part of Capital. So the whole idea of an independent urban music radio station went out the window.

I was a little pissed off that we didn't get the licence, but I came to understand the politics behind the decision. The Academy was associated with the underground, edgier end of black music, with bands like Public Enemy and NWA. Our reputation was a bit too rugged and hardcore for the licensing authority. They needed to play it safe.

We were also a little too white. I never gave a fuck about the colour of the people who worked for me. Our team was always a mix of black and white, men and women – whoever was crazy enough to come along for the ride. But the state-funded radio authorities thought they couldnt be seen to be awarding the licence for a 'black music' station to a white guy. It was disappointing, but Patrick and Yvonne did manage to turn Choice FM into something pretty cool. I can't fault their programming skills. But I never forgot the concept of the Academy Broadcasting Company, and many of the ideas we developed were to resurface a few years later.

Moving on, my next plan was to fulfil my old dream and twin the Academy with the Apollo in Harlem. It made perfect sense: Brixton and Harlem, the Academy and the Apollo. I thought we could not only link our two brands, but also organize transatlantic tours, bringing the best US music over here, and exporting the hottest acts that London had to offer.

The previous owner of the Apollo, Guy Fisher, had now been given his life sentence for racketeering, and the venue was in the hands of some more approachable people. I flew a couple of cool guys, Phin Donelan and Alex Foster, to London to check out the British scene and see what we could work out.

At first it went well. We quickly became friends, and I thought they could see the potential in what I was talking about. They certainly seemed to dig the West World and Metamorphoses club nights. Then it was all brought crashing down by Fleetwood Mac and a publicity-hungry glamour model.

I thought a great way to impress the Americans would be to take them to the Brit Awards at the Albert Hall. At considerable personal expense, I booked us all a box to enjoy the show. Unfortunately, this happened to be the year that the ceremony was presented by Mic Fleetwood and Samantha Fox. It was an epic, unmitigated shambles. Autocues malfunctioned, leaving the awkwardly matched presenters to garble and stammer through half-remembered dialogue. Guests and prizewinners were presented in the wrong order,

The Academy Broadcast Company taking a break
on the venue roof. Myself, Kate Archer, Jeremy Azis,
Dave Loader, Mark Over, and Roger Collyer

leading to the train-wreck spectacle of people bounding out onto
the stage flashing their awards ceremony smiles, only to be frantically pulled back by bewildered stage managers.

The home crowd seemed to accept all this with a very British
sigh of resignation, and could appreciate the absurd humour of the
situation. To the Americans it looked like a pathetic flop. I could
see Phin and Alex looking less impressed by the second, as each
new catastrophe unfolded.

Eventually I couldn't take it any more. I drew the curtain round
the box, and sent Johnny to grab us a couple of bottles of champagne and a big bag of something Columbian. I thought it best if
we concentrated on having a party, and forget the disaster occur-
ring around us.

But the damage was done. After that night the guys at the Apollo
became hesitant at the thought of twinning themselves with any

London institution. After seeing the cock-up of what was supposedly the biggest awards ceremony in British music, they wrote off
the whole country as a bit of a joke. I suppose it served me right
for taking them out of Brixton in the first place. Lesson learned.

Looking back on my years at the Academy, one of my very few
regrets is that I never had an older, wiser head around to bounce
all my crazy ideas off. We were so young, wild, and inexperienced
that while we produced some amazing energy and creativity, I can't
help thinking that if we'd had some real veteran there, someone
who really knew how the business worked, they could have pulled
all my mad thoughts together into a coherent package.

For instance, one of our West World nights had a Batman theme,
based on the old, camp Adam West TV show. It was great fun, with
lots of absurd costumes, and people going crazy whenever the DJs
dropped the classic *na-na-na-na-na Batman* theme tune.

In the run-up to the night we had printed up some T-Shirts
with the famous Batman logo on it. Naturally, the Warner Bros.
legal department had something to say about us using their copy-
righted trade marks. Over the course of our conversation they
actually offered to sell me the exclusive UK licence to all Batman
merchandise for £10,000. At the time I was only concerned about
my club night. I wasn't interested in brand licensing or anything
like that, and I never really got back to them. Needless to say, just
over a year later the Tim Burton movie came out starring Michael
Keaton and Jack Nicholson and was a smashing success, completely
relaunching the entire Batman franchise.

Any wise, experienced businessman would have told me, 'You
know what, for ten grand just buy those rights and stick them

in your back pocket. You can always sell them on down the line, and you never know what could happen.' If I had sprung for that £10,000, I would be a very, very rich man today.

There were countless little instances like that. In my dealings with the Apollo, or the Radio Licensing Authority, some kind of Richard Branson character, even an Alan Sugar type who really knew business, could have guided me through.

My ideal would have been someone like Chris Blackwell from Island Records. We met once about a *Big World Café* performance by one of his great international acts. He was always someone I sincerely admired, having built up his music empire by his own sweat and ingenuity from the boot of his car. This was another occasion when someone convinced me to wear a suit, and then of course Blackell himself sauntered down in shorts and a T-shirt. I was floored by his wealth of experience, and the sheer depth of knowledge he brought when speaking about the industry, as well as his obvious and undiminished passion for music. If I had had an inspiring figure like that around during these years, then perhaps a higher proportion of my off-the-wall schemes would have come to fruition.

To be fair though, I did pull off more than enough craziness to keep things moving, and moving fast. And life was about to get very wild indeed. There was something completely new on the horizon, something so profoundly revolutionary that it would change not just music, but society, forever. We were about to experience the birth of rave.

PART THREE

REVOLUTION ROCK

EBENEEZER GOODE

1989 was a seismic year for British popular culture. We emerged from the doldrums of punk's slow dying and found ourselves blinking and confused at the highwater mark of tacky Thatcherite consumerism. The mainstream watchwords of the day – individualism, greed, and selfishness – inspired some people, but left too many out in the cold. Not everyone fitted in to Thatcher's 'Essex Man' vision of the New Britain, with his mobile phone, safe commuter-belt home, shiny new car, and utter disregard for his fellow being.

Young people were looking for a way to express their distaste with the craven, aspirational model of life that was being forced down their throats. The knowing, self-conscious rage of punk proved inadequate to the task. Johnny Rotten had screamed 'no future' back in 1976, but now that the future had arrived, the kids were forced to look elsewhere for inspiration. They found it not in revolutionary anger, but in love and community. Or at least, 'love' and 'community' as approximated by a thumping kick-drum looped at 120 beats per minute.

All through that glorious 'second summer of love', every weekend saw young people throughout Britain calling semi-secret phone numbers, receiving carefully guarded details, and converging in their tens of thousands in fields to dance like mad, fuelled by the wave of new drugs flooding the market.

It was a crazy time. You'd get handed a flyer with some cryptic line about a 'big rave in the Oxford area' that weekend. You'd phone the 0898 number and buy your ticket, then have to wait till the night itself to call yet another number in order to receive the details of where the event was actually being held. It meant a huge act of trust, and a lot of sitting in cars around the M25 on a Saturday night, making frequent trips to the phone box to see if the location had been released.

But when you eventually got there, my god was it magnificent. Thousands of people dancing to these pulsing beats, with lasers shooting everywhere like an alien landing. It was a truly universalist movement. People would turn up from Eton to Peckham, and everywhere in between. Black, white, yellow: it didn't matter. Race and class became suddenly, and beautifully, irrelevant; we were there to dance. No one had ever experienced anything like this before.

By the time the cops would show up, responding to the bewildered residents of rural England, there was absolutely nothing they could do. If you've got upwards of 20,000 pilled-up ravers going crazy in a field, then three police vans turn up with 25 cops, it becomes a joke. They're basically there to manage traffic. It would have been madness for the cops to try and break up one of those gatherings.

Not that the police, in those early days at least, would have had too much trouble to deal with. Rave was never about getting pissed and having a fight. It really was centred around love, peace, and getting high. In many ways, the early rave scene was the absolute antithesis of the football hooligan culture that had been Britain's national embarrassment throughout the late 70s and 80s.

This was an inspiring time on many levels. All over the world things were changing at a thrilling pace. In Tiananmen Square, student protestors were standing up for their rights. Throughout the Eastern Bloc, regime after oppressive regime crumbled like the desiccated husks they were. Walls were torn down, tyrants were deposed, and people, especially young people, celebrated their freedom on the streets. I truly believe there was a sense of 'something happening', that kids in the UK watched all this unfold and felt that in their own small, hedonistic way, they were part of a global movement pushing towards independence and unity.

The authorities, of course, had no idea how to handle all this love and anarchy. They started getting twitchy. The Thatcher government had established its Iron Lady image from confronting striking miners and militant unions. Now it seemed the establishment couldn't get to grips with a bunch of kids dancing in a field. As if on cue, the British tabloid press went into the type of manufactured, self-righteous frenzy that only the British tabloid press can manage. Led by the *Sun* and the *Daily Mail*, the hacks did their best to stoke the moral panic about this new subculture, as if acid house spelt the end of civilization as we know it. This whole, hyped-up media fuss was really very silly, but it must have sold a lot of papers.

Personally, my first exposure to this new phenomenon came through our West World club nights. Our VIP area played host to Shoom, a travelling club run by the DJ and innovator extraordinaire Danny Rampling.

Shoom is generally credited as the first proper acid house club in the UK. It was Schoom that first used that famous smiley face logo – which came to symbolise the entire movement – for their flyers. They were the spark that kicked it all off. At West World, I started noticing that Shoom was quickly becoming the main attraction of the night, with people queuing up to dance to the strange new music blasting from within, rather than the expensive big-name acts I had booked for the main space. Of course I was intrigued, it was my job to be.

Through the Shoom crowd I got to know pretty much everyone involved in the emerging scene, from the Ibiza Four – Rampling, Paul Oakenfold, Nicky Holloway, and Johnny Walker – to era-defining rave promoters such as Jeremy Taylor, 'Tin Tin' Chambers, Tony Colston-Hayter, and Jarvis Sandy; and, of course, the 'two Normans': Norman Jay and Norman Cook, the latter later adopting the moniker Fatboy Slim.

Obviously, I worked a lot on weekend nights, but I still managed to make it down and party at raves in various fields and warehouses around the South of England. I loved it. There was a genuinely fresh vibe at these gatherings. Everyone seemed authentically cool, and committed to having a good time with a minimum of aggravation. Which, after six years of putting on shows in Brixton, was a massive relief.

But there was one very obvious reason why everyone was so nice and loved-up at the raves. Ecstasy.

With the possible exception of reggae and marijuana, never have a musical movement and a particular drug been so inextricably linked. It was everywhere. Those little pills fuelled a generation and defined an era. It was pretty amazing stuff. You'd see huge tat-tooed Millwall and West Ham fans, who a year earlier would have been tearing chunks out of each other on some stadium terrace, arm in arm dancing to the Shamen with a load of hippies. White kids who had only ever nodded along forlornly to The Cure in their bedrooms suddenly realized it was all right for them to actually dance. People turned on, tuned in, and let go. All inhibitions went out the window. For those few hours everyone was best friends, and we all had a great time.

Norman
Cook AKA
Fatboy Slim
on the decks

But like so many idealistic counter-culture movements, that joyous original rave scene carried within it the seeds of its own destruction. Those happy little pills didn't just come out of nowhere. In fact, they were supplied and distributed by some extremely nasty people.

The hardcore criminal gangs who ran the drugs trade saw before them a completely unregulated, unprotected market awash with money. All those capitalist, Thatcherite principles that the kids thought they had been rebelling against began to reassert themselves with a vengeance.

And it wasn't just the drugs. If you have twenty thousand people in a field, all of whom have paid £15 a ticket, you're talking serious amounts of cash, all stuffed into black bin bags and there for the taking.

Disturbing rumours began circulating around the scene. I began hearing stories that, after all I had been through in Brixton, struck an all too familiar chord.

There was a well-known promoter named Joe, who ran Labrynth, a fantastic, hard-edged techno night. He was a larger-than-life character on the dance circuit, and had been down to the Academy quite a few times. The Labrynth crew had put together a big warehouse rave out in the East End, and had been approached by the local gangsters about doing the security, much in the same way that I had originally been approached by the Mob all those years ago. Joe refused, and tried to front these guys off. On the night of the party, a group of men in balaclavas burst in and attacked the loved-up ravers with machetes. Joe himself had been held at gunpoint.

Hearing about this, and other events like it, sent shivers down my spine. Of course the gangsters would want a piece of the action!

Most of the rave promoters were actually well-educated public school boys from nice homes. By and large, the majority were a bit like me: the eccentric tearaway black sheep of quite wealthy families. But most of them hadn't been lucky enough to find a hard man like Pat, with his private army, to protect them. These idealistic party kids were never going to be a match for the hardened criminals that ran the underground entertainment industry. They couldn't even see the kind of sharks that were circling their little scene. I, however, knew from bitter experience exactly who they were dealing with.

The real prize, however, was always going to be supplying the pills. Some very ruthless elements were getting mixed up with this naively utopian clique. The gangsters were taking control.

Time and time again I saw the same pattern being played out: a gang of dealers would attach themselves to a certain promoter. The promoters, of course, needed someone to supply the dope to make their party go off, and were happy to oblige. But once the gangsters had inveigled their way in, there was no getting rid of them. What were the soft middle-class kids meant to do against guys like that? The balance of power would gradually, but inexorably, shift away from the idealist promoter trying to put on a good party, towards the hard-nosed criminals, whose sole concerns were squeezing out as much money as possible, and eliminating any competition.

I knew the type of people that my mates from the scene were getting involved with. Seeing these arrangements develop was extremely worrying. I had experienced the depressing inevitability of how situations like these resolved themselves. It didn't take a genius to realize that it was only a matter of time before people were going to start getting seriously hurt.

6 A.M.

Just as my initial excitement about the new scene was becoming tinged with this creeping worry about its increasingly powerful criminal elements, I was invited to one of the strangest meetings of a career largely made up of very strange meetings. All I was told in advance was that I was going to speak with a 'private security company'.

I walked in and sat down across a desk from a muscly guy in a dark suit. He had a piercing stare, a military bearing, and he got straight to the point.

'Hello Mr Parkes,' he began. 'It seems like some of your friends have been getting themselves involved with some very, very vicious bastards.'

Well, that was one way to get my attention. Naturally, my first response was to wonder how the hell this guy knew who I was, who my friends were, or what they might or might not be involved in.

Things only became marginally clearer as the conversation went on.

It seemed that this 'private security firm' was entirely made up of ex-SAS and SBS officers, who had followed a career path fairly typical for elite soldiers, and ended up going into business for themselves. Their current assignment was to investigate the organized crime gangs infesting the rave scene. Through a conversation peppered with implication and innuendo, I gathered the impression that these hard-arses *may or may not* have been working with various government agencies that *may or may not* officially exist.

One thing they were very clear about was that they were uncovering more and more evidence of some extremely serious criminal elements taking control of the entire dance movement. I knew a lot of the names they were dropping. We were talking about some genuinely horrible people: *bullet-riddled-bodies-found-in-the-boot-of-a-burned-out-car* kind of people.

This security firm wanted a simple favour. They knew I had access to a lot of the movers and shakers of the rave scene. All they needed was for me to introduce them, undercover, to some of the promoters and party organizers who passed through the Academy.

This put me in a profound quandary. The last thing I wanted to do was to help the authorities crack down on the rave scene. I loved those parties in the fields. I knew that even talking to these guys could be seen as selling the underground out to 'the man'. That wasn't my style at all.

On the other hand, the kids organizing the raves had no concept of the kind of monsters lurking in the shadows of their hedonistic movement. They were moving into deadly territory and didn't even know it. I didn't need any reminders about exactly what they were up against.

I also knew that, while for now it might have been a matter of raves in warehouses, if these gangsters went unchecked, it was only a matter of time before they turned up on my doorstep, posing a real threat to myself and everything I had built. This was no idle worry; the violence was spreading. The way things were going, it was a question of when, not if.

'Look, Mr Parkes,' the SAS guy assured me, 'we have no interest in interfering with people putting on parties; that's kiddies' stuff. We're after the serious criminals.'

'We'll make an agreement,' he continued. 'You introduce us to your contacts as a company that can help with their security needs, and we'll protect them. When the violence kicks off, they'll need people like us around.'

I agreed to help.

It didn't take much. An introduction here, a backstage pass there, and that was that. Nothing really seemed to happen for a while, and busy as I was, I forgot about the whole affair.

Gradually, though, the police began to gain the upper hand in the running cat-and-mouse battle they had been fighting with the rave organizers. I'll never know whether this had anything to do with the guys I introduced to my friends on the circuit, but some of the raves began to run into problems. These were more than just routine hitches: a secret location would suddenly become not so secret, a sound system meant to be moved from a warehouse in east London would get impounded, the 0898 number operating a ticket hotline would get cut.

The rave crews operated in absolute secrecy. To stay one step ahead of the cops, only a handful of guys would ever be aware of the logistical details for setting these parties up. For the police to start busting them, they must have infiltrated and had people on the inside.

The SAS lot that I had spoken to had promised me they were only interested in hardened criminals, not rave promoters. But when dealing with the authorities, you never know who you can trust. I was probably only one amongst hundreds of contacts, but even now, I sometimes question whether my intervention may have contributed in some tiny way to the police crackdown on the rave scene. I very much hope it didn't; those parties were glorious. One thing I am absolutely certain of, though, is that, knowing the direction in which the scene was headed, and the species of characters that were becoming involved, I have never, ever regretted my decision.

Late in the summer of 1989, I was flipping through a stray copy of the *Daily Mail* that one of our tech crew had left lying around backstage. My eyes flicked over yet another histrionic rave story, as ever predicting society's imminent implosion, and castigating the police's perceived inability to stamp the phenomenon out. All of a sudden, one of those tiny light bulbs flicked on in my head.

I dusted off my old suit and booked an appointment with the Commander of Brixton police. Sitting across his desk, I laid out my idea: 'Look, you have a problem with these illegal raves; I have

There was nothing like the energy of that early rave scene

a solution. Make them legal. Give me a licence till 6 a.m. If we bring rave to the Academy, then you'll know it'll all be relatively safe and contained, the country folks will stop complaining, and, best of all, you'll kill all this media hype about failing to stop illegal parties.'

I half expected to be laughed right out of the office. So I was amazed at how receptive the police chief actually was. We ended up having a long discussion on the details of how my scheme would function. I was forced to improvise a fair bit, as I hadn't worked things out that thoroughly. Though the chief was very enthusiastic, he said he would obviously have to consult his superiors.

I will never know if my idea was simply a mutually convenient solution for the police's 'rave problem', or if some senior mandarin opened my file and decided to reward me for my previous co-operation. Either way, the call came through. I was issued the UK's first ever 6 a.m. licence.

The country's first legal all-night raves opened at the Academy and were an immediate, smashing success. All the major dance promoters brought their parties to us: Energy, Megadog, Raindance, Pendragon, Future, Return to the Source et al. These were some amazing nights. Now that they didn't have to piss all their effort up the wall playing guerrilla tactics with the police, the party promoters could put serious time and thought into their laser shows and light displays. Many of them got extremely sophisticated.

On New Year's Eve we threw a mega all-night party to see 1989 into 1990. As midnight approached, Adamski was pumping out his banging techno to the loved-up crowd as the lasers zoomed off in every direction. MC Daddy Chester was leaping around the stage like a demented whirligig, his dreadlocks flying behind him, getting the entire place hyped up. He raised the mic to his lips and shouted, 'I love technology. I love riddim! We take the sounds of 1989 and rrriiippp it uuupppp in the 1990s.'

I watched from the corner of the stage as the crowd heard this and went completely mental. It seemed like a very special moment. Johnny and I hugged like a couple of pilled-up nineteen-year-olds. There was a real sense of a new age dawning, that we were witnessing the birth of an uncharted era in popular culture. It was incredibly exciting for the whole team at the Academy to know that we were right at the vanguard of this new movement. We were leading the way.

Bringing rave to Brixton further cemented the Academy as the UK's cutting-edge venue. No one could touch us. Eventually, other venues received late licences as well, decent places like Bagley's Studios in King's Cross, or the Brixton Fridge up the road from us; but they were always following in our wake. I even got to resurrect my Academy Broadcasting Company dream, and we produced a series of rave-themed TV shows called *Dance Days*.

Our reputation only grew as time went on. We became the venue of choice for the 'rave bands': the groups that took dance music out of the fields and warehouses, and put it at the top of the charts. Everyone from The Prodigy and The Chemical Brothers to 808 State and The Orb hit their performing peak with epic gigs on the Academy stage.

And when the great dance-rock innovators of the *Madchester* scene exploded out of the Hacienda onto the national consciousness, there was only one venue they would come to for their big London shows. The fact that we could keep partying till 6 a.m. blew their already fairly well-blown minds. It takes quite a lot to get a Mancunian musician to admit a London venue might have one up on their northern dance Mecca, but The Stone Roses, New Order, and Happy Mondays all become devoted Academy converts.

Even the old 'crusty' trip-head vanguard got involved. Hawkwind, the original psychedelic freak-out band, launched a series of annual all-night psych-fests, with great titles like *The 12 Hour Technicolor Dream*.

And in a way it did feel like we were re-

He Bangs the Drum: The Stone Roses playing the Madchester scene's London home-away-from-home

enlivening the long-dormant spirit of the late 60s. The original 'summer of love' had had its era-defining 'happenings'; we had rave. With the possible exception of the punk explosion of the mid 70s, I don't think anything had seemed so joyous, so exciting, so full of adventure since.

EBENEEZER BAD

Working the raves represented a whole new learning curve. Just when we thought we had finally been getting a handle on how the late-80s music business functioned, everything was transformed overnight.

There were the small practical differences, like the discovery that a venue's bar take at these events was next to nothing. At a rave you basically sold 5,000 bottles of water, then people refilled them at the taps. Some industry guys even tried to sell me a purple dye to put into the tap water, so people would get turned off and buy more bottles from the bar, but that seemed unnecessarily cheap, even by music business standards.

But by far the greatest revelation of being the dance music's flagship venue was the vicious new level of criminality that it brought into play. By now, we were well used to dealing with the local Brixton heavies, but with the raves we found the entire game changing around us.

In a way, we had been very lucky at the Academy thus far. We had managed to walk a fine line, or at least fall between the cracks, of the competing forces of London's criminal underworld. We were always just a little too big for the local Yardie types to really try and take us over. Though capable of extreme violence, guys like the Railton Road boys were too disorganized for such a complex operation. They could make life extremely dangerous, but trying a serious, sustained move on us would have brought too much heat from the cops. Meanwhile, the serious, established organized-crime firms of London had always regarded Brixton as just too messy a place to get involved with. So for years we had managed to occupy the space left by this delicate balance of power.

With the raves everything changed. Selling Ecstasy at a venue like the Academy became a multi-million-pound business. It was too big a prize for the heavy gangsters not to get involved.

It was only ever a question of maths. If you have 5,000 punters in a rave, at early 90s prices, you could usually count on each of them spending about £20 on pills over the course of the party. That's £100,000 a night. Multiply that by two weekend nights, four weeks a month, and you've got roughly a £10 million a year industry.

With numbers like that, it was inevitable that the big organizations would come to claim their piece of the action. People like the infamous Addams family from north London, and their type of big-league mobsters. These were ruthless, highly organized, and heavily armed professional criminals. They made the local Brixton mobs look like kids squabbling in a playground.

With players like these, there was never any question of speaking in innuendo and insinuation along the lines of 'maybe we could help you with security'. If they wanted something, they took it.

A friend of mine, Davey Hines, had built himself a cool little bar up at London Bridge. He poured his heart and soul into the place, and it had finally started to become a bit of a success. Then one evening, as he was doing his end-of-night stock check, a couple of men walked in wearing big gold rings and long leather coats. 'Nice place you've got here. We're taking it. Make sure you leave the keys on your way out.' There was no recourse for Davey; no possible discussion or argument. He could give up his bar and live; or try and keep it and die. He slid the keys across the table and walked out: heartbroken, but alive.

These were the type of people we were now dealing with. Many of the rave promoters had had similar experiences. Guys would walk into their offices and just say 'right, we're taking a 50 per cent stake in your business'. There was never a choice involved. The thugs with the firepower made the rules.

It was exactly this scenario that I was trying to forestall when I agreed to help that private security agency, and whoever was behind them.

But there was still the drugs business. There was no avoiding that part of the deal. The pills were as central to the rave scene as the music. The new players in the game were a different league from anything we were used to dealing with. Not only were they were raking it in, they acted with the breathtaking arrogance of the true gangster: the one who knows he is untouchable.

Learning the rules of this new dynamic involved some rough lessons.

We caught a guy with about £10,000 worth of Ecstasy. He was obviously one of the big fish, so Pat and I decided that it would be politic not to hand him over to the cops. He was obviously heavily connected, and we thought we would offer a gesture of goodwill to the big firm that he was part of and let him go. We did, however, have to take his drugs off him; they went straight down the toilet.

But we made a serious mistake. We didn't flush the pills in front of him.

About forty-five minutes later I was with Pat at the front door when a car screeched up. This same guy jumped out, with three heavies backing him up. He marched straight up to me and barked, 'Right, I want my fucking drugs back.'

'Sorry mate,' I replied, 'they're down the toilet.'

The guy wasn't having it. He hadn't seen the pills get flushed, and automatically assumed that we had taken his product to sell ourselves. No amount of argument could convince him otherwise. That's the problem with dealing with serious criminals, they always assume that you're just as crooked as they are.

I tried to calm the guy down and explain that we had done him a huge favour in not turning him over to the cops. He didn't give a shit.

He looked Pat and I up and down, pointed at each of us in turn, and said in a cold, decisive monotone, 'Right: you're dead, and you're dead.' Then he got back in his car and sped off.

You could tell he meant it. He was too brazen not to. To drive up to the door of a major venue, look someone like Pat in the eye, and tell him he's a dead man takes some serious brass. To pull that kind of stunt, you need to know you have some extremely heavy back-up. We had an idea of who this dude's crew were. They were people who could bring considerable firepower into play.

I had to think fast. This could not be allowed to escalate.

Then I remembered something. When we had caught the guy, he had had a backstage pass on him. I knew from the colour of his wristband that he must have come through the stage door on the promoter's list.

I motioned for Pat to follow me, and we strode back inside. As we passed, I snatched the printed guest list off our doorgirl's clipboard. We went straight up to the guy who was promoting the night, and Pat physically dragged him into my office.

I held the guest list up in front of the promoter's face. Then, reaching into my wallet, I pulled out the card I had for the Head of Criminal Intelligence at Scotland Yard.

'All right, listen up,' I snarled at the promoter. 'We've just caught someone with ten thousand pounds' worth of pills. Their name is on this list. Now, that person has just seriously threatened my life, and those of my crew. So you listen to me. This list is going into my safe. If one hair is harmed on me, or any of my people, it's going straight to the man on this card.' I made sure the guy could see the Scotland Yard logo before going on, 'His team at the Flying Squad will shake down every single name on this list until they find the fuckers. We'll make all your lives a living fucking nightmare.'

At the mention of the cops, the promoter's face turned white.

'Or', I continued, 'you go and make some phone calls, right now. You make this problem go away. I know every venue owner in London. Do you ever want to throw another party in this city?'

The poor guy almost shat himself. He nodded frantically, and sprinted out of the office. About twenty minutes later he crept back with a whipped-dog expression, and assured me that the issue 'had been taken care of'.

But that list stayed in my office safe until the day I left the Academy. The whole episode taught me another important lesson: if you're going to flush a major drug dealer's stash down the toilet, you make damn sure they see you do it.

Like all good economists, gangsters make their calculations based on only two human emotions: greed and fear. The mobsters who ran the rave business were no different. They could come on just as brazen with their propositions as they could with their threats.

A couple of guys came to see me, looking to book six Saturdays, the first of each month over a half-year period. I knew these people were shady characters, but in this game, who wasn't? I'd at least hear them out.

We talked over their plans, and it all seemed fairly legit. They could talk the showbiz language, and sounded as if they knew what they were doing. They certainly seemed to have the finances to pull off an ambitious run of nights like these.

As the conversation drew to its natural conclusion and we got ready to draw up contracts and seal the deal, one of the guys leaned in a bit closer.

'Just one more thing,' he rasped in a clandestine hush. 'What's your stance on drugs?'

I took a moment to think about how to best respond to this.

The truth was that my 'stance on drugs' could best be described in one word: *sensible*. Of course I knew the stuff was everywhere. I'd be an idiot not to. With rave in particular, it was glaringly obvious what was fuelling the entire scene. My only policy was to keep my own hands clean. If the punters wanted to get high, then good luck to them, but we would confiscate any pills we found; and heaven help any of our security staff if Pat found them pocketing bribes to let dealers into the venue.

Back in the early, carefree days of the Academy we had been able to be far more relaxed about the whole issue. In those days, if our security guys confiscated something in their front-door searches, they would drop it straight into a chute leading directly to a drawer in our box office. We used to have a lot of fun dividing up the haul at the end of a night, having these completely surreal conversations.

'Are the red pills uppers or downers, I've forgotten?'

'No idea, but I'm not bloody touching them.'

'Fair enough, more for me. I guess you can have this block of hash, then.'

All the while, passing around ziplock bags and cardboard wraps, full of every herb and powder under the sun. It was a good laugh after a stressful gig.

Occasionally, if I was at my usual spot by the doors and I saw some kid getting his little bit of dope taken off him by a bouncer, I would wait till he was through the security cordon, then nip around the back of the box office, tap him on the shoulder, and hand him his baggie back with a conspiratorial wink. You should have seen the way those kids' faces would light up. Not only had I just made his night, but I knew he was going to go straight off and tell all his mates about how the Brixton Academy was the coolest venue in the world. I'd usually offer a bit of free advice: 'Look, if you're going to try and sneak dope into a gig, it's probably not the best idea to have a pack of King-size Rizla, with little bits torn off, in your shirt pocket.'

But rave, with its attendant criminality, had completely killed that naive, wink-and-nod, laissez-faire approach. Things had got deadly serious.

And now here I was, with a couple of nefarious characters asking me straight out about my 'stance on drugs'.

I decided honesty was the best policy. 'Look, if we find drugs on people, we take them away. If we catch people selling stuff, we call the police. But this is a rave. I'm not a fool; I know what goes on. But if you guys have an interest in that side of things, I don't want to know about it.'

The two men looked at each other. One nodded to the other. Evidently I had said whatever it was they were looking for.

The second man laid a briefcase on my desk, flipped open the catches, and slid it over to me. I lifted the lid to see neat stacks of £20 notes all wrapped up like little parcels, filling the case to the very brim.

This was quickly becoming more Hollywood than Brixton.

'What's this?' I asked, though I could hazard a guess at the answer.

'That's one hundred thousand pounds,' the guy replied without missing a beat. 'That's your cut. You just tell your people to let us get on with what we're doing.'

Looking down at £100,000 in cash is a peculiar sensation.

I stared at the briefcase in front of me. It was one of those moments in which you can truly see a fork in the road: two very different trajectories for your life laid out in stark contrast.

Thus far, despite every temptation and provocation, I had kept to my cast-iron rule that all my personal business at the Academy stayed strictly legal. But: a hundred grand sitting there for the taking, simply for doing nothing? There's no one in the world whose heart wouldn't beat a little bit faster. Wouldn't you at least pause for thought?

It could be so easy. Just take the money. If this was £100,000 just for looking the other way, think of what I could make down the line? In that moment, everything hung in the balance.

Then I came back down to earth.

I closed the lid of the briefcase, snapped the locks shut, and slid it back across the desk.

'Thank you for that, but I'm going to have to decline. We're happy to put on your parties; but it's your job to keep any drugs business out of sight, not mine.'

The two guys looked at each other in disbelief. They seemed to accept my decision, even if they did think I was insane. We ended up doing their raves at the Academy and experienced no more or less drugs nonsense than usual. I suppose they must have got away with whatever it was they were up to.

I am indisputably a much poorer man for that decision. I have never doubted for a second that I made the right choice.

'We wanna get loaded. And we wanna have a good time': Primal Scream's legendary Brixton all-nighters.

This was only one of countless points over the years at which I was tempted to dip my toe in those waters, to take a payment, to skim a little off the top. But I would always realize that when it comes to crime, you either do it or you don't. There are no half measures. Once your toe is in that water, you're swimming. And the sharks will always bite you in the end.

Closing that briefcase, and every time I turned my back on an offer like it, is without question the reason I am still alive today.

SORTED FOR ES AND WHIZZ

So my decision was made. We were staying legit. Which meant Pat and I spending a good deal of the next few years chasing drug dealers all over the building.

It was difficult actually to catch them at it.

Anyone who has ever been to a rave will know the type: the guys dressed in nondescript T-shirts and baseball caps, walking around muttering 'pills ... you need pills?' in a hushed, paranoiac whisper.

And, as anyone who has ever actually bought pills at a rave will know, the guy who approaches you is never the guy actually holding the drugs.

You hand over your money; the dealer disappears. Then, after a few minutes, if you're lucky, he returns with the product. Often it won't even be the guy you spoke to who comes back, but a completely different, unidentifiable goon in a baseball cap. You suddenly realize you've been watched the whole time, one dealer pointing you out to another. It's a little creepy, but you tell yourself that's just the way it works. You slam back your little happy pill, and get on with having the best night of your life.

There's a good reason the dealers need to have those kinds of procedures in place. They are usually being watched and followed by people like Pat and me.

The crooks were smart. They had their systems, and every time we cottoned on and busted a few of them, they would change up their strategies. Little things could make life difficult for us. Their upfront salesmen would swap clothes halfway through a night to throw us off the scent. Suddenly, the guy we had been following all evening, as he worked the upstairs market, would disappear – only to resurface an hour later having taken up position by the men's toilets.

All these tricks had one singular purpose: to protect the guy holding the stash. We'd track the dealers in a constant, cat-and-mouse game around the Academy. Sometimes we'd get them; most of the time we wouldn't. Years later when I saw the fantastic TV show *The Wire*, I laughed out loud as I watched how the cops would have to spy on the street dealers to figure out where the real stash was being held. This was exactly the same game that drove Pat and me mad for years at the Academy.

The dealers were cynical and ruthless. One of their favourite tricks was to get girls, usually posh girls, to carry their dope, on the assumption that pretty, smartly dressed white women were less likely to get searched.

There was always a certain type of well-brought-up middle-class young woman that liked to hang around with the 'bad elements'. They were probably just picking up a 'bit of rough' as part of some youthful rebellious phase. Most of the time I'm sure they just grew out of it, but sometimes it could mean real trouble. Coming from the background I had, I could spot these girls a mile off. Even when they tried to dress down, there was something in the way they carried themselves: a certain kind of skinniness, that peculiar air of entitlement. I could just tell.

I remember one in particular. I spotted her across the upstairs balcony, and had her pegged immediately. She couldn't have been any more than sixteen, obviously some nice, north London public school darling. She was dressed in the baggy jeans and bomber jacket that were de rigueur at the raves, but carried a Prada handbag.

When we picked her up and brought her to my office, even I was surprised. In that handbag, she was toting about £15,000 worth of Ecstasy. The poor girl immediately broke down in floods of tears. I asked her where she was from, and she managed to stutter out 'Huh ... huh ... Hampstead.' Of course, where else?

I tried to explain things to this girl. 'Look, I know these pills aren't yours. I know you're holding them for someone else: but whoever that is has put you in serious trouble. You are so naive. You have no idea the kind of people you're dealing with. They don't give a shit about you. All they care about now is that they've lost their drugs. You're in real danger. Not from us in here, but from whoever gave you this to carry.'

This girl was in bits. She obviously had no idea about the world she was dealing with. Her fun little flirtation with danger had just turned into something that could destroy her life.

If I had had my way, we would have just let her go. But there were two problems. First of all, an undercover detective had been hanging around backstage while I questioned the girl, so now the police were definitely involved.

But, more important, this girl not only needed to get arrested, but needed to get arrested very publicly. Whatever dealer she was protecting had actually to see her being led away by the police. Otherwise, he would assume that she had stolen his dope, and she could wind up dead.

I never found out what happened to that poor girl. As I watched her being taken off, I hoped that any prosecutor or judge would have the sense to see that she was a naive, if foolish, victim in this scenario, and let her off with a slap on the wrist. A drug bust on that scale could carry serious prison time, and she didn't deserve that. There would be no sense wrecking her future over a stupid teen-age blunder. Even today, I often wonder how that case turned out.

As time went on, and the drug pushers grew more powerful, they also became ever more unscrupulous. As if they weren't making enough money already, they began cutting their pills with all manner of chemicals and household poisons.

This didn't just mean disappointment for the punters, who instead of getting the rush of loved-up euphoria they had paid for would find themselves woozily vomiting in a corner. It meant serious problems for us.

The ravers would usually take their first pill of the night as they were lining up to get into the club at about 10 or 11 p.m. Obviously, this meant they would avoid any problems with our security checks, but also that they could get straight into the action the moment they were inside. By about 2 to 3 a.m. those pills would be wearing off. People would start looking for the next hit to see them through till dawn. Pat and I used to call it the 'lunchtime rush'.

What this schedule meant was that if there were something dodgy in the pills on a particular night, we could have 15-20 people dropping over roughly a 45-minute period. This happened with frightening regularity. It could get disturbing. People would be rushed to our paramedics in pretty awful states: twitching, vomit-ing, mid-seizure, the works.

I used to insist that our medical teams take off their yellow and green high-visibility vests. People under the influence would associate them with police, and refuse to tell the truth about what they'd taken. We'd get brought some guy covered in sweat, his limbs jerking uncontrollably, and his eyes fully dilated and zooming all over the place, and his mates would try and give us the old 'no, he's only had four pints of lager' routine. In those situations you need the truth, and you need it fast. It's a real testament to our medical team that we didn't actually have anyone die over those years. There were more than enough extremely close calls.

There was one incident that especially scared the shit out of me. Bang on cue, at about 3 a.m., some girls brought in their friend who was in a bad way. To look at her, you'd guess this girl was about twenty-two or thereabouts. It turned out she was fifteen. She'd taken a load of sketchy pills, and washed them down with a few pints: never a good combination. We eventually got her stabilized and sitting up, then called in an ambulance to take her to Casualty. Before she left, I grabbed one of her friends and made her give me the girl's home phone number. I could at least make sure her parents weren't left in some horrifying panic when she didn't turn up the next morning. I dialled the number, and some guy in Epsom, Surrey, picked up.

'Hello, this is Simon Parkes, the owner and manager of the Brixton Academy. I don't want you to worry, but your daughter was at the venue this evening, and has had to be taken into Casualty. She is OK, and is in very good hands –'

Before I could even finish my carefully prepared spiel, the voice on the other end of the line cut in. 'Oh, hello Simon.'

I was taken aback. 'Umm, hello, who is this?'

'Chief Inspector Borrell here.'

Oh Christ. A cop. And not just a cop – a cop I knew well. This guy used to be high up in the Brixton police, but had obviously moved on to greener pastures.

This was just what I needed: a police chief's daughter, fifteen years old, full of pills and booze, collapsing in my venue.

'I'm really sorry to have to tell you this,' I stammered, 'but she has taken some pills, and I believe she was drinking as well.'

I braced myself for the blast of outrage. In my mind's eye I could already picture the letter informing me that my licence had been revoked.

'Oh yes,' came the calm reply, 'thanks for letting me know. It's the second time this month. I'll go down and pick her up in the morning.'

Instances like that could mean real trouble for a venue. But ultimately, we had done the responsible thing: patched the girl up, sent her to hospital, and alerted her family.

Not every venue manager would have been so dutiful. In more recent years, things have gone particularly rotten.

In an effort to 'protect the public', or at least to be seen to be 'protecting the public', successive governments have brought in ever-stricter licensing laws. A few years back, they instituted a system whereby, if there are too many calls to a particular club, the police can shut that venue down without notice.

This was obviously meant to encourage club owners themselves to take stronger action against drug pushers on their premises. In reality, like so many government initiatives intended to protect people, it has ended up putting them in more danger. Under the new system, if someone gets sick in a club, the venue operator is just as likely to think, If I call this person an ambulance, it will mean another tick on the record against my premises. Their first priority isn't helping the poor sod, but getting him out of the venue.

All too often what will happen is that a couple of security guards will push a drug casualty out the door and dump them a couple of blocks away from the club. If they're lucky, they end up on a park bench, and someone finds them and calls an ambulance. If they're not, they're discovered the following morning, in a seriously bad way, lying next to some backalley wheelie bins.

In these matters as in so many others, the tighter the controls, the greater the scope and incentive for sharp practice. In clubland, criminality and narrow self-interest will always win out; the road to hell forever paved with legal interventions.

In an area like Brixton, it was never going to be only the gangsters who figured out how to make the rave business work for them.

An informal arrangement developed between our team at the Academy and a few of the local police officers. When they needed their drug crime statistics to go up for a particular month, perhaps if they had an upcoming budget review or something similar, we would get a call.

On a certain night, if we caught a few low-level dealers, guys with maybe twenty or thirty pills on them, not the serious mobsters, we might let them go with a warning. We might even let them go without confiscating their drugs first. But we would always let them out of a particular exit on the side of the building. They would wander off, not quite believing their luck in getting away *and* getting to keep their product, only to be pulled over for a 'random' stop-and-search by the cops a block or two away from the venue.

These police, of course, knew exactly which exit to watch. If someone was let out through those particular doors, it meant they were carrying. The only stipulation was that they follow the pusher until they were just far enough away that no connection could be drawn to the Academy.

It was fantastic. The police loved us, and owed us a favour, but also the word went out on the street that 'the people from the Academy were OK guys'. It made the criminals that tiny bit more peaceable towards my staff when they did get caught.

Meanwhile, the cops not only got their busts, but made themselves look super-sharp at picking out dealers for random street searches. I'm not sure how strictly kosher arrangements like these might have been, but they were definitely very Brixton.

Hosting Britain's first legal raves, and setting ourselves up in the vanguard of that movement, was the jewel in the Academy's crown as the coolest venue in Britain. It was an incredibly exciting explosion of energy and creativity.

As time went on, however, I began to notice that the further rave got from its underground origins in the fields and warehouses, the more it became a business like any other. The promoters, who had been forced to be so inventive and revolutionary when they were working in the shadows, now realized that they didn't need to keep coming up with cool new ideas to sell tickets. All that was required was to shoot a few lasers about and stick some big-name DJ on the flyer. People got complacent. The scene gradually began to feel tacky.

As I wandered around the raves that by now we were putting on almost every Friday and Saturday, I began to miss the individualist, bespoke spirit of my late-80s club nights. Dance parties like Shoom, Energy, and Pendragon had seemed like the natural heirs to the extraordinary underground phenomena that were West

World, Metamorphoses, and the Mad Hatter's Ball. The new dance scene that was now emerging seemed more about just cramming as many punters as you possibly could into a space, then turning up the bass. All those quirky, one-of-a-kind club nights that I loved so much, with their unique styles and word-of-mouth buzz, were being swept away in an ever more monotonous kick drum loop.

No matter how repetitive it got, though, the dance scene was definitely popular. My job was to put on the nights the kids wanted to come to – and they wanted rave. So all-night techno became the regular weekend fixture at the Academy. The uptake was incredible. Those nights kept the venue full, without the constant hardscrabble hustle of the early days.

But just I was just getting used to my new rhythm of life as London's 'King of Gigs', my whole Academy dream was very nearly snatched away from me, by forces that had nothing whatsoever to do with the world of music.

CAUGHT BETWEEN LLOYD'S OF LONDON AND SADDAM HUSSEIN 1

As 1990 drew to a close, like everyone else in Britain, I was keeping my eye on the TV news. And I was getting nervous. There were half a million Allied troops lined up on the Iraqi border, and everyone knew that war was coming.

At that point no one knew that Desert Storm would only last a few weeks. My worry was that when the war did break out, the American bands that made up such an important part of the Academy's programme wouldn't be able to fly.

There were more than enough domestic acts, and of course the raves, to keep the venue ticking over, but I thought it might be wise to drop in to see my bank manager, just to let him know there might be a slight dip in the cash flow during the early part of the coming year.

At this point the Academy was performing outstandingly well. Our profile and cash flow showed consistent growth. We were £120,000 into a £250,000 overdraft, but all the numbers lined up to show we were the quintessential model of a successful small business. I saw this meeting simply as a professional courtesy, giving the bank a heads-up.

I was completely unprepared for the reaction I was to get.

That meeting sticks in my memory because it took place on a Monday morning after one of the longest, most trying, weekends of my Academy career.

The weekend had kicked off with back-to-back all-night raves on the Friday and Saturday. That kind of schedule is exhausting at the best of times, but on this Saturday, I also managed to wind up with a very impressive black eye covering half my face.

We had a cool and exceptionally pretty girl named Giselle working our VIP bar. I watched as she was approached by some hulking, rough-looking guy. He said something to her. She said something to him. He must not have liked her response, and poured a pint of beer over her head.

This not only offended my chivalrous instincts, but I wasn't having my staff assaulted by anyone. I sprinted after the guy as he wandered off. I grabbed him by the shoulder, spun him around, motioned with my thumb, and shouted, 'You're done, get out.' It was only then that I managed to get a proper look. Shit. I hadn't realized quite how big he really was. Something in his demeanour told me this guy wasn't going to go quietly.

Then he swung at me.

I saw it coming just in time, and managed to duck the punch. Then, not quite knowing what else to do, I launched myself at the guy, landing so awkwardly that I ended up holding on to his back like a limpet, with my arm around his neck. I don't think he was expecting that manoeuvre, and he came crashing down, right on top of me.

Our security guys sprang straight into action. It took eight of them to pull this character off me and get his arms pinned behind his back.

We frogmarched him down to the foyer. Then, just as we were pushing him through the doors, he broke free, spun on his heels and gave me a fantastic right hook, straight into the cheekbone. There was no ducking this one. Pat and Big John immediately caught him again and dragged him outside. I'm fairly sure his evening didn't come to a pleasant end, but I was still left with a real peach of a shiner on my left eye.

When one is preparing for an early-morning appointment with the bank manager, it's never ideal to be coming off consecutive all-nighters, with half your face covered in a deep, purple bruise.

An even worse position to find oneself in, the night before that meeting, is kneeling on the floor, covered in spurts of arterial blood, cradling a stranger as he screams in pain from a gunshot wound to the belly.

That is precisely where I wound up at the end of this particular weekend, as we got ready to welcome Shabba Ranks to the Academy stage.

This was well before Shabba had transformed himself into Mr Loverman and smoothed out his sound for a pop audience. In late 1990 he was still very much a roughneck Jamaican Dancehall star. We knew we could expect a hard-edged, rude-boy crowd for this gig, but that Sunday things got seriously out of hand.

I had been standing in my usual spot, monitoring the crowds as they streamed through the front doors. As the time came for the support act, Shinehead, to finish their set, I got ready to nip backstage and check everything was running smoothly for the band changeover.

Just as I turned my back, I heard a commotion break out at the security cordon. A strange but familiar smell filled the air. My eyes started burning uncontrollably. Through the tears that came welling up, I could just make out some sort of punch-up kicking off between my bouncers and a group of local hoods. A few of these guys were wielding bright orange canisters. Oh Christ: not the fucking CS gas again!

By now our security team had the experience to deal with situations like this. Pat had them drilled to military precision. In seconds reinforcements had arrived from all over the building. But just as the cavalry was piling into this melee, my radio crackled to life.

I heard the frantic shout that I'd been dreading for the past seven years. 'Gun shot. Gun Shot! Auditorium. Stage-left. One man down. Gun shot, GUN SHOT!'

Well, goddamn. Didn't it all have to go down at once?

My eyes shot over to Pat. He jerked his head as if to say, 'You go on Boss, I'll take care of things down here.' That was all I needed. I was off.

I sprinted through the auditorium, pushing through the crowd, my eyes still streaming from the CS spray. As I neared the stage though, all thoughts of the pain in my eyes and throat immediately disappeared. To my horror, I saw three of my security guards standing in a protective semicircle around a prone figure. He was lying in a twisted foetal position, blood pouring steadily through his fingers as he clutched at his abdomen. Fuck. A gunshot death on the premises? Venues get shut down over incidents like this.

I grabbed the guy's left leg and, with two security guards, lifted him through to the backstage area. He was still bleeding heavily and screaming in pain as we frantically brushed the plates off one of our catering tables and laid him out.

The only reason the guy didn't die right there on that table was that our head paramedic was ex-military. He had served in the Falklands, and was used to gunshot wounds. There was a desperate few minutes as we struggled to get the victim stabilized before the ambulance arrived. It was only the professionalism and quick thinking of our medical team that saved his life.

The second the victim was stretchered off to the ambulance, I turned back inside to try and sort out the chaos and piece together what had happened.

I set Pat to start interrogating the witnesses. We worked out that the shooter had done his business, then slipped out of a side door. When the police had shouted at him to stop, he had squeezed off a few rounds at them before disappearing. This escalated the situation in a serious way. The Old Bill don't take kindly to getting shot at. Within minutes, I had very senior officers demanding I shut down the whole gig in order to get their forensics team to work.

It was up to me to persuade them that this was the worst possible move they could make.

'Look, the last thing you need at a Dancehall gig like this is to panic the crowd. If you guys let it be known there's a gunman on the loose, people are going to go crazy. It'll be a public order disaster for the whole area.

'Besides,' I continued, 'the spot you're after is right by the women's toilets. There have been hundreds of people walking through it already. It's a contaminated crime scene as it is. The best thing we can do is to go on with the show, and then your forensics guys can come in, once we've got everyone out in an orderly manner.'

The cops reluctantly accepted this, and we got Shabba Ranks onstage to do his thing. Meanwhile, I tried to figure out what the real story was.

It turned out that the guy who had been shot was the promoter's brother. The second I heard that, everything clicked into place. I remembered that this promoter had been unusually insistent on having some of his own security staff in the backstage area.

They had known there was going to be some kind of trouble tonight, and they hadn't told me. The whole CS gas attack at the front door had been a diversion. This was no random shooting. This was a proper hit: professionally planned, set up, and executed. It was only the expertise of our paramedic team that had foiled the attempted assassination.

I was furious. I had just had all the carpets backstage redone, and now they were covered in some low-rent gangster's blood. Couldn't these guys shoot each other in the privacy of their own homes?

On a more serious level, I also felt very let down. The Academy was the only major venue in London that would touch Dancehall music with a ten-foot pole. I had always gone out on a limb to give guys like these a chance, and still they brought their Kingston street bullshit in here?

Pat and I figured this must have been some dispute in Jamaica that had carried on over here. If it had been a local Brixton issue, our guys on the street would have picked up on it and given us some intelligence to watch out for trouble on the night. Either way, it was a kick in the teeth for me personally, and bad PR for the Academy, because, of course, the shooting was covered on the news. It was yet another black mark against Brixton in the media for us to overcome.

Once the show was over I ended up having to hang around till 5 a.m. while the cops combed the venue for evidence. They found three more bullets and a few cartridges. In the end, though, they never tracked down the shooter. The whole incident became just another episode of dirty, haphazard violence in the history of the Jamaican music scene.

As the sun came up over Brixton that morning, I crashed out, thankful to see the back of this pain-in-the-arse weekend, and desperate to squeeze in a couple of hours' sleep before my scheduled meeting with the bank.

Little did I know that my real troubles were only just beginning.

I walked into my bank manager's office that Monday morning completely exhausted. My throat still stung with the drip of the CS gas, and that big blue shiner was still spread across my face.

But I wasn't worried. I knew the numbers were on my side. Any glance at the Academy's books would show a well-run business, with consistent year-on-year growth, and excellent advance bookings for the next two quarters. In my head, this meeting was a formality, just a check-in to let the manager know that the geopolitical rumblings in the Persian Gulf might create a slight disruption.

The bank had other ideas.

What I didn't know was that in the midst of the 1990 property crash, all banks had radically changed their policies. My details went into a computer. The bank manager looked at the results and simply said, 'No, sorry, we're calling in your overdraft.'

'I beg your pardon,' I stammered in incomprehension.

'I'm very sorry,' he continued, in that clipped, emotionless tone shared only by bank managers and James Bond villains, 'we shall need you to repay this £120,000 within one week from today.'

Seven days to pay back £120,000, without notice. I was stunned. The Academy had the cash, but only just. Most of our money had already been advanced out to promoters as part of my Box

Office scheme. If I paid the bank now, I would have serious trouble operating day to day, let alone booking new bands and club nights.

I was in a panic. I knew I needed advice from older, more experienced business minds. The young loonies that surrounded me at the Academy were great at thinking up new ideas for clubs, but not for conducting complex disputes with Lloyds Bank. In desperation, I turned to the wisest guys I knew, guys familiar with the Academy, and who I knew I could trust: Jim Millar and Bob Scaddon from Watney's brewery.

I phoned Jim and Bob's office in Mortlake and, in an avalanche of information, relayed to them how the bank was demanding our entire overdraft back with no warning.

Jim and Bob were completely unfazed. These guys had been around the block, and they were well used to, as they put it, 'banks acting like turds'.

'Look,' said Jim, 'it's easy. We've already lent you seven hundred and fifty thousand pounds last year for that Schedule of Works. We'll just lend you an extra hundred and twenty thousand to take care of this bank nonsense. In fact, we know you're running a good business, why don't you take two hundred and fifty thousand pounds from us and bring your entire loan to a neat million pounds. That will give you some ready cash to manoeuvre with, and will show your idiot bank manager that we have the confidence to lend you a million quid. That should get him off your back.'

That was all I needed to hear. I marched back into the bank with a letter, signed by the board of Watney Combe and Reid, approving a £250,000 loan. At this point Watney's were part of the huge conglomerate Grand Metropolitan, a bigger company than Lloyds Bank itself. There was no doubt that they were good for the money. The only stipulation was that, as Watney's were currently involved in a large pub swap with Courage, worth a couple of billion pounds, the money would take six weeks to clear into my account. I was absolutely sure that Lloyds would find this arrangement acceptable. Any reasonable person would. But I wasn't dealing with reasonable people. I was dealing with banks.

'No, sorry,' said the manager, 'we must insist on the £120,000 being paid in the next four days, or we will have to freeze all your accounts.'

My blood went cold. This was ridiculous. I had the money as a cast-iron guarantee, leaving aside the fact that the Academy itself was an excellent business. If these pricks froze my accounts, I wouldn't even be able to pay the electricity bill. How was I meant to run the gigs we already had booked? I mean, Lenny Kravitz has a good voice, but he would struggle to get the Academy crowd going with an unamplified, campfire-style sing-a-long.

If I thought I had been in a panic before, now I knew the real thing. In my mind I could see my wonderful Academy being stolen by some soulless, impersonal arsehole of a bank. After surviving beatings, death threats, and a shooting, the thought of having the whole thing destroyed by some suit typing numbers into a computer drove me into a frenzy.

I went back to see Bob and Jim at Watney's. If the bank's actions drove me to despair, they drove Jim and Bob into a rage. These two weren't the types to let bullshit like this pass. The three of us put our heads together, came up with a plan, and went to war.

The scheme we devised was wonderfully simple, brilliantly devious, and completely legal.

As part of my original £750,000 loan from Watney's, the brewery had taken a charge on the Academy building as collateral. So we waited for the four days to pass, and, as threatened, the bank froze my accounts. The repayments on my loan stopped going out to Watney's, and Jim and Bob immediately sent in the receivers to take possession of the venue.

At the same time, we set up a company called Magstack Ltd, whose major shareholder happened to be a trust on the Isle of Man called Simon Settlements. I began taking the legal steps to declare myself personally bankrupt. Watney's then lent Simon Settlements £800,000 to rebuy the Academy, and I, acting as Simon Settlements, hired myself as a manager to run the place.

It was a brilliant little stunt. I still owned and ran the Academy, but on paper I was penniless. Lloyds Bank, on the other hand, was now completely exposed on that £120,000 which they had made such a hassle about in the first place. You can't shake a hundred and twenty grand from a man when he's been declared bankrupt. The bank manager was absolutely furious when he saw the trick we had pulled, but there was nothing he could do. We had him in checkmate.

But that was nowhere near the end of this little drama.

Jim, Bob, and I were plotting all these moves in absolutely secrecy. We had to. We knew that Lloyds would try everything in its power to block us. But in a strangely flattering testament to what I had achieved thus far, the Brixton Academy going bust was a big enough story to make the national news. People started to talk.

My first job was to shut down the industry gossip mill.

We still had a lot of extremely big bookings coming up. It was essential that I assure my contacts, from London to Los Angeles, that everything was in hand – that these shows would still go ahead. I also needed to keep my channels open and continue making bookings for later that year. There would be no point making all these schemes to rescue the Academy, only to have it stand empty for six months.

It didn't take long for the industry insiders to realize what we were up to. The word that the Academy was here to stay spread around the business pretty quickly. However, as the dust was settling, it was very interesting for me to see which people reached out and offered to help, and who suddenly stopped returning my calls. In show business you only really learn who your friends are in times of crisis. A whole lot of the guys who used to call me to scam guestlist spots suddenly didn't want to know. But then some dudes, like Steve Sunderland from the live sound company Audiolease, would phone up and say, 'Hey let's organize a series of Save the Academy gigs, you can use our sound systems for free.' It was very enlightening on a human level.

In the meantime, quite a few property developers, and other assorted sharks, began circling, with their eyes on getting hold of the building itself. It fell to Johnny, Pat and I to discourage these shifty characters from making an offer.

The first call we made was to our old friends at the 12 Tribes of Israel. They were more than happy to help. We moved a dozen of their deepest, most hardcore Rastas into permanent residence at the Academy. Every time a potential buyer came to view the building, Pat would greet them out front with all his south London charm, then swing open the main doors to reveal these giant dreadlocked characters glowering through a thick cloud of smoke.

The buyer usually backed out of the building pretty quickly. Only to find a gang of kids off the local estates, all employed by me as assistants and runners, sitting on the hood of their car, showing off their best Brixton 'come and have a go' grimaces.

It worked like a charm.

When we knew one particularly eager property agent was coming down for a viewing, Pat and I snuck up, drilled a load of holes, and ran a hosepipe into the auditorium ceiling. When the guy came in and immediately asked why there was water pouring from the roof, Pat gave a world-weary shrug. 'Leaks, mate; leaks. We done everythin' we could, but nothin' can stop the water in this place.'

Needless to say, no one put in a bid. The plan that Bob, Jim, and I cooked up had worked perfectly. We had managed to sidestep the bank's efforts to shut us down. The Academy was still mine, and I was still at the helm.

But there was one more twist to come in this tale. Things were about to take a turn for the absurd.

CAUGHT BETWEEN LLOYD'S OF LONDON AND SADDAM HUSSEIN 2

It may sound from all this as if I took the decision to declare myself personally bankrupt a little lightly.

It's true that I did develop a certain devil-may-care attitude to all the momentous financial manoeuvres going on around me. I was still young and hubristic enough to believe that bankruptcy wasn't really all that big a deal. My only concern was keeping hold of the Academy. Nothing else mattered.

But there was another, much more significant, reason for my insouciance. Throughout early 1991, as we played our financial chess with Lloyds Bank, I was certain I was going bankrupt anyway due to another, very different, Lloyds: Lloyd's of London.

As children, our grandfather had made my brothers and me 'Names' at the Lloyd's of London insurance firm. Now Lloyd's was going down, and we were getting sucked under with it.

Lloyd's of London was an institution established in the merchant coffee houses of seventeenth-century London. As Britain's commercial empire spread across the globe, wealthy traders and aristocrats would agree to underwrite each other's shipping ventures. However, this firm didn't function as a traditional, limited liability, shareholder company. It was much more an old-fashioned gentleman's club. You didn't actually have to put any money in; this was such an exclusive little society, it was assumed you were good for it. Crucially, these arrangements were made on an *unlimited liability* basis.

The system had worked well for Lloyd's members, or Names as they were called, for a few hundred years. It made some people very wealthy, and some very wealthy people even wealthier.

Then came the deregulation of the financial industry. The company, like the rest of the City, was infested by a new breed of cynical, avaricious wide boys. These wolves ran circles around the old-timers, who ran things on a handshake and an assumption of gentlemanly conduct. They manipulated the lax systems in place, insuring, reinsuring, chopping up and reselling policies. At the end of it all, their toxic debts ran into billions of pounds.

When it all, inevitably, came crashing down, the crooks who set the whole thing up vanished into thin air. The rest of us got saddled with their debt. It was one of the great stitch-ups of financial history. Thousands of people lost their life savings in this debacle. I was one of them.

It had come as quite a shock when, in early 1991, I opened a letter telling me that I owed Lloyd's of London £700,000. Then, a few weeks later, another letter arrived, demanding a further £750,000.

I used to joke that I seemed to have underwritten every major disaster of the past ten years: from the Piper Alpha oil rig explosion to the Brink's-MAT gold robbery, and about half the asbestos claims racking the American insurance industry.

So the whole time that Jim, Bob, and I were working out our schemes and machinations to outfox Lloyds Bank, I was happy to declare myself personally bankrupt in order to save the Academy. I was going broke anyway.

Lloyds Bank, however, weren't at all happy with our little shell company manoeuvre. They knew we had played them for fools.

Their retaliation was to come after me personally. Things got nasty. Their first move was to seize my beloved flat in Lancaster Gate. I remember clearing out my beautiful little bachelor pad the day the bailiffs arrived. I left one roll of toilet paper in the middle of the empty floor as a symbolic gift for them. If you're going to act like such shits, you're going to need some bog roll.

The thought did cross my mind that the whole dispute came down to a £120,000 overdraft. I knew they would get well over that for my flat. I could just picture my bank manager looking smug, thinking he had turned a nice little profit on the whole affair.

But what neither me, nor the bank, realized was that my flat was also collateral for my Lloyd's of London obligation. By seizing my apartment to cover their £120,000, Lloyds Bank had made *themselves* liable for my £1.5 million debt.

I'd love to say this had been an ingenious plan of mine all along. In fact, I didn't even realize what was going on until the bank called me in for a meeting at their head office. The branch manager that I had been dealing with was nowhere to be seen. Instead, as I walked in, wearing my scruffy jeans and T-shirt, I was met by two very senior executives.

These guys tried a classic 'good cop'/'bad cop' routine. At first they came on all obsequious, saying, 'We've reviewed your case, and we think it's absolutely outrageous how the bank has treated you.' The first guy offered me a cheque, then and there, for the original £120,000. I could see it sitting there on his desk, £120,000, made out to Simon Parkes. Quite tempting for a guy who has just declared himself bankrupt and been forced out of his home.

Then the other suit cut in with, 'Of course, there is the small matter of this charge from Lloyd's of London, which will, naturally, have to be transferred back to you.'

That's when the penny dropped. It suddenly clicked why the bank was suddenly being so accommodating.

I burst out into hysterical laughter. 'You know what,' I gasped, 'you guys have actually done me a massive favour here, I was just beginning to get worried about that whole Lloyd's of London thing. I'm sure you can handle it just fine.'

At this point, the 'bad cop' exploded. I was sure he was about to hit me. I secretly rather hoped he would, it would have been nice to finally get some kind of honest emotion from these fuckers. His partner had to physically restrain him. I walked out of their office unmolested, but very satisfied with how karma had worked this situation out.

Of course, Lloyds Bank took me to court. The case dragged on for months. I used to cycle up to the court from the Academy and watch all the suits battle their disputations, dressed in my lucky Tour de France cycling shirt.

I couldn't resist a touch of schadenfruede as I watched the Lloyds executives' faces twist in rage as the judge found in my favour. They immediately demanded the right to appeal. The judge replied, 'May I suggest you seek the advice of some of my learned friends, before putting this man to any more of your trouble. I think you've done quite enough.'

He then turned to me and asked if I had incurred any expenses from the case. I smiled. 'About twelve pounds fifty for photocopying m'lud. They can keep it.'

From the outside it must have looked as if I had pulled off some brilliant financial manoeuvre. But I have never really thought that way. It was all just luck, and some bad karma for the bank. That initial meeting with the bank manager had been a simple professional courtesy on my part, a bit of good manners to let him know about a potential dip in cash flow. Their greed and intransigence managed to turn it into a £1.5 million liability.

Most important to me, the Academy was safe. My position there was secure, and the bookings kept coming in like never before.

And, most ironic, at the end of it all, the Gulf War that had sparked all my original concerns was over in under a month. Not one of the US bands had to cancel their shows.

ALT DOT ROCK

It seems that every few months, some veteran music critic or other writes a book about one of the 'golden ages' of popular music. There have been countless tell-all accounts of beatnik 50s jazz, the various late-60s countercultures, and, of course, mid-70s punk. I believe that once enough time has passed for the requisite amnesia and mythmaking, the early 90s may well claim its place amongst those other hallowed eras. From our vantage point at the Academy we witnessed a breathtaking explosion of talent in those years, across an unprecedentedly diverse range of musical genres.

In Britain, artists like Goldie, The Orb, The Chemical Brothers, Orbital, Primal Scream, The Prodigy, and The Stone Roses were pushing the supposed boundaries between rock, dance, and pop ever further. These radical innovators, often working out of their bedrooms, took the volatile energy of the rave scene and used it to create soundscapes no one had ever dreamed of.

Meanwhile in the USA there was an explosion of flair and creativity in guitar-based rock music, creating a renaissance in that genre unlike any since Patti Smith, Television, and The Ramones had conquered Lower Manhattan in 1976. From Kurt Cobain to Kim Deal, this 'Steve Albini moment' in American music was the most radical sound we had heard in decades.

Both these transatlantic cultural currents found their expressions in one UK venue: the Brixton Academy.

We had already established ourselves as the only big hall that

Why so
Mellon Collie?
Billy Corgan
of Smashing
Pumpkins

could accommodate the UK dance movement as it moved out of the underground and into the charts. You couldn't really do a rave in the Hammersmith Odeon; the seats would get in the way.

Likewise, the new wave of American guitar bands were specifically looking for something edgy and wild. These acts represented the birth of a whole new movement, a weird, self-contradictory genre that we came to call 'Alternative Music' or, as MTV put it, alt.rock. This mutant hybrid, simultaneously the creation of underground, punk-inspired, musicians and ultra-corporate entertainment executives, became the sound that defined an era. While often selling millions of records, these new bands consciously, perhaps self-consciously, defined themselves against mainstream pop culture. When they came over to the UK, that kind of spirit was never going to work at a place like the Albert Hall: that was Eric Clapton territory. For the new breed of self-proclaimed Yankee rock rebels, the Brixton Academy was where London began and ended.

The first indications I got of the new energy brewing in American music came via awesome breakthrough shows by Faith No More and Red Hot Chili Peppers. These bands had been releasing records and playing high-octane, underground gigs all over the West Coast since the mid 80s. They had toured tirelessly as steady, hard-working groups, but neither had gained any significant recognition beyond their own insular scenes. Now, seemingly overnight, both bands had put out albums that had rocketed up the Top Ten. The world had once again woken up to quality rock music.

When Faith No More played the Academy, I stood by the side of the stage and watched the crowd go mad in a way I hadn't seen at a rock show in years. The band, in turn, also seemed fired up by the Brixton crowd. They had played the Hammersmith Odeon the previous night and been completely disappointed by the tame, bland atmosphere. All that pent-up energy exploded on the Academy's giant stage. Mike Patton ran around like an electrocuted madman; the band were tight as hell; and the kids went wild. When some of the crowd started a chant adapted from the English football terraces, which must have sounded ludicrous to American ears, FNM immediately took it as the title for the live album recorded that night. *You Fat Bastards: Faith No More Live at the Brixton Academy* was a big hit in the States, and set the Academy up as the place for US indie bands to play in London.

Frank Black: like a passive-aggressive indie teddy bear, but what a sound! The Pixies were perhaps the 'Academy band' par excellence.

But this was just a harbinger of the invasion to come. My instinct that something wild was bubbling away under the surface in guitar music was confirmed not long after, in one of the all-time greatest gigs of my Academy career.

The Pixies didn't look or talk like a classic rock band. Frank Black was a chubby, passive-aggressive, indie teddy bear, and the rest of the band were shy to the point of awkwardness. They dressed more like truckers than rock stars, barely speaking to one another, let alone anyone else. But the second they got onstage, my god did they explode.

Sonic Youth: reinventing what rock 'n' roll could do

I was in awe. This was rock 'n' roll, but not as we knew it. Between Frank Black's tortured yelp, Kim Deal's snaking basslines, Dave Lovering's frantic pounding on the drum kit, and the weird noises that Joey Santiago coaxed out of his guitar, there was a sheer, white-hot intensity to their performance that was unlike anything any of us had ever seen. To me, the very fact that a band this original and out-there could sell out a 5,000-capacity venue and inspire such obvious and intense devotion in their fans had to mean that something good was cooking in the musical cosmos.

There was a strange magic between The Pixies as a group and the Brixton Academy as a venue: some connection that seemed to unite the place and the band. When they did their 2004 reunion tour and announced a four-night run at the Academy, those shows turned into the fastest-selling gigs in the venue's history.

The Pixies seemed to open the floodgates. From that point on, bands poured in from the States, each one managing to push traditional rock 'n' roll in radical new directions, and all of them with a collective spirit of artistic exploration and rebellion. And they all came straight to Brixton. I hadn't seen that kind of explosive sense of purpose in rock music since bands like The Clash and The Smiths, and I absolutely loved it.

We put on incendiary shows by everyone from Dinosaur Jr, Jane's Addiction, Smashing Pumpkins, and Butthole Surfers to The Jesus Lizard and Fugazi. Rage Against The Machine played one of the fiercest sets I ever saw at the Academy for an Anti-Nazi benefit gig, while Pearl Jam and Alice in Chains brought their own brands of distortion-drenched Seattle melancholia to the Brixton crowd.

Late 1992 saw another of the concerts that still stands out as a career highlight at the Academy. It was a freezing December night when we brought in a double headline bill of Pavement and Sonic Youth. These two bands had achieved a measure of commercial success on the back of the MTV-friendly grunge scene, but they were in a completely different class from the other American sludge-rock bands around. For one thing, neither was from the Pacific Northwest. These groups brought a very different type of sophisticated, urban cool into play. Between Pavement's hyper-literary, surrealist, slacker indie, and Sonic Youth's ultra-sharp, experimental New York art-noise, there was an electrifying feeling in the Academy that night. The way Sonic Youth's twin guitar attack made their instruments scream in unheard-of ways, while still producing recognizable songs, was completely astounding. Watching from the side of the stage, we truly felt we were witnessing something *new*: guitar bands pushing the limits of music in the way that people spoke about Jimi Hendrix or the Velvet Underground having done a generation earlier.

I wasn't the only one left totally blown away that night. I have it on good authority that both Graham Coxon of Blur and Johnny

Brixton, born and bred:
David Bowie's homecoming gig at the Academy

Greenwood of Radiohead were in the crowd at those gigs, taking careful notes. The influence of that Thurston Moore/Lee Renaldo guitar mayhem on both their subsequent work is all too palpable.

These new acts were the hottest, most innovative bands in the world. And the fans flocked to see them. We did one sold-out show after another. It was hard to resist a little bit of self-satisfaction as I thought back to all those smug industry tosspots telling me with absolute certainty only five years before that I would 'never get a rock band to play Brixton'. Now, there was nowhere else any rock 'n' roll band worth the name would even consider playing.

My newfound confidence was confirmed by the one member of the British rock aristocracy who was guaranteed to have his finger on the pulse of any fresh movement in pop culture. David Bowie, perceptive as ever, realized that the era of glitzy, ego-driven solo stars was over. The new energy was focused around bands. The kids wanted groups of guys with loud guitars. So, as only a legendary solo star like Bowie could, he put together a group of guys with the loudest guitars around: the two brothers, Hunt and Tony Sales, who had played with him and Iggy Pop back in the late 70s.

And when Bowie toured with Tin Machine, he knew they had to play the venue that the new rock bands, and their fans, considered edgy and credible. It was pretty thrilling for me to bring an icon like the Thin White Duke to the Brixton Academy. This was a guy whose music I had grown up listening to, now playing my own venue; and damn could that band make a noise.

One of the major things I enjoyed about putting on shows with this new wave of American guitar bands was that the support systems that surrounded them – their labels, management, and agents, et cetera – were actual professionals. No member of Pavement's entourage was going to resort to serious violence over some last-minute renegotiation; The Jesus Lizard might play aggressive basslines and wolf down mountains of pharmaceuticals, but you could be reasonably sure that no one was going to put a bullet in a member of their crew over some underworld dispute thousands of miles away.

After all the criminal bullshit I had had to put up with over the years, this simple professionalism came as a blessed relief. I've never talked to Pat about it, but I'm sure it must have been a load off his mind to go back to chasing stage divers rather than dealing with death threats from murderous gangsters. The promoters who ran the Alternative scene in Britain were people like Simon Moran at SJM, Bob Angus at Metropolis, and especially the brilliant Dave McLean at Riverman. These were guys who had come up through my unique Box Office deal. I knew them, they knew me. We could do business with a minimum of hassle and double-dealing.

But I couldn't get overly complacent just yet.

The left-field American rock scene wasn't the only revolution shaking up the music world in this era. A major portion of our business was still tied up with the unstoppable growth of the UK dance scene, forever fuelled by Ecstasy and controlled by the mobsters that supplied it. But there was another American import whose surging popularity in this era was to change the face of popular music forever. Hip-hop was about to cross the threshold from its origins as the soundtrack to edgy urban black rebellion to become the dominant sound of American, and hence world, music.

I loved the energy and groove of hip-hop, but I was never allowed to forget how the scene operated. The rules that governed the rap game still applied. Brixton was still Brixton; and hip-hop meant gangsters.

POOR OLD SINSEMILLA JOE

You'd expect the catering rider for the two biggest rap stars on Earth to run to more than three letters. But there it was on the page, in black and white, in front of me: 'Catering requirements: KFC.'

Wow. I had Snoop Doggy Dogg and Dr Dre coming to town, both megastars riding on the back of multi-platinum records, and all they wanted was Kentucky Fried Chicken? Well, that was fine by me. I had budgeted at least £3,000 a night for catering, as rappers were increasingly becoming more demanding than the rock bands. Now I could put most of that right back in my pocket.

I would have paid a little extra though, just to have seen the look on the guy's face at KFC on Brixton High Street when my runners walked in, slapped £500 on the counter and said, 'Give us everything.' It eventually turned into such a palaver that we had to have a convoy of guys running down the back alleys between KFC's back door and our stage door, passing bags of fried chicken to each other, hand to hand, like some kind of United Nations food drop. Pat and I had a good laugh watching them go for it. Backstage at the Academy turned into an apocalyptic fried chicken graveyard, and the smell was pretty overpowering. But all credit to Dre and Snoop's entourage, they polished off the lot.

1993 was an exciting year to be promoting hip-hop shows. The Academy was still the natural UK base for the big US stars. Our early gigs with the original wave of badass rap innovators like Public Enemy and NWA had established us as the only UK venue that most of the American rap power players had even heard of. On my trips to the States, I had become good friends with the movers and shakers of that business, guys like Russell Simmons and Lyor

Snoop Dogg: Doggy Style '93

Cohen at Def Jam Records, who were real music biz pioneers, and always sent me their hottest acts.

But in 1993 everything changed. It was in this year that rap made the leap from hot youth subculture to major global industry. For the first time we found black rap acts outselling white guitar bands. It felt genuinely revolutionary, and was a thrilling moment to be a part of.

If there were two records that simultaneously typified the unprecedented new popularity of hip-hop, they were indisputably Dr Dre's *The Chronic*, and Snoop Doggy Dogg's *Doggy Style*. These albums smashed the charts, both going platinum several times over. For millions of white kids across the heartlands of the USA, not to mention Europe, it was these two records that represented their first exposure to rap music. I'm sure Dre and Snoop still giggle to

314

themselves, thinking of the terror they must have inspired in so many middle-class parents, as those albums blasted out of their children's bedrooms.

And now we had the men of the moment coming to the Academy for a double headline show. I was absolutely determined to show them that Brixton could hold its own against any US crowd.

Judging by the raucous atmosphere of the gigs, we pulled it off. The crowd were totally caught up in the moment, bouncing their heads with their hands in the air; and despite being high as kites and full of KFC, Dre and Snoop Dogg were complete profession-als, ripping up a couple of fantastic shows.

It wasn't until a few weeks later that the whole thing unravelled, and I found myself in the centre of a shitstorm of dirty hip-hop politics and thuggish Brixton gangsterism.

I was upstairs in the office when I got a call from the woman at reception, 'Simon, there are two officers from the CID to see you.' I didn't think anything of it as I made my way downstairs. I had long ago come to accept that the CID coming in and out of the Academy to run surveillance from our roof was just something I had to go along with.

I walked down into the lobby and saw these two officers who I knew quite well. I assumed they had stopped in to ask some routine favour, so I was very surprised when they came out with, 'Simon Parkes, we have a warrant for your arrest. Anything you say or do can and will be used against you.' I was sure this must be some kind of joke. So, keen comedy act that I am, when they asked, 'Have you got anything to say?' I piped up in mock outrage and cried, 'Stop hitting me officer.'

I thought it was hilarious, and later, when it was read out in court, it got quite a chuckle. But I stopped laughing when I saw the expressions on their faces. Oh shit. These guys are for real. 'OK, look, you'd better come back to my office and tell me what this is all about.'

First off, here's some background: I had co-promoted those Dr Dre and Snoop Dogg shows with our old friend Darren B, of the Railton Road boys, and an equally roughneck associate of his, Cyrus Mewshaw. Their street empire had grown ever more powerful over the past few years. They had become major players in the Brixton underworld. Darren and his pal Cyrus were serious bruisers: at least 18 stone apiece, heavily connected, and with nasty reputations they could live up to.

I knew both these guys. We had co-promoted quite a few shows over the years, and a wary mutual respect had developed. They knew which lines not to cross with me, and I knew which questions not to ask them. When they came to me with the idea of bringing Dre and Snoop over from the States, I knew immediately it would represent a major step up for their operation. Promoting such a huge show, with American stars, would massively boost their Brixton rep. Thus far, I had always appreciated how these guys used their underworld clout to keep any Brixton street trouble out of the gigs we organized; so, I thought, What the hell, I'll give them a shot at the big time. We struck a co-promotion deal, and I agreed to forward the £30,000 deposit to book the acts.

So on my next trip to LA, I stopped in for a meeting with Suge Knight at Death Row Records. There have always been a lot of rough stories flying around about Suge, but I always quite liked the guy. Obviously, he is a heavy character, a *real* heavy character. He made the thugs down in Brixton look like kittens. But I always saw him as refreshingly no-nonsense. He kept his mind on the money and cut through all the false niceties, which made him easier to do business with. He wasn't a dude you wanted to mess about with, but then I made a point of playing straight with everyone, it's how I survived. Besides, I told myself, anyone who had reputedly dangled Vanilla Ice off a 22-storey building, and *not* thrown him off, must have at least some restraint in his character.

So Suge and I made the deal, one of many I did with him over the years. I would run the show through our box office, and take care of the contracts. Darren and Cyrus would be in charge of selling tickets through the specialist record stores like Red Records in Brixton, still an important market for a gig like this. They would also use their street connections to ensure there was no gangster bullshit on the night itself.

It should all have been so simple.

But flash-forward a few months, and here I am sitting in my office with these two CID geezers explaining to me, off the record, why I'm being charged with extortion and racketeering ...

The story played out like this.

It turns out that before they came to see me about co-promoting the Dre concert, Darren and Cyrus had gone around Brixton leaning on various small business owners to try to extort the money for the deposit. One of the guys they had tried to intimidate was this local character named Sinsemilla Joe, one of the faces who did the rounds in the neighbourhood.

Sinse Joe was a nice little guy. A committed Rasta, he stood at a skinny five feet three, with these amazing thick dreadlocks going all the way down to the backs of his knees. Those locks probably made up about a quarter of the guy's bodyweight. He was known locally as a straight shooter, a guy who stayed out of trouble and kept his nose clean. He was also a very hard worker, and had built himself a nice little chain of Caribbean food joints. He'd started in Brixton, but had gradually opened up about five more stores in places like Notting Hill and Wandsworth; anywhere there was a significant West Indian community. He really was a lovely guy, old Sinse Joe; nobody had a bad word to say about him.

So these two thugs, Darren and Cyrus, had gone into Sinse Joe's little jerk joint in Brixton, taken him into a backroom, and 'asked' him if they could 'borrow' the thirty grand to put up the deposit for Dre and Snoop. Sinsemilla Joe was no fool. He knew if he handed over any money to these gangsters he was never going to see it again. But he also knew what refusing the money would mean. It must have been a horrible position to be in, especially for a man who had never put a foot wrong in his life and had worked so hard to build up his little empire.

Putting people under that kind of pressure can lead to very unexpected consequences.

When Darren and his pal Cyrus came back the next week to pick up their extorted cash, the last thing they ever anticipated was for gentle, clean-living Sinse Joe to pop up from behind the counter with a massive handgun and start blasting away at them.

When the cops told me this, the image of a tiny little Sinsemilla Joe firing away at these six feet five monsters with some .44 Magnum, probably about the size of his own arm, almost made me burst into laughter. At the time, though, it wasn't funny at all. Joe got Cyrus in the shoulder, and even managed to clip Darren. Needless to say, the two injured – and very shocked – gangsters scarpered pretty quickly under fire.

So far, so Brixton. But here's where it gets really interesting.

Unbeknownst to Sinse Joe, Darren, or Cyrus, the cops had had Joe's place under surveillance the whole time. They were picking up everything on tape. The Met used regularly to get warrants to bug Caribbean food joints and barber shops. That's where the West Indian guys would let their hair down and talk openly, and the cops could pick up scraps of intelligence about crime in the area.

The police had been after Darren and Cyrus, particularly Darren, for years. So when they heard that original conversation about the thirty grand, they thought, Bingo, we've got these guys on extortion. Of course, they couldn't let Sinsemilla Joe know what was going on. They figured they'd just wait till the money was handed over, then arrest the two gangsters, using the tapes as evidence. They certainly weren't expecting Sinse Joe to come out shooting, and were probably just as surprised as Darren and Cyrus themselves.

So where did I fit in to all this? Well, in that original confrontation, when Darren and Cyrus were first leaning on Joe for the £30,000, they had said he could either give it to them in cash, or as a banker's draft made payable to 'Simon Parkes'. This triggered the police's imagination. Suddenly, in the case they were building, they decided I must be the head of the whole operation, the bloody Brixton Godfather. So I end up under arrest, with no idea what's really going on.

All this goes to show how amateurish and naive thugs like the Railton Road boys were. They didn't even want their banker's draft made out to 'the Brixton Academy'. I was the face they knew, so they dropped my name. Coming from the world they did, these guys just had no comprehension of how legitimate banking worked.

If I had had a choice I probably wouldn't have chosen to co-operate with the police on this. Darren and his crew weren't guys you wanted to be testifying against. But I had no option. I had been mentioned on tape, now I was in the mix. I had to play along in order to clear my own name.

It didn't take much for my lawyers to explain to the police exactly how the gig had been financed. The paper trail on my end was absolutely transparent. I had transferred the money, through none other than Coutts Bank, to Suge Knight at Death Row Records – who, at the time, was on bail for some tricky business of his own out in the States. Out of the whole affair, I was the only one who wasn't actually a criminal.

However, I still had to go down to the Old Bailey to testify. Not too pleasant with Darren and Cyrus staring me down from the dock with their blank, ruthless scowls. But I knew that even they must realize that my evidence was purely factual. I didn't materially affect the case one way or another, so there was no need for them to come after me.

It was Sinsemilla Joe I felt sorry for in all this. He'd been caught on tape shooting at these villains. The cops had him on attempted murder. If he didn't turn Queen's Evidence in their case against Darren and Cyrus, he was going down for a very long time. In the West Indian community, co-operating with the police in any way, especially testifying against 'one of your own', no matter how awful they were, was completely forbidden. It was something you didn't do, ever, under any circumstances.

So Sinse Joe became a pariah. He was finished in the eyes of his own community. People he'd known his whole life stopped speaking to him. He certainly had to kiss his little fast-food empire goodbye. I felt terrible for poor old Sinsemilla Joe. I had got to know him quite well as we hung around the Old Bailey during the trial. He really was an honest, gentle soul, who meant no harm to anyone.

And to top it all, Darren and Cyrus got off scot-free. We sat there speechless as their lawyers persuaded a court that these two hardened gangsters were really 'community organizers' trying to put together concerts for the youth of Brixton. On the police tapes, they were heard asking Sinse Joe if they could 'borrow' the £30,000. In a court transcript, it's hard to convey adequately the menace and terror of Darren asking you if he can 'borrow' money.

So the story was spun that these two 'community workers' had asked Sinse Joe to 'borrow' some money, then had gone back to his place the following week to buy some patties and jerk chicken for lunch, whereupon Joe had gone psycho and opened fire. They made old Sinse out to be the bad guy, and the hardened career criminals came out smelling of roses.

It was unbelievable, but it worked. They walked out of court without a speck of dirt on them. The CID guys were furious; they'd sweated for months over this case.

God only knows what happened to Sinsemilla Joe. He was obviously finished in London, and with the Railton Road boys on the loose he could hardly go back to Jamaica; they would have people out there too. I hope it turned out all right for him in the end. Some guys are just too nice, or too unlucky, for Brixton.

At any rate, a few years later Cyrus Mewshaw's body was found in a car, riddled with something like 19 bullets. It goes to prove that, even in show business, sometimes people eventually do get what they deserve.

FIGHT
THE POWER

It wasn't just the Brixton troublemakers and the CID that were keeping me on my toes in this era. During 1992–3, there were even more significant undercurrents at work.

Just as the Academy was settling into a steady rhythm of sold-out rock gigs during the week and sold-out raves till 6 a.m. on the weekends, a fresh challenger was coming up on the London scene. I had totally destroyed Rank at the Hammersmith Odeon; I had seen off the threats from both the street gangsters of south London and the suited gangsters of the City of London; but now a new power was emerging in UK music. And this wasn't just any power: this was Vince Power.

Vincent Power was born one of eleven children in an impoverished village in County Waterford, Ireland. About the same time that I was shovelling pig shit up in Lincolnshire, Vince was escaping an apprenticeship in artificial bull insemination on an Irish farm and running away to London. He worked in house demolition before building up enough money selling second-hand furniture to follow his dream and go into the music business. Just as I was establishing the Academy, he was converting a disused boxing gym in Harlesden, a rundown north London neighbourhood almost as rough as Brixton, into a small but excellent venue called the Mean Fiddler.

Vince is probably the most consummate music biz operator I have ever met. He's certainly the toughest. Stocky, crop-haired, and concrete-jawed: one look at the guy and you knew he could handle himself. Everyone was terrified of Vince. People assumed that as an Irish bruiser, he must be heavily connected with the IRA. Personally, I don't think he was hooked into any terrorist network; Vince was hard enough on his own. But he was also smart enough not to do anything to dispel the rumours. In the circles we moved in, it could be very useful to let people go on thinking you had some serious firepower backing you up.

The Mean Fiddler was born out of Vince's love for country-and-western, but before long it had grown into a proper little rock 'n' roll club. But the masterstroke that really established Vince in the UK music business was that in 1989 the Mean Fiddler Group took over the organization of the Reading Festival.

Throughout the 80s and early 90s, there had been no reason for any rivalry between Vince and I. With a capacity of under a thousand, the Mean Fiddler was a tiny venue compared to the Academy. There was never going to be any competition there. Vince ran his festival in the country, I ran my venue in Brixton. We stayed out of each other's way.

Then, around 1993, things began to change. As so often in the music biz, it all started with a really nice guy getting fucked over.

Ollie Smith had founded the Town & Country Club up in Kentish Town in the mid 1980s, creating a very decent live music venue out of another beautiful old art deco cinema building: something I could certainly respect.

Ollie was a sweet guy. He had worked like a demon to build up the Town & Country, which was a real labour of love for him. There was a slight touch of friendly rivalry between the two of us. With a capacity of around two thousand, Ollie would very occasionally pitch an agent such a good deal that a touring band might go for a two-night run in Kentish Town rather than one night at the Academy. With only half our space, though, Ollie was never a real threat to me. We became quite good mates over the years.

Then, towards the end of 1992, Ollie started confiding in me that he was getting worried. The freehold lease on the Town & Country was held by the giant construction firm Murphy & Sons, whose depot occupied the area behind the venue. Now it seemed there were plans afoot to redevelop the Town & Country building into a supermarket. This would have been very lucrative for Murphy's, but Ollie was understandably distraught at the idea of having his beloved venue turned into a Sainsbury's.

He fought back by starting a Save the Town & Country Club campaign, which gained support from some big stars. Even Keith Richards lent his voice in solidarity.

Rumours began circulating that Ollie's very public campaign had enraged old Mr Murphy by jeopardizing his supermarket redevelopment scheme. We began hearing stories of a petty tit-for-tat war between the two. Murphy banned Ollie from using the car park behind the venue, making load-ins for concerts impossible. So Ollie struck a deal with the church next door, allowing bands to pull into their driveway and load gear in from there. In turn, Murphy apparently made the church an offer to completely redo their roof, if they cancelled their arrangement and stopped helping the venue out.

Ollie put up a plucky fight, but it was always going to be a losing battle for him. In the end, the entire redevelopment proposal was cancelled as the building was listed as a heritage site, but that wasn't enough to save poor Ollie. He was sent packing back up to Leeds, where he promptly founded another Town & Country Club, with the same great energy as his place in London.

That's when Vince Power stepped in.

Traditionally, Kentish Town is as much an Irish ghetto as Brixton is West Indian. The story went that Vince came to see old Mr Murphy, and over a few pints of Guinness the Kerryman and the boy from Waterford worked out a classic Kentish Town backroom deal.

Whatever was concocted, Vince ended up taking over, doing the place up, and reopening it as the Forum. I went to see Ollie's last gig at the Town & Country. Appropriately for the area, it was a storming show by Van Morrison. I was also invited to the debut concert of the newly opened Forum. Just to rub salt in poor Ollie's wounds, the very first gig Vince put on there was another Van Morrison show.

This new alignment in north London had wide ranging consequences, even for us south of the river.

With over double the capacity, and all of the street cred, the Academy was always going to be a greater venue than the Forum. But Vince had a secret weapon in his arsenal: the Reading Festival.

This was back in the day, before multiple 'music and lifestyle festivals' began popping up every summer weekend in the UK, all competing for corporate sponsorship and the attention of middle-class thirty-somethings and their children. Back then, there were only the two biggies, Reading and Glastonbury, and they were for rocking out in the mud, not prams and organic falafels.

Controlling Reading gave Vince enormous leverage on the industry. He could offer agents a much-coveted slot at Reading, on the condition that the bands do their warm-up shows at the Forum rather than their natural choice, the Academy. Now, for the first time in years, I had some credible competition to keep things interesting.

The cloak-and-dagger backroom machinations of this rivalry were to shape the rest of my time at the Academy.

It worked out like this: between September and May, the Academy would always be on top. Then, during the summer, as Reading crept closer, Vince would kill us on the bookings. The agents and promoters were all petrified of getting on the wrong side of Vince Power, both in terms of losing precious festival slots for their acts, and of possibly losing teeth if they pissed him off too much.

Vince and I played a constant game of brinkmanship behind one another's back, each trying to sweeten the deal and poach the best gigs from the other, without giving away the shirt off our back in the bargain. We each had our own currency to trade in. Vince had Reading and a violent temper. I had the bigger venue, and Johnny and my personal charm.

Despite the competition he represented, I always genuinely liked Vince. He was obviously a great businessman, but beyond the hard-arse image, also a funny, larger-than-life guy. There were two things in particular I admired about him. The first was that anyone could tell a mile off that he had got into this game out of a genuine love of live music. He had that authentic spirit written all over him. The other was that he absolutely hated agents, especially the established big-power agents that ran the industry. These were both character traits I could very much relate to.

Vince and I couldn't have come from more disparate family backgrounds, but I think we recognized each other as born mavericks.

Despite our fierce business rivalry, we became very good friends over the years.

Every few months we'd meet up at the Jazz Café in Camden, which Vince also ran, for a dinner, a glass of good wine, and a laugh about the music industry. These nights would invariably end up with the two of us, a little bit tipsy, in hysterics over which one of us had poached what bands from the other. 'How the hell did you get The Charlatans off me ... you offered them *how much?*'

When playing this kind of behind-the-scenes chess game with a guy as sharp as Vince Power, you had to be constantly on the lookout for openings and opportunities.

One of my favourite steals from Mean Fiddler occurred when I got taken to see an unknown, but much-whispered-about, group called Jamiroquai at the Orange, a 200-capacity toilet-circuit venue in north Kensington. Within seconds of them kicking into their opening number, all my doubts about their mind-bendingly awful band name disappeared in a wave of sugar-coated funk-pop mayhem. These guys were going to be stars. It wasn't even a question. You put that frontman with that rhythm section, and it's a foregone conclusion: no doubt about it.

I made some surreptitious enquiries about album release dates and touring schedules, only to discover that Vince was about to announce a flagship London concert to promote Jamiroquai's upcoming record, at the Clapham Grand.

I could feel in my guts that these guys were bigger than that. The Academy was already quite plugged into the whole acid jazz scene that was just emerging with acts like the Brand New Heavies. In many ways, those guys were the successors to the more muso-ish end of the Metamorphoses/Soul II Soul phenomenon that Johnny Lawes had fostered at the Academy in the late 80s. It made a lot of sense that that crowd would find their audience in Brixton.

I knew I had to move fast, before Vince went public with his Clapham show. Just as the gig was finishing, I found Jamiroquai's agent, a friendly guy called Colin Davie, pulled him into the men's toilet, and asked him straight out how much Vince was offering as a fee.

'Eight thousand pounds,' came the reply.

Virtual Insanity: Jay Kay of Jamiroquai

'Bring them to the Academy three months later and I'll double that,' I shot back.

Colin looked at me as if I was crazy. These guys hadn't even had a hit yet. And I wanted to have them at the Brixton Academy only a few months after their first big London show? Usually promoters shy away from doing more than one gig per year with a band in the same city. I was talking about bringing this lot, completely untested, straight to the big leagues. In conventional music biz terms it was, as Jamiroquai might put it, virtual insanity. On the other hand, from Colin's point of view, I had just offered to double their fee, and hence his commission. We shook on it then and there.

Johnny also thought I was crazy. I got the usual 'you must be off your fucking head' line, but I didn't care. I knew the second that Jamiroquai released a major label album, they would go stellar. Let Vince piddle about with these guys in a 1,000-capacity venue, his concert would just be advertising for mine. Besides, I was curious to see what kind of show an overactive adrenalin junkie like Jay Kay could pull off on our giant stage.

I had to resist a bit of smugness when I was proved absolutely right. We announced our Academy show the day after Vince went public with his Clapham gig, and completely killed him on sales. Of course people were going to come to see a band like that at the Brixton Academy instead of the Clapham Grand.

As the promoter of this show, the beauty of it was that I had booked Jamiroquai at exactly that golden moment before their album came out and they became huge stars. We sold out the gig, with 5,000 people paying £13.50 a ticket; and I had only offered a £16,000 fee. Only a few months later, with a hit in the charts, they would have been able to demand far more. We made an absolute killing on the night.

Needless to say, Colin Davie didn't stay Jamiroquai's agent much longer after that. They were picked off by David Levy, who by now had gone to work at the large agency ITB. He brought them back to the Academy a few times over the years.

This was a particularly satisfying instance when I managed to get one over on Vince Power. I have absolutely no doubt that he could recount any number of stories in which he outfoxed me, probably without me even knowing it.

IN BLOOM

After a year or more of this sort of backroom wheeling and dealing, a possible solution to the Power struggle suddenly occurred to me. Vince had started with a festival and acquired a venue to go along with it. I needed a festival to complement my venue.

I was sure that with the right team, I could create a new summer festival to rival Reading and neutralize Vince's ace card. It was extraordinarily ambitious, but definitely the next logical step. Yet again, the Academy crew geared up to pull off the seemingly impossible.

My first call was to Dave McLean from Riverman Management. Dave was not only extremely well connected in the alternative scene, but I had given him his first big breaks with my Box Office advance scheme, and he loved the Academy. He was also one of the few guys I knew in the business with real integrity and a sense of loyalty. There was a lot riding on my new idea. I had to be absolutely sure that anyone I worked with wouldn't sell me down the river to one of my rivals.

Our first thought was to bring the travelling American super-tour Lollapalooza over to Britain, making the UK the 51st state in the musical union. This roving alt.rock circus was a monster of an organization: essentially a mini-Glastonbury that moved to a new American city every weekend for the entire summer. All the logistics were already in place; why not just bring the whole thing over to Britain?

Dave and I flew over to the States to meet with the festival's two founders: the veteran manager Ted Gardener and Perry Farrell, legendary frontman for Jane's Addiction.

Perry Farrell was a familiar face from when Jane's Addiction had played the Academy. Even then he had come across as what the English politely call an 'eccentric'. Now, as he greeted us in the California sun with a wild-eyed, Syd Barret stare, I could only conclude that several years

Nothing's Shocking: Perry Farrell of Jane's Addiction

of rock stardom had blasted his mind right out into the stratosphere.

The Americans seemed pretty excited about our idea, and convinced us to stay out there for a while. We ended up joining Lollapalooza for an extraordinary couple of weeks on its West Coast tour.

My god. If I had thought things could get debauched backstage in Brixton, nothing had prepared me for the mayhem that was a Lollapalooza tour in the early 90s. I suppose I should have expected it. If you put all the hottest bands in the world together on the road for four months, things are pretty much guaranteed to go a little Hunter S. Thompson.

I think I must have partied with just about every major rock star of the period in those few days. We could never quite be sure who was actually there to play, and who was just along for the ride.

As they tend to, things got weirdest in Los Angeles. The concert was held in Inglewood, a poor, violent, and predominantly black and Latino district. The organizers had built a kind of strange military-style camp to protect the white middle-class rock kids that poured in. It reminded me of American prisons from the movies: huge walls, with watchtowers and heavily armed guards along the perimeter. Inside it was a total rock 'n' roll carnival, but even as we were going mad in our compound, one could still glance at the walls and see the searchlights raking out into the surrounding area, searching for possible intruders. It was a very different approach to putting on a gig to anything we did in Brixton, but a great party nonetheless.

We got back to London with extremely sore livers, but very excited about the potential of what we could do with Lollapalooza UK. It was a pretty revolutionary idea, and could have wrought profound changes in the music scene on this side of the Atlantic. As I set about striking deals, however, and getting the paperwork in order, the plans started to unravel over in the States. It was difficult to stay abreast of the situation from Brixton. It wasn't easy keeping track of Perry Farrell at the best of times, but it began to get harder and harder to extract straight answers from the Americans.

I had far too much riding on this festival idea to put control in anyone else's hands, particularly if those hands were a touch on the shaky side. One morning I looked over at Dave and asked, 'Do you think we'd be better off ditching Lollapalooza and just doing our own thing?'

'Thank god you said that,' he replied. 'I was starting to worry.'

I poured the coffee, and Dave and I started bashing out ideas to create our own, brand-new summer festival.

Later in his career, Dave McLean would go on to find considerable success by discovering and managing the band Placebo. At this stage, though, his major claim to fame was that he had been the first UK industry player to have noticed, and supported, a young Seattle punk group called Nirvana.

Dave had driven us all crazy for months with his obsessive, evangelical praise for this new band. Then, when he finally brought Nirvana over for their first UK show and dragged me down to see them play for four hundred people at the Camden Underworld, I understood in an instant exactly what he had been banging on about. Nirvana played with a furious energy unlike anything I had felt since The Clash. It was utterly amazing. Here, at last, was a band that really *meant* it.

Over the years, Dave had maintained his personal relationship with the band, still acting as their UK promoter even as they had rocketed off to become the biggest band in the world, and the most significant musical voice of their generation. Nirvana's rise happened so fast that it had surprised even many of their earliest supporters. It's a strange thing to say about a band as emotively raw as Nirvana, but their trajectory reminded me of U2, leaping from small club gigs to the stadiums over the course of one album. In the end, as we were all to witness, the kind of emotional dislocation this crazy journey entailed may not have been the best thing for the band, but it also meant that Dave McLean, their 'man in the UK', likewise found himself suddenly catapulted into the upper echelons of the game.

Nirvana was our ace card as we cut a deal with Chelmsford Council to use Hylands Park, a grand estate not far from London, and arranged meetings with the team behind the Scottish festival

T in the Park, and the great Irish promoter Dennis Desmond. Ambitious, detailed, and very secret plans were laid for a new festival, to be called In Bloom. We named the whole thing after the seminal Nirvana song, track two on *Nevermind*, and lined up Kurt and the boys as our first headline act.

Once Nirvana were involved, the old music biz sharkbait effect kicked straight in: every other major guitar band wanted their name on the same poster as their Seattle grunge idols. We put together an incredibly strong bill, including the hottest bands of the time: Smashing Pumpkins, Green Day, Beck, Soundgarden, and Hole, amongst many others. It was incredibly exciting. I knew this festival could blow Reading out of the water. If I could pull this off, it would radically tip the balance of power in the UK music business and shoot me straight to the top. Hence the imperative for secrecy: I also knew that if rumours of these arrangements got out too soon, then not only Vince Power but many other promoters as well would do everything they could to sabotage this threat to their primacy.

Eventually, the deals were finalized and the contracts were signed. Dave and I got down to plotting how to make the launch of In Bloom a real event, something to shake up the entire scene. Our first move was to book Nirvana for a four-night run of shows at the Academy that April. The master plan was to announce the launch of the festival, with a huge media blitz, using the gigs to maximize publicity. It all seemed to fall into place perfectly. We had everything set and ready to rock.

But the gods of showbiz had other plans. Once again, things were about to get dramatic.

'OH DEAR GOD, PLEASE SAY COURTNEY DID IT'

When you have the biggest band in the world booked to play your venue in three weeks, it's always going to be hard work.

When you also happen to be using those gigs to launch a major new summer festival, put your arch rival out of business, and take over the UK music industry, it can get quite seriously hectic. At moments like these, you don't need any extra stress and worry. What you certainly don't need is the lead singer of said band checking into a hotel in Rome and necking a champagne-and-Rohypnol cocktail.

Nirvana were scheduled to play four nights at the Academy starting on 3 April. The shows had sold out as soon as they were announced. So in early March, when the news came in that Kurt had overdosed and was in a coma in Italy, it was one of those minor-heart-attack moments that showbiz can sometimes throw at you.

But in this line of work you learn to roll with the punches. Singers get 'tired and emotional' all the time. You make a few phone calls to the right people; check in with David Geffen; make sure the promoters are all right: and everything can be handled.

Most of Nirvana's upcoming live dates were cancelled as Kurt flew back to rehab in Seattle. The Academy shows were far too important to call off, but they were postponed, making ours the opening dates of the band's European tour. We simply sent out a message telling everyone that their tickets would still be valid, and got on with the usual mayhem of running the venue, and making our plans for the In Bloom festival.

Then the world ended.

On 8 April 1994, I woke up with a minor hangover, but nothing too serious. Somewhat groggily I brushed my teeth, put the kettle on, and flicked on the morning news. Bang. There it was: the top story on every channel. 'Kurt Cobain, lead singer of Nirvana, has been found dead at his home of a gunshot wound to the head.'

That didn't half snap me wide awake. Those reserved, measured tones that British newsreaders affect are probably intended to be calming, but at that moment they made me want to put my foot through the TV screen. Jesus Christ, I'd better get to work and find out what was going on.

It was only on the drive down to Brixton that the full gravity of the situation hit me. I had already advanced all the box office money for the upcoming Nirvana shows to put together In Bloom. If we were going to have to refund every Nirvana ticket, it would come to over a quarter of a million pounds. This was the inbuilt danger of my high-risk business model. It had served me extremely well up to now, putting the Academy way ahead of the competition; but it meant that when the shit hit the fan, the walls really got splattered.

The office was already in a state of panic by the time I arrived. My phone was ringing off the hook with frantic messages from all over the world: the US, Europe, Japan, even panicked voices jabbering at me in Spanish from South America. In LA it was still

Courtney Love ... 'Dear God, please say she did it'

the wee hours of the morning, but news like this could get even the jaded A&R men out of bed. Everyone at the Academy, and seemingly the entire extended live music community, seemed to be looking to me to tell them what was happening and what they should do about it. Amidst all the background noise of rumour and counter-rumour, it wasn't even clear yet what had actually happened in Seattle.

And the details were what really mattered to me. The question of what actually happened could determine the entire financial future of the Academy.

It came down to this: we were insured for murder, but not for suicide. If it turned out that, as a lot of people were claiming, Courtney Love had shot Kurt, then our box-office money was covered. With murder we were safe. But if it was proven to be a suicide, we were out on our own, totally exposed. This was serious. I was a big fan of both Hole and Nirvana. So even I was a little shocked to catch myself praying, 'Oh dear god, please say Courtney did it.' Showbiz does funny things to us all.

It was Dave McLean I really felt sorry for. He turned up at the Academy later that morning, ashen-faced and heartbroken. Dave had a real friendship with Kurt, and a heavy emotional history with the band. He had spotted their potential light years before anyone else, when they were still criss-crossing the American Northwest in an old beaten-up transit van. Now, four years later, Nirvana were global megastars; Kurt Cobain was dead; Dave McLean was sitting in my office with shaky hands; and I was looking at an empty venue, and a whole lot of problems.

Amidst all this madness, as I was running around like a blue-arsed fly, trying to keep the whole ship from sinking, Pat lumbered up to me with a fistful of Nirvana tickets saying, 'Oi boss, you reckon these will be worth something someday?'

Pat was a fanatical hoarder of Academy memorabilia. The guys and I used to rib him that he was like a proud granny saving her grandchildren's school work; quite funny, seeing as Pat was a 250-pound monster who would break you as soon as look at you, but right now I had other things on my mind.

'Yeah Pat, maybe. Whatever.' And I was off on another frantic transatlantic crisis call.

As the day went on, it became increasingly clear that Kurt's death would be declared a suicide. So it now looked as if we were exposed to the tune of £250,000. In my mind's eye, I could see the sharks beginning to circle. The constant phone calls and meetings got steadily more desperate as we struggled to try and keep up with the unfolding events.

It wasn't until late afternoon that Johnny passed me a phone, whispering, 'Simon, it's Radio One on the line. Zoe Ball wants a live interview.' Oh great, just what I need. By this point in the day, I was a complete wreck and in no state to be chit-chatting on the radio. But I thought, What the hell? At the very least, I can get a bit of publicity for the venue out of this.

Zoe started asking me all the usual questions about Nirvana and Kurt, and what they meant to music fans: all the stuff that has been repeated ad infinitum ever since. Then she threw in some simple question about what the vibe was like right now down at the Academy, and something clicked.

I don't know where it came from, but suddenly the image of Pat asking me if those tickets might be worth something flashed through my mind. I didn't have time to think about it, but I found myself saying, completely off the cuff, 'Well Zoe, you know, it's absolutely extraordinary, we've had Nirvana fans from all over the world frantically calling us trying to buy tickets for these concerts. People from America and Japan are offering us over £100 for Nirvana tickets, as a piece of history.'

In the office I could see Johnny whip around and give me a 'what the hell are you talking about?' look. I shrugged and winked, 'just go with it, man'. At that point I would have said anything. I was just throwing stuff out there to see what would happen.

And something did happen. Later that evening Johnny came striding into the office and slammed a copy of the *Evening Standard* down on my desk. The front page was filled by a huge picture of Kurt at his kohl-eyed prettiest, but on page 6 was a prominent story about how crazed Nirvana fans were getting into a bidding war over Brixton Academy concert tickets. My wild claim had been picked up on the news wire, been passed through the Chinese-whisper machine of the popular press, and gone global. All over the world it was being reported that Nirvana fans were paying hundreds of dollars to own tickets to 'the shows that Kurt would never play'.

Within hours the calls started coming in. People suddenly started to believe there was a sacred Kurt Cobain artifact to be had, or at least a piece of rock history to be sold on for a profit.

Well, as ever, if there's one thing the music business teaches you, it's how to spot an angle. And at this point my back was to the wall. So Johnny and I sat down and started making some phone calls of our own. Over the next few days, ads started appearing in *Loot* and the *NME* offering to purchase Nirvana tickets for massively inflated prices. We were inventing a market. In this game sometimes you have to let supply create demand.

Somehow this wheeze of Johnny's and mine worked. The trickle of calls coming in grew into a flood. Anguished American teenagers, Japanese kids barely able to pronounce the words, East End geezers trying to turn a quick buck: people were phoning our box office, desperately trying to buy tickets for concerts that would never take place. They were offering way over the face value of the tickets themselves, sometimes upwards of £150.

The hysteria only snowballed over the following week. People who had tickets were holding on to them instead of asking for refunds, and people who didn't were frantically trying to buy them from us. We had to hire extra staff for the phones just to handle the traffic.

I don't know how we did it, but in the end fewer than 20 per cent of ticket-holders demanded a refund. To those that did, we were happy to refund a ticket for £13.50 and then immediately sell it on for £100. Of course on those four nights we missed out on a large bar take, but on the other hand there were no expenses such as security and paying bands. Not only did we not go under because of Kurt's death, bizarrely we ended up turning a profit on four gigs that never happened.

But the real fallout from Kurt's death went way beyond anything that could be fixed by a clever scam.

Although my quick thinking had saved the day at the Academy, the loss of Nirvana destroyed in one fell swoop all our grand plans for the In Bloom festival.

It was the coup of having Nirvana as a headliner that had drawn in the other bands, their agents, and the venue at Hylands Park. Dave and I frantically tore through our little black books, going to all the other groups with whom we had a personal relationship. The Beastie Boys, Soundgarden, and Rage Against The Machine were all very game for taking over that headline slot, but none of them were quite big enough to tie the whole thing together in the way we needed to launch a major new festival.

Just as fast as they had rushed to illuminate themselves in Nirvana's reflected glow, the agents now began scurrying away with their acts. Images of rats and sinking ships were never far from my mind.

The disintegration of In Bloom was a real blow for me. Not only was this intended to be my secret weapon against Vince and Mean Fiddler, but I had almost begun to feel that the Academy couldn't get much bigger. Once you're able to book bands like Nirvana for four nights, how much higher can you really go? My question was always 'What's next?' The challenges of a new festival would have kept things fresh.

And, just to add an extra sting, the agent Martin Horne went on to sell the entire package *sans* Nirvana to Vince Power for Reading the following year..

Looking back, it is hard to overstate how seismic an event Kurt's suicide was, both for the music world and for myself. At one stroke it removed the centralizing focus of American guitar music, and condemned us all to years of shoddy imitators. Meanwhile in the UK it left the field open for the homegrown talent to assert itself with that strange amalgam of fey art-pop and laddish swagger that became Britpop.

Over the years I've read a lot of people talking about Kurt Cobain as 'the last rock star'. Obviously, this is largely melodramatic nonsense. The business churns them out, and chews them up, in its own inscrutable rhythms. But in some ways the description resonates. It is hard to think of anyone since who has shaken it up as profoundly as Kurt did: a star who could not just sling together a killer tune but really, truly, believe in it as they played. There has certainly been no one who has managed to galvanize an entire generation as he did. These days, as the line between musicians and crass celebrities becomes ever more porous, and hit artists as often as not come off TV 'talent' shows, a phenomenon such as Nirvana may not even be possible any more. You can claim that he only ever stung them into disillusioned slacker apathy, but Kurt Cobain became the focus of his fans' imagination and energy, of their collective projected fantasies, in a profound, and perhaps unrepeatable, way. And maybe, in the end, that is what killed him.

Well, that and the smack.

For me personally, the effects were a little different. Though I had somehow managed to manoeuvre us out of our immediate crisis, the real collateral damage in the wake of Kurt's death was below the surface. Beginning with the unravelling of all my painstaking plans for In Bloom, in many ways what happened to Kurt was an early trigger of the processes that would lead me to leave the Academy altogether.

FUMÉE

As upset as I was about the collapse of my plans for In Bloom, I could always console myself with running the best venue in Britain. There was still plenty of fun to be had.

The first thing I did to cheer myself up was to buy myself a slick new Aprilia motorcycle. Riding a motorbike proved to be tricky with only one arm, so I had a fancy prosthetic limb made.

While it was odd to feel completely symmetrical for the first time in my life, this new appendage proved to be fun for more than just speeding around south London. Nothing throws people off their guard at the start of an important business meeting quite like walking in, taking off your motorcycle helmet and leather jacket, then plonking your arm down on the table in front of you and saying, 'Right then, let's get down to business, shall we?'

Likewise, if some trendy new restaurant opened in town that I thought might be good for impressing women, I would go there once and check my arm into the cloakroom. Then, when I left that evening, I would deliberately leave it behind. Once you've been the guy who calls up and says, 'Hello, I think I may have left my arm in your cloakroom last night,' you'll never have trouble getting a table again.

But motorbikes and false limbs were never going to be enough to hold my attention for long.

Amidst all the big-name rock bands and sold-out raves we were putting on, I began to miss the quirky, bespoke atmosphere and word-of-mouth buzz of our old club nights. The grunge bands and superstar DJs brought their own crowds; there was little wit or challenge required to fill the venue. Where was the thrill of the unknown, the strange magic of a West World or a Mad Hatter's Ball?

So I hooked up with three of the best loonies I knew, Carden Harper-Taft, Fintan Mcalindon, and Matthew Smith, and we created the mad creature that was Cinema Fumée. The idea was a sort of hybrid of a cinema, a nightclub, and a piece of performance art. People would come to see a film but would get an entire, immersive experience. The press, as is their way, latched on to the idea of 'a cinema where you can smoke', but it was so much more than that. As our slogan went, we set out to put the 'sin back into cinema'.

One of my favourite Fumées was when we did a surf-movie double bill of *The Big Wednesday* and *Point Break*. Through Lynn Franks we cut a deal with a surf supply company, and had all these amazing Baywatch-style girls wandering around the Academy in bikinis, along with a big mechanical surfboard ride in the foyer. Best of all, we found this crazy stuntman who rigged up an apparatus so that, just at the critical dramatic climax of one of the movies, he shot out on a surfboard, flew through the air above the auditorium and over everyone's heads, before crashing into a safety net behind the screen. No one had seen anything like that before, and people were truly amazed.

Cinema Fumée nights always had a theme, and as ever I enjoyed getting all the little details exactly right. When we showed one of the Cheech and Chong stoner classics, the tickets were printed on packs of rolling papers. We were probably asking for it, but I hadn't seen the venue that hazy with smoke since the last big 12 Tribes of Israel Rastafari gathering.

Carden, Fintan, Matthew, and I made a fantastic, off-the-wall team, constantly trying to push each other's ideas that little bit further.

Many of our flyers for various Cinema Fumée nights advertised that we were showing the cult 70s road movie *Vanishing Point*. In reality we never actually screened that film. *Vanishing Point* was our code, for Fumée insiders, that we would be showing an illegal movie. In this era, Stanley Kubrick's *A Clockwork Orange* was still officially withdrawn from circulation. When we screened it, we turned the upstairs balcony of the Academy into the Korova Milk Bar.

When Oliver Stone's *Natural Born Killers* came out, its UK release was delayed by the moral gatekeepers at the British Board of Film Classification. Over in France, however, they weren't so squeamish. I got a friend, studying in Paris, to smuggle the cans of film over on the ferry, and we screened the movie, with Woody Harrelson's Southern white-trash drawl strangely complemented by the French subtitles.

Just as with West World, our little underground buzz got picked up by the media, and started attracting attention from some unexpected places. I was very pleasantly surprised when I got a call asking me to do an interview for American radio. What I wasn't prepared for was the DJ throwing the questions open to his listeners. In this era, the US was just starting to come into the grips of the anti-smoking lobby. The entire radio spot turned into an endless harangue by various fanatical anti-tobacco activists. I tried my best to explain patiently that it was only a bit of fun; that there were 4,000 cinemas in the UK, and that anyone who wasn't into smoking was welcome to go to any of the other 3,999. But after several of these hysterical call-ins, even my good manners and understated British charm were getting stretched. When one particularly fevered Californian woman claimed that by allowing smoking at my little movie night I was 'trying to kill her', I couldn't stop myself from responding, 'Well, you're lucky that I'm five thousand miles away, or I probably would try and kill you.' After that bombshell, the DJ drew the interview to a fairly sharp close.

Inevitably, as with anything transgressive and fun, the authorities took exception. The Federation Against Copyright Theft swooped in, thinking they had uncovered some crazy underground film distribution network. It didn't take long for the man from FACT, who actually turned out to be quite a good guy, to figure out we that we weren't some back-alley, pirate video operation, but actually were doing something very cool.

However the impulse behind the bust came from some very high-up executive at Warner Bros. There was a fairly lively exchange of letters between us. We treated his dry business lingo and legal threats as a bit of a joke, signing all our correspondence as from the 'the Four Fumeteers'. In the end they tried to sue us for £60,000. We walked into court all dressed as the guys from *Reservoir Dogs*. The judge burst out laughing and fined us £200 for being cheeky. Even so, to avoid any further legal hassle, it seemed best to take Cinema Fumée out of the Academy and into other venues.

BEYOND BRIXTON

As part of my never-ending quest to keep things fresh and interesting, I even began to venture outside the bounds of SW9.

Two East End geezers who Pat knew had taken over an old art gallery on Sloane Avenue, striking a deal with the owner to run the place rent-free as a vodka bar. These guys had soon realized they were a bit out of their depth in well-heeled Chelsea, so they asked Pat to introduce them to his 'posh mate'. We met, they handed me the keys, and I started setting up the coolest bar in London.

I was after something like the ultra-hip lounge-dive bars I had been taken to on the Lower East Side of New York. I brought in Carden Taft's girlfriend Joe Lawrie, who did set design and art direction on music videos, and we kitted the place out like some kind of *Bladerunner*–Andy Warhol–David Lynch fantasy world. My favourite little touch was when we drove up to Greenwich Market and bought a load of fashion mannequins. We sawed them all in half, then Joe attached seats, turning them into barstools. So, when you first walked in and glanced around the place, for a few seconds it would look as if everyone sitting at the bar was actually standing, but naked from the waste down. You could always spot people doing these wonderfully shocked double takes, before they realized what was going on.

We hired some fantastic barmen, and models from the music video world to act as hostesses. Sushi was just starting to get trendy in this era, so we cut a deal with a great guy named Jeremy, who ran an excellent restaurant called Nippon Tuk next door. We knocked a hole through our wall into his kitchen, and offered the best sushi in town to our guests at the bar. NyLon opened with a bang. It was ultra sleazy in all the right ways: very debauched, and very fun. In no time we had lines stretching around the block.

NyLon became a big hit with the mid-90s celebrity party set, the kind of Hugh Grant and Liz Hurley type crowd. I had no idea who most of these people were, but I liked that my bar was popular, and was more than happy to have hordes of extraordinarily stunning women swanning around.

I even spotted Pippa there one night, my saviour from the Bunny Wailer gig, beautiful as ever. This time, I finally managed to find her at a moment when she didn't have a boyfriend hanging around. I wasn't going to let the opportunity slip by. I asked her out, and the rest, as the cliché goes, is history.

Then, one afternoon I got a typically overexcited phone call from Dee, our beautiful maître d'. She joyously informed me that I '*must* get a copy of today's *Evening Standard*'.

There we were on the front page of the magazine section: a big feature entitled 'NyLon: The Sexiest Bar in London'. I was as horrified as Dee was euphoric. What we were doing was completely illegal. We had no permission to be in the premises, let alone a drinks licence or anything like that. I frantically scanned the article, praying my name wasn't mentioned. It wasn't until the very last line that I spotted it: some awful sentence like, 'And just to add a frisson of gritty cool, the bar is run by Simon Parkes, owner of the famous Brixton Academy.'

A few days later I got the call I had been dreading, but very much expecting. 'Well, well. You've been a very cheeky bastard, haven't you?'

Now, that's what I call an opening line. I laughed out loud. Maybe this was someone I could do business with? 'I think we'd better have a chat,' I offered.

'Yes, I think we'd better,' came the reply.

I went down to see the owner of the building with my solicitor in tow. The owner turned out to be a property lawyer who had acquired our little spot in the same crash that had got me in trouble with Lloyds Bank a few years before. Since then, no one had even put in an offer for it, and the space had been standing idle. The conversation warmed up a bit when this guy realized that the head of my lawyer's firm was actually an old family friend, and that the two of them played tennis together at the ultra-exclusive Queen's Club. Welcome to doing business in London.

'Look,' the guy explained, 'you've actually done me a favour here; that space has been empty for years, and you guys are finally creating some interest in the building.' He paused. 'But you're going to have to pay me some bloody rent.'

'How much did you have in mind?' I asked.

'I think a hundred grand a year would be fair.'

I gently explained that a sum like that would make it impossible for me to operate. Then I made a counteroffer. 'How about we give you five hundred a week, cash, in a brown paper bag, and no questions asked?'

'Make it a grand,' he responded, 'and we can call it a deal.'

We called it a deal.

Which left me with another problem. We were attracting a lot of attention, with queues an hour long and major press write-ups, but we didn't even have the correct licence to sell drinks. I walked into Old Brompton police station expecting to get thrown out on my arse.

Then, as I opened the door to the Licensing Department, who should I see behind the desk but Plum, the old box office girl from the Academy, who I had rescued from the tear gas attack with John Curd all those years ago? Life is a funny old game sometimes.

With a wink and a nod, Plum advised that what the council didn't know could do no harm, and made it possible for us to keep the bar going. We got almost a whole extra year out of it, and a lot of very wild times, before some guy came in and offered a load of money to turn the space into yet another high-end clothes shop.

North London was still supposed to be Vince Power's territory. Aside from the little patch of Eire he had the run of with the Forum in Kentish Town, his other main stomping ground was Finsbury Park. Every year he would put on an Irish-inspired folk and rock festival up there called the Fleadh, as well as the odd one-off event.

One evening I happened to run into this sweet Rastafarian guy called Stevie 'King Jah' Collins, who I knew from the old reggae days down in Brixton. It turned out that Stevie had moved up to Finsbury Park to start a community centre for black youth. As we were chatting he happened to mention that, as part of his community work, he held a licence to put on an all-day music event in the park itself.

This got my mind going. Stevie and I chatted a few more times and put together an idea whereby I would do a big rock gig with INXS headlining; then my team would help run the production for a reggae all-dayer as part of his community action brief.

I have to admit that my main impetus for all this simply was to see the look on Vince's face when I told him I was doing a big gig in Finsbury Park; but the plans actually came together very nicely. I was a huge fan of Ian Dury and the Blockheads, so I got in touch with their manager, Bob Gold, who was keen to sign them up as the support act. I also arranged a very slick financial system whereby advance sales through Ticketmaster would end up paying the deposit for the band. It was fairly complicated, but I ended up making the same money work for me in a number of different ways. I was pretty pleased with myself for working the whole shebang out.

We brought in the Australian beer company Castlemaine XXXX, who were very keen to associate their brand with fellow Aussies INXS and sponsor an INXXXXS event. This chimed in neatly with Saatchi & Saatchi, who came up with the advertising slogan 'Drink to INXS in Finsbury Park'.

Then, just as we were about to go public with a high-profile launch, things started to go a bit shaky with the Antipodeans. INXS's manager called me up, saying they might not be able to play, as two of the band were brothers, and their grandmother had just died. This was in February. The gig was in July. Without wanting to sound insensitive, I replied that I was sure that the two musicians were professional enough to recover sufficiently over the next five months to play one concert. The conversation ended awkwardly, and after this, one issue after another seemed to come up. INXS's team in Australia were starting to act very funny indeed.

I did some digging around the music biz gossip channels and learned that Tim Parsons from MCP, INXS's usual promoter, was putting huge pressure on them not to play the gig with me. Tim was a good guy, and the two of us got on very well, but he was pissed off with me for pinching one of his best bands. Fair enough. For all I know, Vince Power had also found out about our mini-festival and was throwing his considerable muscle around to try and protect his turf.

Eventually, it got to the point where INXS's manager came out straight and said the band just weren't going to play the show.

Jim Morrison meets Crocodile Dundee: Michael Hutchence of INXS

'Well,' I responded, 'I've already paid out forty thousand pounds in deposits and insurance for the venue, and you're letting me down very badly.'

'Yeah, and what are you going to do about it?' he demanded.

'What I'm going to do about it is I'm going to sue you.'

'Yeah, yeah,' the guy laughed in derision, 'I've heard that one before.'

'Actually, I've got a million pounds in litigation insurance, and I'll take you to the cleaners.'

That raised the stakes.

'If you try and sue me,' the guy grandstanded, 'you'll never bloody work in music again.'

The old hackles came up. This guy was threatening me. Well, bring it on.

'Mate, I run the Brixton Academy; I've been threatened by real gangsters. Don't push your luck. There's no way I'm getting done for forty grand here. So you'd better start coming up with some bloody solutions, and fast.'

That made him pipe down a bit. Inevitably, we struck a compromise. We'd call the Finsbury Park gig off, but when INXS came back through Europe on tour that autumn, they would play the Academy for free.

This time they were as good as their word, and there was nothing any other music biz player could do to sabotage us. INXS showed up that October and, I have to say, played a fantastic gig. I wanted to be grown up about the whole affair and show the band that I didn't hold their management's nonsense against them. So I laid on a very lavish backstage lounge for them, with all the best catering and booze, etc. The INXS guys responded to all this, and went all out with their onstage theatrics, with Michael Hutchence giving it his full Jim Morrison meets Crocodile Dundee routine.

But there was another twist to this tale. The guest list to the INXS Academy gig read like a who's who of hip London celebrity. There was the Aussie contingent, led by the tiny but perfect figures of Kylie and Dannii Minogue, as well as the usual gaggle of actors, musicians, and people just famous for being famous. But for some reason, at this show there was also a large crowd of big-name tennis players. I found myself looking around my rock 'n' roll venue and seeing faces like Boris Becker, Pat Cash, and Steffi Graf: very odd indeed.

More significant, two of the names on the list that night were Michael Hutchence's girlfriend, Helena Christensen, and the British tabloid darling and TV personality Paula Yates.

Now, I've never been a fan of crass celebrity culture, but we used to have paparazzi outside NyLon all the time, waiting for the huge stars like Madonna, who would often make an appearance.

Murder Ballads: Kylie Minogue and Nick Cave must have been one of the unlikeliest pairings in music history, but somehow it worked

I had got to know some of these guys, and would occasionally tip them off if there was a particularly celebrity-heavy night at the Academy. It suited me very well to have pictures doing the rounds of famous people hanging around Brixton and *not* getting stabbed. The paps would sometimes make the journey down, but they were generally nervous about hanging around Brixton with their flashy, expensive cameras.

That night I got right on the phone, saying, 'Look, you guys want to be here right now, we've got Kylie going mad, and partying with half of bloody Wimbledon.' I don't know if that sounded too outlandish, even for those jaded hacks, but they gave me the old, 'yeah guv, we'll see what happens', and never showed up.

More fool them. This night was a gossip-snapper's dream. Helena Christensen had been hanging around the Academy all afternoon as the band soundchecked, before disappearing back off to the hotel with Hutchence. But that evening, just minutes after INXS came offstage, Christensen ran out of the venue in tears. And at the end of the night, Michael Hutchence left the building with Paula Yates.

I have no idea if their affair began at the Academy that night, but within a fortnight it was plastered all over the TV and the tacky British gossip press. If those paparazzi had made the trip down to Brixton for the gig, they would have certainly got themselves a scoop to keep their vampiric editors happy for a long while.

BACK TO BRIXTON

Despite the fact that when she had first met me, a massive Rastafarian had had his hands wrapped around my throat, Pippa would often joke that I exaggerated the dangers of my job, claiming that she had saved me from the worst of what Brixton had to offer.

It wasn't long before Brixton gave its answer.

It was a Buju Banton gig: the type of roughneck Dancehall show where we knew to expect a lot of cash through the box office, and at least a bit of trouble. In a Bunny Wailer-esque move, Buju waited till the venue was full, then demanded the balance of his fee in cash before taking to the stage. Only he took things a step further, refusing even to leave his hotel and come to the venue until he got his money.

I had heard stories that Banton had tried what the Jamaican music biz gangsters call a 'renegotiation' at the Forum a year before. This is a Kingston street gambit whereby an artist waits for the venue to fill up, then simply demands another few grand or they won't go on, leaving the promoter either to pay up or to face the wrath of the fans when he can't deliver the artist they've paid to see.

As much as I wasn't one to be blackmailed, I really didn't have a choice. There was no time to think things over or plead for reason. I jumped on my motorbike, with ten grand in cash, and sped over to his Kensington hotel, weaving through the rush hour traffic.

I walked into Banton's suite to be greeted with the death stares of his hard-arse entourage, and the smell of the salt fish that his private chef was cooking up. Considering Buju Banton is now serving a ten-year sentence in Florida on firearms and cocaine smuggling charges, this was not a man you wanted to be messing with. Tonight, though, we were lucky, and Banton didn't try any gangster bullshit. I handed over the agreed fee, and we got him onstage for his show.

But the craziness of this night had only just begun. Just at the peak of the gig, when the crowd was going mad, I received another urgent call that some detectives from Brixton CID needed to see me. By now, this kind of message no longer sent me into a panic, but I still hurried down to see what was going on.

It turned out that the cops had picked up some intelligence that we were going to be the target of a major armed robbery later that night. They wanted to use the opportunity to lay an ambush for the thieves, who were part of a hardcore criminal gang they had been pursuing for several months. It all sounded quite exciting, and I agreed to help out. It was only polite, seeing as the cops had taken the trouble to give me the warning.

What we obviously couldn't do was have a load of heavily armed, special-unit Met police trooping through the Academy on a crowded Ragga gig. Anyone carrying dope would have panicked and run off, and I would have lost three-quarters of my audience. So we came up with a plan.

On the dome that covers the Academy's entrance, there is a small trapdoor that leads straight to the box office. We regularly used it to smuggle out bags of cash, saving us the obvious security concerns of walking through a crowded gig with our evening's take. Tonight we switched the game, using the trapdoor to smuggle people in, instead of cash out.

A squad of special unit, So19 armed police commandos shimmied up the wall of the building and dropped through the hatch, into our box office. I have to admit I became a bit of a gung-ho schoolkid at the sight of their Heckler & Koch sub-machine guns. It was incredibly exciting. They had another squad of plainclothes guys out on the street tracking the suspects, and we followed their progress on the radio. Eventually we got the message that the four villains had pulled up in a car and were waiting half a block down from the building. The armed police guys jammed their ammunition magazines into their guns and slid back the bolts with loud metallic clicks. The tension started to rise.

Then, just as everyone was silently gearing up for the big moment, our ears glued to the radio waiting for the signal, we all jumped at a loud knock on the box office door. Pippa's unmistakable voice rang out. 'Simon, are you in there?' Oh shit. Not now! I threw open the door and grabbed her. 'Get in here.' Pulling her into the back room, I made her lie under the desk, covered in my flak jacket. If there was going to be a shootout, I wasn't having my girl getting caught in the middle of it. Pippa did her best to look unimpressed, but I think she secretly found it all quite exciting as well.

We waited. Nothing happened. The suspects sat in their car outside, we sat in our box office: they with their sawn-off shotguns, we with our automatic assault weapons. My heart was beating like a drum 'n' bass tune.

Then the radio crackled to life again. The so-called robbers were pulling away and leaving the scene. Something must have spooked them. They had called the job off.

By now I was so hyped that I found this result quite disappointing. I had a fairly good idea who these robbers were, and thought that them getting dramatically busted at the Academy would send out an unmistakable message to the rest of the criminal community. I was all for jumping on my motorbike with a rucksack full of cash, and luring the bad guys into another ambush·elsewhere, but the cops said it was too risky an option. They couldn't afford a public shootout around Brixton, and couldn't take the gamble of me getting hit in the crossfire.

It was a timely reminder that no matter how many giant rock acts you put on, Brixton will always be Brixton. It was also some good ammunition for me the next time Pippa started to poke fun.

LIKE A
ROLLING STONE

In the pantheon of popular music there are the stars, there are the superstars, and then there are *the legends*. On 29 March, 1995, I found myself standing at the side of the Brixton Academy stage watching Bob Dylan sing 'Like a Rolling Stone'.

It is hard to describe the sense of pride and joy I felt at that moment. I had seen Dylan perform this song once before: when I was seventeen years old and almost got my friends and I expelled

I Shall Be Released: Elvis Costello joins Bob Dylan onstage

from school by sneaking down to the huge festival at Blackbushe. Now Zimmerman himself was playing my venue, shaking my hand after the soundcheck, and croaking, 'Thanks for having us down, man'.

Then, just as I thought the moment couldn't get any better, Dylan murmured something about welcoming a 'special guest' to the stage, and Elvis Costello strode out into the spotlight to join him in closing the gig with 'I Shall Be Released'.

Watching these two songwriting giants harmonize on that beautiful chorus, I felt something profound shift in my feelings about my entire grand adventure with the Academy, and everything that I had been through with it. I had known for years that we had grown into something special, that we could attract the biggest stars in modern music. It now felt like things had elevated another level still. We had moved from the stellar to the legendary.

It didn't stop there. No one can sing 'Like a Rolling Stone' quite like Bob Dylan; but the Rolling Stones could make a damn good try.

Believe me when I tell you, the single most frustrating position in which a venue owner can find himself is to have the greatest rock 'n' roll band of all time booked to play your hall, but not be allowed to tell anyone about it.

When the agent John Giddings first told me the Stones wanted to close their massive Voodoo Lounge stadium tour with an 'intimate club show' at the Academy, I almost leaped out of my skin. Only a band like the Rolling Stones could call playing to 5,000 people a 'club show'. By now, I had had quite a few of my musical heroes through the Academy, from David Bowie and The Clash on down, but this somehow felt different. This was the Stones.

The only condition attached to the gig was that it was to be kept absolutely secret. The show was intended to be a private party for the band, their mates, and a few 'superfans'. The group would have a guest list of 1,000, using the entire Academy balcony as a giant VIP section, while tickets for the auditorium would go on sale with a surprise announcement the night before the gig itself. A great party combined with a clever marketing strategy: what could be more Stones?

I wasn't even allowed to tell my staff, lest someone leak the story. I was forced to go around saying, 'Look, just be prepared, next Wednesday is going to be massive.' Even my closest friends like Pat and Johnny would beg, 'Oh come on, just tell us who it is,' and I would have to refuse. My bar managers tried to wangle the information out of me, claiming they needed to know how much beer to order. 'Plan on a lot; then double it,' was the best guidance I could give. The Stones' team was very clear. If one word got out about the gig, the whole thing would be called off. I wasn't about to risk Vince Power poaching this one off me!

The show remained a secret until the Tuesday night, when the announcement went out on the radio. By 9.30 a.m., Wednesday morning, the queues for tickets were snaking around the block from HMV Oxford Street, causing major traffic problems in the West End. The lucky few who managed to get a ticket had a luminous band locked on to their wrist. They had to live with this bracelet overnight. We were under strict instruction: anyone without a wristband wasn't to get in. The Stones' management weren't taking the chance of any forgeries or fakes slipping through.

Even I was only allowed two names on the guest list. In my own bloody club! So I ended up hiring my own brothers, and quite a few of my mates, as extra security staff and runners. They'd never have forgiven me for not getting them into this gig.

Mick, Keef, and Woodsy bringing the
Voodoo Lounge to Stockwell Road

The day of the show itself was also an education. If I thought
I had seen big productions before, this was another level entirely.
Truck after truck rolled up to our back door, disgorging mountains
of equipment, along with a legion of techies, road crew, and management staff. It really was like watching some World War Two
movie of the US Army steaming into battle. Their efficiency and
professionalism were absolutely incredible. Everyone knew exactly
what their job was, when they were meant to do it, and how they
fit into the beautiful juggernaut that is a Rolling Stones tour. Their
design team went all out, transforming the entire upper floor of
the Academy into the Voodoo Lounge itself. I got a shock to see my
own venue morphing into the image of some New Orleans bordello
from a Dr John song. It was an extraordinary piece of set design.

Then, just as this whole giant mechanism was clicking into
place, the spirit of rock 'n' roll reared up to throw in a bit of chaos.

At about 3.30 that afternoon, the tour manager came sprinting up to me and breathlessly gasped, 'We've got a problem.'

It seemed that Keith Richards' limousine was on its way into town, and had got stuck in a massive traffic jam on the A3. This was pretty serious. The soundcheck was scheduled for 4 p.m. In an operation this complex, the itinerary was timed down to the minute. Any delay would throw the entire machine into chaos.

The poor tour manager was in a panic, and his team were at a total loss about how to handle this.

I reckoned I might have a solution.

I raced over to Brixton police station and had a word with a senior officer I was on good terms with there. I explained that if there were a major delay to proceedings, then all the A-List celebrities on our guest list were going to roll up to Stockwell Road in their limos only to have to wait around for an hour, making them easy pickings for the predatory Brixton hoods.

The police chief seemed to take my point, and went to have a word with the Traffic Division.

After a few minutes he returned and said, 'All right, the boys down in Traffic have agreed to send out a team of outriders on motorbikes to get Mr Richards to the Academy ... on the condition that all the blokes who go out receive passes to the concert tonight.'

I burst out laughing. Bloody cops. Still, there was little else to be done, and I quite admired the chutzpah. Sod the Stones' management and their wristbands. If the police could get Keith to the venue on time, why shouldn't they come in and enjoy the gig?

What I wasn't expecting was for them to send about 14 bloody riders. That's more than most foreign heads of state get. Everyone in that unit probably got a free ticket to the gig that night. The cops pulled a fast one on me there, but it was damned impressive how quickly they managed to usher the errant Stone into town.

I went out to oversee things as the limousine pulled up to our back door with its cavalcade of police motorbikes. I was very excited to meet Keith Richards; what music fan wouldn't be? I was also amused at the idea of the old rock 'n' roll pirate being escorted in by the cops. How different from the late 60s, when the Met were busting the Stones every chance they got,

But when the driver swung open the limo door, it wasn't Keith Richards who I saw. Instead, I was presented with the spectacle of the snooker player Alex 'Hurricane' Higgins, very deep in his cups, attempting to clamber out of the car while maintaining his grip on the bottle of brandy clutched in his hand. He was followed by yet another snooker player, Jimmy White, in a similar state of flailing intoxication. Only then did Richards himself emerge, only slightly more elegantly wasted.

His team was on him in a second, manoeuvring him straight towards the stage, where the soundcheck had only just got under way. Richards seemed blissfully unaware of all the fuss his traffic trouble had caused, floating above the neurotic stressing of his crew with the nonchalant cool of the true rock star. In fact, he seemed pretty detached from everything that was going on. One wondered whether he even knew there was a gig that night. But the second they got him onstage and strapped on that famous black telecaster, some deeper force seemed to possess him, and he came instantly to life, hitting every chord with that signature Keith Richards swagger.

This was something I noticed about Keef, both that night and a few years later when I was taken to see him playing solo for two hundred people at the Marquee Club. No matter how wasted he seemed, no matter how far gone on his own special trip, the second that guitar was in his hands, some primordial muscle memory kicked in, and you realized he knew exactly what was what the whole time. It was you who had to catch up with him.

The gig was magnificent. That special Brixton Academy energy loop between artist and crowd was in full effect, pushing each to ecstatic heights. It must have felt amazing for the band, after so many years playing giant stadiums, to receive the full concentrated intensity of the Academy crowd. And what song did they drop right in the middle of their set? None other but their own version of 'Like a Rolling Stone'. It was the second time a generation-defining musical icon had performed the number on my stage in the space of a few months.

That concert is regularly included on lists of the 'Ten Best Rolling Stones Shows of All Time'. I had diehard Stones fanatics coming up to me saying, 'I've been to over three hundred Rolling Stones gigs, and I've never seen anything close to this.' It was another one of those moments that reminded me why I had set the Academy up in the first place.

The Voodoo Lounge in the upstairs bar was packed with a guest list that only the Rolling Stones could command. Every giant of music from Rod Stewart to Joe Strummer was there, as well as some more surprising faces, such as the author Salman Rushdie, freshly emerged from hiding in the wake of *The Satanic Verses* furore. I suppose a booze-soaked Rolling Stones gig was the last place one would expect to run into jihadist assassins. Besides, they would have had trouble getting wristbands.

The last bit of trouble we had that evening came later, when we had to remove Hurricane Higgins from the building for getting aggressively lascivious towards Rod Stewart's coterie of young blondes. You had to be pretty out of control to get yourself kicked out of the Voodoo Lounge, but that wild man of snooker managed it.

But the overwhelming feeling of the whole experience was that of the true old spirit of rock 'n' roll pulsating through the building's very bricks: a really magical night.

The Academy was on a roll; and it didn't end with the Stones.

In this era there was only one hotel in Los Angeles where anyone who was anyone in showbiz would stay: the Mondrian on Sunset Boulevard. A few weeks after our Stones gig, I flew out for one of my regular trips to La La Land.

The night I arrived I found myself wide awake at 5 a.m., my mind spinning with jet lag. I thought, What the hell, I'll go burn some energy in the gym before my round of meetings starts.

This being Los Angeles, by 5.30 a.m. the gym had started to get quite busy. I was pounding away on a treadmill when some muscle-bound guy in a tight-fitting T-shirt and white headband got on the machine next to mine. Just as I was starting to huff and puff, and he had barely broken a sweat, he turned to me and, in that classic LA way, smiled. 'Hi, I'm Jordan Carter. I run the House of Blues club on Sunset. Aren't you the guy from that Academy venue over in London?'

It was quite the flattering surprise to be recognized in a city five thousand miles from home. Though I suppose there couldn't have been that many other one-armed Englishmen hanging around LA showbiz hotels.

Shaking hands across two treadmills going at different speeds can be a very awkward manoeuvre, especially for someone with only one arm, but somehow we managed. A typically LA conversation ensued, with us talking business as we moved from exercise machine to weight bench, pausing our industry gossip to wipe away sweat, or swig from neon-coloured energy drinks. We agreed to meet for breakfast upstairs; then he would show me around the House of Blues, which was virtually next door to the hotel.

By sheer chance, as we sauntered through the lobby on our way out, the band Simply Red happened to be checking in at the front desk. They all recognized me from their Academy gigs back in the day, and greeted me warmly with big hugs all round. This, of course, only made me look cooler in the eyes of my new mate, as he went on to give me the tour of the famous House of Blues rock club.

Then, amidst all the LA showbiz chitchat, he said something that really did get my attention. 'You know who you should think about getting? Bruce Springsteen. He's touring in Europe in a few months.'

'Come off it.' I laughed. 'Bruce Springsteen plays stadiums.'

'No,' the guy replied, 'he's doing a solo, acoustic tour; only playing club shows for the new record. You should think about it.'

I did more than think about it.

The second I got back to the hotel, I put in a long-distance call to Johnny at the Academy and told him to gather some intelligence about what Springsteen was up to with the new album, and which venues he was in discussions with in Britain. The call back came about thirty minutes later. Johnny gave me the lowdown on the Boss's new stripped-back, acoustic direction, and said his people were in the midst of arranging a gig at the Albert Hall.

I sprang into action. Racing back to Jordan at the House of Blues, I managed to wangle a fax number for the Springsteen management team. I then rushed back to my room and scribbled out a fax on the hotel stationery entitled *10 Reasons Why Bruce Springsteen Should Play the Brixton Academy Instead of the Albert Hall.*

I laid it out in bullet points. My central thrust was that the

The Ghost of Tom Joad:
an incredible one-off solo show by the Boss

Albert Hall was where old dinosaurs went to die. If you wanted
to be where the action was, it had to be the Academy. Further, if
Springsteen was really calling his new album *The Ghost of Tom
Joad*, named after the itinerant hero of John Steinbeck's masterpiece
The Grapes of Wrath, then he should remember that a character
like Joad would never have been allowed even to set foot in the
Royal Albert Hall. Tom Joad's successors were to be found on the
streets of Brixton.

I wasn't expecting much for all this effort. It was always going to be a long shot. But if I could get the Rolling Stones, I might as well take the chance before my luck changed.

Somehow I made it happen. The Boss came to the Academy for an amazingly powerful two-night run. It was just him on a bar stool, with one spotlight and an acoustic guitar. Not many performers can command a huge stage like the Academy's with no backing band or showbiz trickery. But Springsteen brought such intense presence and passionate delivery to his performance that the audience was utterly captivated. They hung on his every note in pin-drop silence. I even broke my own rules and we made these our very first seated shows at the Academy. It was indisputably the right move. Springsteen played for almost three hours, his energy never failing, creating a sense of intimate communication with the audience that was incredibly moving.

SHOW ME
THE MONET

A few days before the Springsteen concerts, my mate Jeremy, who did the sushi for Nylon, took me aside to ask a favour. He had a good friend from the States who was on his way over to London. This guy was a fanatically devoted Springsteen fan, and was desperate to get into the gigs, which had long since sold out. Was there any chance I could swing some guest list spots as a personal favour?

'Sure Jeremy, no problem man. Just keep that sushi coming.'

It was no hassle for me. I stuck the guy on the list with a plus one, reserved him two seats down at the front, and thought no more of it.

Then, a few days later, I got an excited call from Jeremy. 'Hi Simon, listen man, that friend of mine was blown away with the Springsteen tickets. He says it was the best show he's ever seen, and he wants to thank you.'

'Don't be silly Jeremy. You know I'll always help a mate out, if I can.'

'No,' Jeremy continued, 'he insists. Listen, do you like art?'

'Of course I like art. What kind of question is that?' I asked, a bit confused.

'OK,' continued Jeremy, 'tomorrow morning at 8.30 a.m., a car is going to pick you up from the Academy. Don't ask questions, just be ready.'

Now I was intrigued. What the hell was all this about?

The next morning I duly dragged myself out of bed and was picked up outside the Academy at the appointed time. The car drove towards the river, then along to Pimlico, before pulling up outside the Tate Gallery.

It turned out that the guy who I had put on the guest list for Springsteen was some vastly wealthy American dude, who had contributed about fourteen Monets to the big French Impressionists exhibition that was the Tate's flagship show that season. At this guy's insistence, the entire gallery was opened an hour early, just for me. I was whisked straight past large queues that were already forming outside, and into the cool silence of the gallery.

It's an amazing way to see great art: all alone, unrushed, and uncrowded by chattering tourists and their cameras. This was a special little moment of peace in the maniacally unpredictable whirl that was my life.

Perhaps inspired by the delicate beauty of the paintings, and the unfamiliar stillness of the moment, I started daydreaming, in my way, about what I should do next with the Academy. How could I make it grow and expand? What was the next step?

For the first time in my life, I found I didn't have an answer.

This was a shocking new feeling. Pausing to reflect, I was forced to ask myself: if you've had Bob Dylan, The Rolling Stones, and Bruce Springsteen across your stage over the past several months, how much bigger can you actually get?

I found the question troubling. The idea of not having a new challenge to overcome didn't sit well with me. I always need something to push against.

Not wanting to follow this train of thought to its obvious conclusion, I did my best not to think about it, and just let the playful colours of Monet and Degas wash over me.

That moment of reflective tranquillity didn't last beyond the exit of the Tate Gallery gift shop. Once those doors closed it was back to the pandemonium of Brixton.

1995 was a glorious year at the Academy. It wasn't only the legendary giants of rock that were passing through. This era saw incredible, career-defining, gigs by bands as varied as Pulp, Stereolab, The Prodigy, and my favourite of the new crop of emerging British talent, a shy group of introverted Oxford intellectual types called Radiohead.

Their album *The Bends* had just been released as part of their grand effort to rise out of the pigeonhole of forever being 'that band that played the song "Creep"'. Seeing how utterly they entranced the crowd at the Academy, it should have been obvious to anyone that they were always destined to be so much more than that. Radiohead ingeniously combined the angst-fuelled intensity of American grunge with a uniquely British sensitivity and songcraft, creating something strikingly original and irresistibly powerful. Their performance at the Academy was spectacular. To look at, you wouldn't think that these five quiet guys had it in them, but once they got onstage they were atomic.

By now, the rock bands had started taking advantage of our 6 a.m. licence as much as the rave promoters. Primal Scream did an amazing all-nighter with the whacked-out godfather of P-Funk, George Clinton, as their support act. This was quickly followed by another fantastic party-till-dawn by The Stone Roses, which Ian Brown has always claimed was the best gig they ever played.

Having been so cruelly deprived of Nirvana, we put on the breakthrough UK concerts by Dave Grohl's new act, Foo Fighters,

The best of Britpop.
Jarvis Cocker of Pulp was always a magnificent performer

as well as extremely loud gigs with Red Hot Chili Peppers, Iron Maiden, and the cartoonishly energetic pop-punk trio Green Day. Paul Weller returned to the Academy for a triumphant three-night run, this time with the man of the moment, Noel Gallagher, in tow.

Amidst all this sweaty, macho rock, though, it was the madcap whimsical poeticism of Björk that most bewitched me. Her old group, The Sugarcubes, had played the Academy years earlier. I always thought they were a catchy band, but nothing prepared me for the mix of passionate experimentalism and gentle sincerity that Björk brought to her solo performance. Throughout the entire show she seemed completely 'in the moment', her concentration never wavering, and her generosity to the audience never faltering. I wasn't the only one utterly captivated that night. It's an amazing sensation to look out over a stage and watch 5,000 people simultaneously falling in love with the same person.

After all that Dave McLean and I had been through with our In Bloom travails, when he came to me saying that he and his partner at Riverman, Alex Weston, had discovered 'the band they had been waiting for', I was keen to help out however I could. After all, the last band he had raved like this about had turned out to be Nirvana.

Placebo needed a showcase to let the record companies see what they were capable of. We set up a stage in the Academy foyer, and they blew all the A&R goons away. It was quite something for Placebo to be able to show themselves off in our beautiful art deco entrance hall. Most bands of that era did their showcase gigs in tiny black-box Camden toilet venues like The Falcon or The Barfly (then still called The Monarch).

By their third song I knew Dave was absolutely right. This band had 'it'. As they finished their post-showcase schmoozing, I winked to their frontman, Brian Molko. 'No worries mate, in eighteen months we'll have you on the main stage.' This was quite something for the singer of an as yet unknown band to hear, and he shot me a look of disbelief. I ended up betting him £20 that my predic-

A tender moment between Brian Molko of Placebo and Michael Stipe of REM

tion would come true. Credit to the guy, when they headlined the Academy a year later he came up and paid me.

Over the next fifteen years, Placebo became Academy stalwarts. They are a classic example of a band who get precious little love from the music press and all the assorted chin-stroking tastemakers of indie rock, but who still inspire absolute devotion in their fans. To this day Placebo hold the record for the most Brixton Academy gigs of any band.

Even as all this fun, joy, and mayhem raged around me, I couldn't get that troubling question from the Tate Gallery out of my head: what next?

Every gig we put on sold out immediately, and our weekend raves unfailingly had lines of people queuing around the block. It was as if we didn't even have to try. We'd already had the biggest bands in the world, so short of using ouija boards to summon the spirit of John Lennon for a Beatles reunion, how much further could I take this thing?

The raves were actually becoming a problem. Don't get me wrong; they were a lot of fun if you were loved up, full of Ecstasy, and dancing till dawn like a Duracell bunny. But if you were working all night, with nothing to fuel you but espresso after bitter espresso, then that repetitive, pneumatic-drill, kick drum thump could become a form of Chinese water torture.

It was getting to feel oppressive, not to mention utterly exhausting. Trust me: you do back-to-back raves till 6 a.m., 48 weekends a year, plus weekday gigs in between, and you start to feel the toll. I began to feel like a grumpy old Victor Meldrew caricature, hiding in my office just to avoid the monotony of that unending 4/4 beat. I had got into this business for the passion and power of live music, for that electric connection between the band and the crowd. Raves, exciting as they could be, lacked the emotional immediacy of a great rock 'n' roll show.

For the first time in my life, I found myself not enjoying work.

It was the council that finally did it, though.

The time had rolled around for us to renew our live music licence. It was no big deal; we had all our paperwork in order, and had filled in the appropriate forms. The deadline for the reapplication happened to fall on a Saturday. We sent the documents off on the Friday, knowing that they would arrive the next morning.

But of course, the office was closed on Saturday. They only opened the envelope on the Monday morning, after the deadline had passed.

I got a call from the relevant officer at Lambeth Council saying that our licence had expired. With a mixture of incredulity and fury, I argued that of course we had got our application in on time. But this guy claimed that as the deadline fell on a Saturday, it was our responsibility to have the documents delivered by the time the office closed on the preceding Friday.

I knew this awful little jobsworth from the past few years of my dealings with the council. He was the classic, textbook example of the mediocre, grey-suited bureaucrat using his position of authority to get in the way of people actually trying to make things happen. I wasn't the only operator in the area to have had trouble with this little twerp, and I knew I was in for a long, tedious fight.

I spent a frantic few days desperately trying to argue my case and appeal the decision. This was serious. Applying for a new licence could take months and would cost a lot of money. If I didn't hold a valid licence, then all the upcoming gigs I had in the diary were thrown into jeopardy. If I went ahead with them, I would technically be breaking the law.

In desperation, I went to the police.

'Look,' I explained, 'next weekend is Notting Hill Carnival. Your resources are going to be stretched as it is, and I've got two major rap gigs scheduled. Most of the tickets have been sold through record stores. I have no way of reaching these people. If the Academy has to cancel these shows, you're going to have a public order nightmare with five thousand pissed-off hip-hop fans all wandering around the area with no way to vent their energy.'

The cops saw my point immediately. They sent a representative down to the council offices with me. He was fantastic, arguing that not only was it essential that the upcoming concerts go ahead, but that the Academy was extremely useful for the police and a major force for good in the area. He ended the discussion with an exasperated, 'Oh just stop being so silly, and give Simon the bloody licence.'

But the smarmy pencil-pusher from the council was unmoved. He had decided on his position, and nothing was going to change his mind. He couldn't have been more officious and arrogant either, just the type of attitude to drive me up the wall. Even when the head of the council, along with the police, came down and advised him to stop being an idiot and give us the licence, he refused.

Eventually I asked him straight out, 'What will happen if I just go ahead with my rap gigs next week?'

'You could be fined, and even go to prison,' he threatened.

'Yeah, well put me in prison then, because I'm doing the fucking gigs.'

I knew Brixton police weren't going to arrest me for putting on concerts that they had advised me to go ahead with. As if cops in this part of the world didn't have better things to be getting on with?

So the shows went ahead and, lo and behold, I didn't go to prison. I brazenly continued to operate, eventually switching back to working on occasional licences, as I had when the Academy first opened, until the whole bureaucratic nonsense could be sorted out.

But the entire episode left a very bitter taste. If you ask anyone vaguely knowledgeable what the single biggest driving force behind the regeneration of Brixton has been, the only answer is the Brixton Academy. After all the energy, love, time, work, and sweat I had put into this neighbourhood, all the jobs I had created, all the visibility and publicity I had provided, the council was treating me like this? They should have been giving me a fucking medal. It was hard to resist the urge to shout a big 'fuck you', and just walk away.

The actual decision came quietly, without any fanfare or drama.

It was about 4.30 a.m., with some rave in full swing. I had an hour and a half to go; then hopefully a few hours' sleep; then back in at 3 p.m. for the same circus all over again. I walked down the side of the Academy, watching the late-night revellers shout at each other and vomit on street corners, the stink of the burger vans in my nostrils.

As I let myself into the back door of the building, it suddenly dawned on me that I had now been doing this for almost fifteen years. I was in my late thirties, and while I was still by and large having a good time, could I see myself doing the same thing when I was pushing fifty? When you're working like I did back then, ten years can slip by in a heartbeat.

There was no flash of revelation, no choir of angels, and not a single moment of doubt. Much like how I had come up with the name 'Academy' all those years before talking to Mike Henley, the thought was just suddenly there in my head. And I knew it was right. 'Fuck it. I'm selling.'

THE BIG IDEA

I started by quietly putting the word out on the industry gossip networks. Many people were shocked that I would want to sell the Academy just as everything was going so well. The guys who knew me best, however, friends like Pat and Johnny, understood immediately. I wasn't built for simply cruising along at the top of the game, with no challenge ahead of me. I've just never been terribly good at boredom.

The first offer I got on the place took even me by surprise. The Academy had only been on the market for a couple of days, and I had yet to really go public with the news. In walked a group of Latin American guys with shiny suits, diamond-encrusted Rolexes, and an air of absolute, indomitable, self-assurance.

As they marched into my office, my immediate assumption was that these guys were gangsters, and not just the local Brixton Yardie types, nor even the big London organized crime firms. When a bunch of Latino guys like these rock up, the only conclusion one can come to is that they are part of a very serious Colombian cocaine cartel.

There was some sinister arrogance about the way they held themselves. They would stare straight through you, regarding everything around them with a proprietorial air, as if it were already theirs by right.

'Hello Mr Parkes, we've heard that your building is for sale.'

This was absolutely the last thing I needed. If these guys were connected enough to know about my plans before I had even put out a press release, they must be linked to some extremely heavy characters. I hadn't kept myself out of the criminal rackets all these years just to make my last big deal with some Medellín mafiosi. I knew exactly how those enterprises panned out: with some poor fucker in the trunk of a car. I had no intention whatsoever of being that fucker.

My only hope was that, as the official news of the Academy's sale hadn't been released yet, maybe I could fudge this?

'Umm ... well ... you see, I'm not actually quite sure what the plans are at the moment, but the building isn't officially for sale right now.'

'Everything is for sale, Mr Parkes. It's just a matter of deciding the price.' The reply came back immediately, without a moment's hesitation, emotionless and cold.

Jesus Christ. Who even talks like that? This was getting into some extremely creepy territory.

As the conversation progressed, things became clearer. These guys weren't Colombian, they were Brazilian. And they weren't cocaine smugglers: they were the Universal Church of the Kingdom of God.

Originating in the favelas of Rio, this evangelical megachurch now had over 12 million adherents across the globe, and was looking for a space to house its flagship London tabernacle. Suddenly it all made sense. Only two sets of people can stare through you in quite the way these guys did: serious gangsters, or people who are certain they have God on their side. My suspicion was that these characters might well fall into both categories.

At least I could be fairly sure that the conversation wasn't going to end with a garrotting down a dark alley. And what the hell? If you're trying to drum up an auction on a building like the Academy, someone has to start the bidding.

I also have to admit that that jobsworth at the council had pissed me off so much over our licence, that part of me got a perverse satisfaction from the idea of turning around and saying, 'Well, if that's how you're going to be, fuck you. I'll sell the whole thing to these weirdo religious nuts.'

So the church had a look around the building and at the relevant paperwork. A few days later they sent through their offer. It was laughable. They wanted the whole shebang for £400,000.

I picked up the phone, and almost as a joke opened with the line, 'I just received your offer. Stick another zero on the end of that number, and we can have a conversation.'

Without pausing for even a second, the voice at the other end of the line simply said, 'OK, that's fine. Shall our lawyers call yours?'

Well, that's one way to conduct a negotiation.

This put things in a very different light. Whatever god these guys worshipped had obviously endowed them with some very deep pockets. I had never really taken this whole idea that seriously. My plan had always been to use the church's interest as leverage in my negotiations with the music biz sharks. But four million pounds is four million pounds. I suddenly started thinking that I might come out of this very well indeed.

Of course, the rumour that 'the world-famous Brixton Academy' was going to close down and become a church sent the media into a frenzy. The local bigwigs, along with various music journalists, started a 'Save the Brixton Academy' campaign. Naturally, they focused on me, the guy who had set the whole bloody thing up, as Public Enemy Number One for wanting to sell it. I didn't particularly mind all the personal attacks. If you're trying to sell a major music venue, that kind of publicity is absolutely priceless.

The local MP for Streatham, the Right Honorable Keith Hill, was heavily involved in this campaign. When I went for a meeting at his offices in the Houses of Parliament, I had to pause halfway through our discussion and ask him, 'So, have you ever actually been to a gig at the Brixton Academy?'

To his very great credit, he answered straight. 'I have to be honest, no, I haven't. But I am very well aware of what a fantastic thing it is for the area, and the community.'

I admired his candour. It would have been so easy for him just to lie. I roared with laughter. 'You know something, you're the most honest politician I've ever met.'

It didn't take me long to realize that the church's schemes were never going to pan out. Leafing through their various documents, I noticed that amongst their proposals for the building they would be offering religious 'cures for homosexuality' and regular 'Pray the Gay Away' services. One look at that, and I knew that a left-leaning, politically engaged council like Lambeth were never going to let this purchase go through.

I can't say I was that upset. Even £4 million could never have cured the heartache of destroying the beautiful thing I had created, not to mention shutting down the best music venue in Britain.

But of course, I didn't tell anyone. Having people continue to believe there was a serious offer on the table was great for business. The moment people thought the end of the Academy might be drawing near, our bookings went through the roof. Suddenly, everyone was rushing to put on one last show at their favourite venue. I wasn't about to ruin a good run like that by letting the truth slip out.

In the end, the cosmos exerted a strange bit of circularity, and the Universal Church of the Kingdom of God ended up buying the Rainbow in Finsbury Park: the very venue where I first snuck down from school to see Chuck Berry all those years ago. Well, at the time, that gig had certainly felt like a religious experience to my teenage soul. No matter how hard they tried, I knew those dodgy, Rolexed charlatans would never be able to exorcise fully the spirit of rock 'n' roll that generations of music fans had infused into the very bricks of that place.

It was amidst the fallout and confusion in the wake of the collapse of the Universal Church deal that I had my next 'big idea' for the Academy's future.

This was another of those little light-bulb-going-on-in-the-head moments that can redefine someone's entire career, or at least their legacy.

Suddenly I was excited again.

My thinking was that in the absence of a festival like In Bloom, or something similar, the only way for the Academy to grow as an institution would be for it join with a group of other concert halls as a single company. This would allow it to become the base for a network of venues across the country.

It seemed so obvious. A company with a string of venues could strike deals for entire tours, not just one-off gigs. We could use this as industry leverage, in the same way that Vince Power used the Reading Festival; but on a much bigger scale.

This could be huge.

It would also entail a much larger organization. No individual player had anywhere near the financial muscle to create something like what I had in mind. This idea would require a Public Limited Company, with its entire requisite panoply of shareholders, stock dividends, quarterly reports, and all the other nonsense that I had gone into music specifically to avoid.

After so many years operating as my own boss, by my own rules, I obviously wasn't going to subject myself now to having to answer to some board room. At any rate, the whole point of this was that I was looking for a way out of the music biz.

But I had a good idea who the right man for the job might be.

I went to see John Northcote at Break for the Border. These guys had done great things with the tiny Borderline Club on Charing Cross Road. They had also just raised enough capital to buy the Shepherd's Bush Empire. I figured John could be just the guy to navigate the divide between the rock 'n' rollers and the financiers.

I explained my grand vision in my usual overenthusiastic torrent of words and ideas. After a few blank stares of incomprehension, the light behind John's eyes slowly seemed to switch on. Over a series of meetings, he came to understand what I was aiming at, and got fully behind the concept. We hammered out a deal.

I sold the Brixton Academy to Break for the Border for £2.5 million pounds. Which, as a 249,999,999 per cent return on my original £1 investment, isn't half bad. One of the key stipulations of the deal was that I would stick around, as an outside consultant, to run the Academy for another eighteen months. It was obvious to everyone involved that I was the only one with any idea of how the whole circus really ran.

MEN IN SUITS

I couldn't have been happier with my new arrangement, at least at first.

I still got all the thrills of running the Academy, but without the crushing burden of sole responsibility. A huge weight was lifted, and I felt I could breathe easier than I had in years.

After putting so much time and energy into the Academy for so long, just stopping overnight would probably have been too much of a shock to the system. But perhaps the strangest feeling of all was getting my life back.

I hadn't been to a New Year's Eve party for fifteen years. I was always working. For a decade and a half, I had been putting in roughly an eighty-hour week, fifty-two weeks a year, in this one building. Every Friday and Saturday, and several weeknights in between, were all spent amidst the booming music and rock 'n' roll madness of 211 Stockwell Road.

I hadn't had a proper holiday, been to a dinner party with mates, bought a house, or any of those other little things that people with 'normal' jobs call 'having a life'.

My friends had all got married, and I had been able to attend maybe three of their weddings; and I had had to sneak out of one to deal with the Brixton riots.

Now all of a sudden I found I could actually take part in all these new experiences. It was all incredibly exotic, and a very pleasant, if disorientating, feeling of weightlessness.

Amidst all my newfound levity and ease, though, there were two trends that I found increasingly troubling.

The first was what was happening to music.

In the horrifying wake of the Spice Girls, the record companies were increasingly focusing their efforts into churning out ever more of these identikit, manufactured girl-and-boy-groups. For anyone who loved music, it was genuinely painful to have to endure these tacky Barbie-doll bands croaking out their turgid, anodyne pop trash – all cobbled together in some songwriting 'hit factory'.

Of course, this had been going on at some level for years. We had all suffered through Jason Donovan's success in the 80s. But now the dynamic seemed to intensify and accelerate at a level that I, for one, had never witnessed before.

From a label's perspective, it made perfect sense. Those pop groups were docile, easily manipulated, and sang the songs they were told to. They sold bucketloads of records, at minimum outlay for the company. There was never any worry about helping artists through 'difficult creative periods' because these weren't creative artists. It was far easier for the label simply to drop the act and dredge up a new gaggle of wide-eyed teenagers to bewitch with promises of pop stardom.

From a live music standpoint, those pop groups were cringingly awful. They may have been pretty enough for the tacky pop magazines, but half of them couldn't sing a note. While studio trickery could fool the fans on record, at a gig they were totally exposed.

These groups weren't created to write albums that fans would cherish for years, but to send one song up the charts, then disappear. I used to book bands by studying the album charts, not the singles. Fans that buy albums are fans that come to gigs. A few giant pop groups aside, people were understandably unenthusiastic about paying to see five wannabe H&M models awkwardly miming for an hour, just to hear the one hit tune that the label had wrung out of them.

It was an awful, corrosive development for music as a whole. And anyone who gives you the weasely old industry lines 'well, Motown was a hit factory too' or 'Stock Aitken Waterman aren't doing anything Sam Phillips didn't do' deserves a smack round the face with the entire Stax Records back catalogue. On vinyl.

At the same time, it seemed that guitar music had somewhat lost its way. American bands were locked in a cycle of diminishing returns as the labels signed one vacuous Kurt Cobain knock-off after another. Meanwhile in the UK, the golden creative moment of Britpop passed, and no one seemed to be stepping forward to carry the torch on from the original innovators such as Pulp, Elastica, Supergrass, and of course the big two: Blur and Oasis.

This whole dynamic was amplified by what my friends and I came to call the 'MTV effect'.

As ever, it was all a question of economics. The old formula was that one punter at a concert meant ten records sold on word-of-mouth hype. On this basis, the record labels had been willing to invest £50,000 in tour support for a band, on the assumption that they would sell half a million albums on the back of it.

The inexorable rise of MTV, and all the assorted copycat 'music TV' stations, threw the old calculations of relative value into chaos. The accountants, who were increasingly calling the shots at the big American labels, looked at the bottom lines and started asking,

'Why don't we take that £50,000 of tour support and put it into making high-end music videos instead?' On a tour you hit a few hundred thousand people; with a successful video you can reach 60 million at a stroke. From a moneyman's point of view it made perfect sense.

But what the record label desk jockeys didn't take into account, or just didn't care about, was the intensity of experience of the audience at a concert compared with that of the kid with MTV on in the background as he does his homework.

No one has ever breathlessly related to me how 'watching that music video changed my life'. I lost count very early on of the number of times people said that about unforgettable shows at the Academy. Though we had done very well renting the venue out for video shoots, ultimately a great gig is a shared emotional moment between an artist and their crowd. With a few wonderful exceptions, music videos are audio-visual wallpaper.

The MTV effect didn't just alter where the labels spent their promo money, it began to dictate what groups got signed at all. Increasingly, the focus shifted from which bands wrote the best songs, or delivered the most intense performances, and became more about who looked best in the videos. Suddenly, every member of these new bands seemed to be these perfect little coiffeured show-poodles. It might work for the videos, but it wasn't rock 'n' roll.

The old tech crews and I developed a joke that it was 'all in the drummer's teeth'. There is absolutely no reason whatsoever why the drummer in a rock 'n' roll band should have perfectly straight, shiny teeth, even if they are American. The second that some new group walked into the venue, and the rhythm section started flashing their expensive dental work, the roadies and I would wink at each other, assuming, usually correctly, that this band had been signed for their inoffensive looks. They hadn't suffered through the hard graft of touring dive bar after dive bar in a shitty old van: the struggle that forges truly great rock bands.

The other development troubling my life, and one that affected me on a far more visceral, day-to-day level, was dealing with the suited businessmen that I now found myself having to answer to.

I had always known that I wasn't built for the world of the Public Limited Company: for board meetings, decisions by committee, and corporate hierarchies. But I had never counted on the transition being this difficult.

Don't get me wrong, not everyone who worked for Break for the Border was some kind of joyless stooge. John, and a lot of the other guys, were generally all right. But the accountants, lawyers, and financiers called the shots now. These were the new gods who had to be propitiated, and it very clearly wasn't for me.

It wasn't just the incident over the IOU for those two grams of cocaine to book Black Grape. There were countless examples of that kind of failure of communication. It all added up to make my job at the Academy excruciatingly difficult.

Not long after Break for the Border had taken over, we did a very successful three-night run in partnership with SJM Promotions. SJM were probably the Academy's best client, and Simon, who ran it, had been with me almost since the beginning.

As these were the days before we all began living on mobile phones and the Internet, each promoter working the Academy would have a telephone in their backstage office, with a £25 per night budget for calls. Many of the bands coming through the venue were on tour, with business to sort out for the next leg of their journey, so these calls were often international.

A few days after our three-night SJM run, one of Break for the Border's accountants came to me and claimed that the band had gone £18 over their telephone allowance, and he would have to raise an invoice with SJM.

I exploded at the poor little twerp. 'There is no way you can raise an invoice for £18. Forget it! If it's £180, forget it. If it's £1,800, then *maybe*.' We had probably taken around £45,000 on hall hire over those three nights, and upwards of £150,000 on the bar. And this jobsworth wanted to hassle my friend Simon over eighteen quid?

It was exactly by avoiding this kind of pedantic, killjoy wankery that I had originally stolen all the business from the Hammersmith Odeon. I wasn't having my own bloody venue making the same mistakes as those old dinosaur companies. I tried desperately to explain to the accountant how this business worked: that if we came on like wankers, then the next time SJM had a great show to promote, they would go straight over to Vince Power at the Forum.

This poor guy was so obviously out of his depth that he stammered out the worst possible response, the one answer guaranteed to drive me completely mad: 'Well, I'll have to take it to the board.'

I wasn't used to decisions made at monthly board meetings. It drove me insane. I was used to thinking on my feet, to finding the angle, and going for it before the next guy got in there; to being cut-throat in business, but generous with the spoils; to the music business as it once was: piratical, volatile, and fun.

It also stuck slightly in my craw that, the second I was out of the picture, every government agency around seemed to be lining up to throw money at the Brixton Academy. Regeneration projects, funded by both local and central government, had been pouring money into Brixton for years. Every single one of my friends operating in the neighbourhood was tapping this resource in one way or another. The entire area had its mouth on the government teat.

The only one that seemed to get shut out of this bonanza was yours truly. Maybe I was too white, or perhaps it was the old stigma of my family name, but every public agency seemed blocked from giving the Academy any assistance.

It actually got to the point of absurdity, becoming a running joke between my black mates and me. I'd get word of yet another failed application, and they'd laugh their arses off and say, 'Simon, you should just be gay. If you were at least gay you'd get the money in a second.' These guys knew how the system worked.

Then, only months after Break for the Border took over, the council handed them £900,000 to do up the front of the building. I was left asking myself: 'Wait a second, I've been asking for help for fifteen years, and you've just gone and given it to a bloody private limited company?' Of course, it was fantastic for the Break for the Border chaps. That extra nine hundred grand went straight to their bottom line, upped their share price, and all the suits took home fatter stock dividends and corporate bonuses at the end of the year. Which must have been very nice for them, but, once again, it ain't rock 'n' roll.

Indeed, rock 'n' roll seemed to be in increasingly short supply. These accountants and lawyers lacked the slightest feel for how the industry actually worked. I'd get a call from the finance guys at 5 p.m. on a Friday, saying, 'OK Simon, we're going for a big meeting in the City on Monday, and we need your projections for the next three months.'

To which I would quite naturally reply, 'I've got an all-nighter tonight, with doors opening in an hour; another all-nighter tomorrow night; and a gig on Sunday. When the fuck am I supposed to sit down and figure out the next three months' numbers? And ... why the fuck didn't you let me know about this last week?'

But the guys in the City were the bosses now. The numbers would have to be crunched. I couldn't help the creeping suspicion that maybe I was being deliberately squeezed out, that perhaps I operated as a little too much of a maverick for this brave new corporate world.

Either way, I was beginning to find operating in this new, commercial atmosphere even more oppressive than doing back-to-back raves every weekend.

POWER PLAY

Things came to a head several months later, when I spied an opportunity to have one last crack at Power.

About the time I was first thinking of selling the Academy, I had been offered the chance to buy the Astoria venue near Tottenham Court Road. Though initially tempted, I reminded myself that I was trying to exit the music business, not launch entire new ventures, and I had turned it down. Naturally enough, Vince Power had stepped in and snapped it up.

Thus, by the mid 90s, the battle lines were drawn so that Break for the Border controlled the Academy and the Shepherd's Bush Empire, while Power's Mean Fiddler Group ran the Forum, the Astoria, and a string of much smaller venues.

Then, amidst all the music business whirl and chatter, I hit upon a plan that could knock Mean Fiddler out of the game, and make us the undisputed kings of UK live music.

It went like this. By 1996 Oasis were far-and-away the biggest guitar band in Britain. They had comprehensively won their manufactured playground spat with Blur, and were so ubiquitous that I stopped turning on my radio for fear that if I heard those opening chords to 'Wonderwall' one more time I might go into a full psychological breakdown.

Now the band's management were looking for a way to confirm publicly their place on the throne, before launching their campaign in the States. All through early 1996, the music business was rife with rumours that Oasis were planning a massive summer event at Knebworth House.

I sensed an opportunity here.

Vince Power's major asset was still the Reading Festival. It was always the ace card he held over us. But I knew how Vince ran Reading. It was an incredibly high-risk financial model, not dissimilar to how I used to operate at the Academy. Every summer Vince was heavily invested. If Reading had even one off year, it could leave Mean Fiddler on the brink of insolvency.

This is where my plan came into play.

If Oasis's management could be convinced to schedule their massive Knebworth shows for the same weekend as the Reading Festival, they would completely destroy its box office. No possible headliner was big enough to go head-to-head with Oasis, and no agent would have the stomach for that kind of fight. Reading would make a huge loss, or even go down entirely, leaving Mean Fiddler in very severe financial straits.

That's when we would step in. With Vince on his knees, Break for the Border would be free to swoop down and buy up his venues at a fraction of their true value. This would put us in total control of Britain's entire live music industry.

It was an ingenious scheme, if admittedly somewhat underhanded. In most other industries, I'm sure this would be considered completely unethical. In ours, it was pretty standard play. I loved Vince as a person; he's one the true legends of British music. But business is business. Not only am I one hundred per cent sure that Vince would have done exactly the same to me in my position, and I would have admired him for it, but I'm sure when he reads this, he'll laugh his arse off.

And it only gets dirtier.

The Oasis team still needed to be convinced to take this fight on.

Luckily, by this time, I knew anyone worth knowing in UK music. Contact was made, and the band's team were sounded out. The reports back were that for £50,000 in a brown paper envelope, the Knebworth concerts could be deliberately set to coincide with Reading, leaving us to pick up the pieces after the ensuing battle.

Never known for their humility, the boys from Oasis, we figured, would be up for outdoing Reading just to have done it. Everything was in place. All that was needed to seal the deal was the cash.

I was buzzing with excitement. This was it. The one. The last big score to take Vince Power down, and put us on top.

But when I took the idea to the board, they looked at me as if I was a raving lunatic.

The suits just didn't seem to understand that this was exactly how the game was played. This was *rock 'n' roll*. I did my best to break it all down for them slowly, taking it piece by piece. I figured that these guys were good capitalists; if nothing else, I could appeal to their greed. Eventually avarice did win through, the light seemed to dawn, and I managed to convince them of my plan's potential.

But out of their lame, blinkered, boardroom mentality, they came up with the most pathetic possible objection: 'But how are we going to justify fifty thousand pounds in cash to the accounts department?'

I completely lost my temper with this stuttering indecision. 'I can raise a bloody consulting invoice for fifty thousand tomorrow, if you need it,' I shouted, 'any one of us can. This is the Brixton fucking Academy; it's not hard to find fifty thousand pounds in cash!'

The suits just didn't get it. One ridiculous hurdle after another was put in the way. There always seemed to be more committees to go to, more bureaucratic hoops to jump.

In the old days I would have put this whole deal together in twenty-four hours, and in six months I would have put Vince on the back foot, and established my team at the Academy as the music biz kingpins. That kind of nimble operating had become impossible in this new era of bottom lines, shareholder meetings, and board approval.

The corporate bigwigs hemmed and hawed, played politics, and argued amongst themselves for too long. They let the opportunity slip by.

As it happened, when Oasis's Knebworth concert was announced, on a different weekend to Reading, 2.6 million people applied for tickets, making it the most in-demand live music event in British music history. My little plan would have been a smashing success.

After the suits' abject failure to take the golden opportunity I had offered them, I decided I was through with the corporate music business. I spent a final few weeks wandering nostalgically around the Academy that I had built from nothing with so much love and sweat, and made plans for a graceful exit.

OUTRO: IN MY LIFE

Every so often, perhaps once a fortnight, Pat will swing by my house for a cup of tea. He'll ease himself into a chair, complaining of some ache and pain or other; and we'll chew the fat like every pair of old mates since the dawn of time, usually talking about our children or, in Pat's case, grandchildren.

It's funny to see Pat adjusting to the role of respectable pater-familias: proudly talking up his brood's marks at school or goals in football; and, of course, bemoaning the worries they cause him. But Pat is still Pat. He may have more lines on his face, and his grandkids' drawings stuck on the fridge door, but when he walks into a room, there is still that unmistakable air of someone you just don't mess with.

Inevitably, he and I always end up talking about 'the old days' at the Academy. My wife will walk in and roll her eyes as we burst into laughter recounting some old war story or other. It's like a bloody Bruce Springsteen song.

Inevitably, when Pat goes, a more reflective mood takes over. I start thinking back on all my mad adventures over the years with the Academy, and trying to work out what it all means.

More often than not, the main question I end up on at these moments is very simple: how the hell did I get away with it?

Looking back with the more experienced eyes of an older man on some of the stunts I pulled, I just think, my God, I must have been a complete nutter. Perhaps it's the effects of fatherhood? When you have a wife and children, you just don't expose yourself to the same kind of risks as you do as a tearaway young blade.

Of course, with hindsight one can see anything one wants. Everything can be made to make sense when you already know how the story ends. Without projecting too much back on the past, though, I think it all comes down to those two key lessons I internalized as a kid: my mum's golden rule about not judging people, and old Mac's hard-learned injunction never to let myself be threatened.

If I had been a more judgemental character, none of this would have ever come off. Prejudice would have got in the way. I first walked into the Brixton Astoria as a wide-eyed kid. All I saw was a beautiful space where I knew I could put on amazing gigs. Brixton just struck me as lively, interesting, and cool. If I had carried any preconceptions about the area's violent reputation, or any street-smart savvy about how London worked, I probably would have walked away at that moment. Any sensible person would have.

Likewise, if some cheeky Rasta turned up at the door of most businesses, demanding to borrow his new boss's car to go and book one of the biggest bands in the country, he would be laughed off the doorstep. But I followed my gut about Johnny Lawes. He seemed like a good guy, so I gave him a shot. He turned out to become one of the most valuable assets I had at the Academy, and a great friend to boot.

It was generally my policy to say 'yes' to everything, and see what stuck. It may well have got me into some scrapes over the years, but it was this underlying attitude that made the whole crazy circus possible.

On the flipside, the laws that governed the jungle of the Brixton music biz proved to be not all that different from the unwritten rules of the school playground. If I hadn't always had old Mac's voice in the back of my mind telling me not to let myself be pushed around, I would have been eaten alive.

Head-butting a Brixton gang leader is generally a quick and easy way to write your own suicide note. When I was in that situation, I knew I not only had to put the guy down, I had to make sure that the Railton Road boys, and every other mobster in the room, saw me put him down.

If I had let John Curd run the front door security on that first rock gig with The Cult, from then on every other promoter and agent would have expected to take the same liberty. It's not that they're bad people, they just work in the music biz. Give them an inch, and they'll take your entire venue.

Of course, the other reason I survived my encounters with the Brixton gangsters is simply that I never became one of them. Despite the countless opportunities, temptations, and provocations, I always kept myself firmly on my own side of the law.

The moment I closed that briefcase with £100,000 sitting there for the taking, my choice was made. And that was only one among so many opportunities.

It would have been so easy to skim a little here, to take a payment there. I had friends in the industry who used to tell me to just unplug one cash register, on one bar, at each gig we did. It would have been the simplest thing in the world to make £1,000 disappear each night. With so much cash moving through the venue, no one would have ever noticed it. The question would never even have been asked. And if you're doing upwards of 100 gigs a year, it adds up.

That was just the tip of the iceberg. There were so many scams I could have pulled, so many angles I could have worked, that it would take a whole new book even to begin going into them.

I could have been a much, much wealthier man than I am today.

I could also be in prison, like so many of the guys I knew back then. Or dead, like a fair few others.

The old line about prostitution always applied. Once you've taken the money, you're in the game. After that, it's just a matter of quibbling over the price. If I had crossed that line, if I had started making plays and running scams, then I would have had to spend the rest of my life constantly looking over my shoulder. There would always be the underlying worry that one day either the police or another gangster would come knocking.

And that was never the point. I didn't set up the Academy in order to spend my time on paranoid double dealing and wringing out as much cash as possible. I wanted to put on great gigs. The whole thing was always about joy and excitement, about rock 'n' roll.

I tried to apply these same standards to how I dealt with the music biz guys, going far out of my way to maintain an honest reputation.

In 1994, the great agent Charlie Myatt, who took care of Radiohead, Supergrass, and just about every other decent band to come out of Oxford, brought The Levellers down for a show. At some point during the night, he teasingly dropped some offhand comment about how I might have *over-capacitated* the venue. I wasn't going to let that stand. First of all, I knew that that's how rumours got started. I couldn't have people running around saying that I had fiddled the books. But also I loved Radiohead, and I wanted Charlie to book them for a show.

So I pulled my team together and made them count every single ticket stub, then arrange them in numerical order. You can imagine what a nightmare that was. My guys must have thought I really was off my fucking head. I then presented the whole package to Charlie, along with the video footage of the front door. 'OK

Charlie, you think I over-capacitated your gig. Here you go, have a look through that.'

Charlie looked at me as if I was insane, and then burst out laughing. 'Jesus, Simon, I was only kidding around.' I knew Charlie had been half joking when he first made the remark, but my rep was my rep. I took this extremely seriously.

Don't get me wrong, I could play the game just as well as the next guy. And when you're playing against characters like Vince Power, you have no choice but to become a wily operator. But it was crucial to me that people knew that when they struck a deal with Simon Parkes, I would stick to my end of the bargain.

So I can say with absolute honesty, and a little bit of pride, that I never knowingly fucked anyone over any more than our industry demanded.

I think, too, that people in the biz came to appreciate that about me. I ended up earning the nickname 'Mr Nice'. Which was amusing to joke about with Howard Marks, when we shared a spliff on the Shepherd's Bush Empire balcony while watching a Catatonia gig in the late 90s. I never normally got high while working a show, but this *was* Howard Marks. We shared the same nickname, after all. Though I did get mine by actually being nice to people, as opposed to buying some random geezer's passport, like that charming old dope smuggler.

Overall, I suppose I thought that trying to be crooked or 'clever' would take too much energy. Energy I could otherwise put into having a good time. I knew plenty of guys who cheated, scammed, and cooked their books, trying to get one over on everyone else. They'd all end up having to run two entirely different sets of accounts. It just seemed like a tremendous hassle, not to mention the ever-present risk of getting caught. Who needed that kind of worry? I think if most of those guys had put the same amount of effort into growing legitimate businesses as they did into gaming the system and stabbing each other in the back, the numbers would have probably evened out in the end. In the meantime, they would have had a lot less stress, and considerably more fun.

It all comes down to the question of what you're looking for out of what you do. For me, it was never about the prize; it was about the adventure.

After I left the Academy I did some work with Dave McLean at Riverman Management, and was then brought in as a consultant to help relaunch the Coronet, another old theatre-turned-music-venue, in Elephant and Castle.

Most important, though, I asked Pippa to marry me, and in a moment of insanity she actually said yes. We walked down the aisle in 1999, and have three sons, Joe, Oliver, and Sam.

Without overplaying the sentimental father role, there is no doubt that, for me, this is the only adventure that could ever have followed and surpassed the Academy. Anyone who has watched their children grow, learn, and become their own people will know what I am talking about. For me, the boys are a source of pure joy. On their good days, at least.

And, naturally, as they are sons of mine, I now spend the vast majority of my time on the touchlines and borders of various sports events. Rugby, football, karate, tennis, swimming, cricket: it never stops. I get exhausted just watching them.

God only help me when they grow up a bit and discover rock 'n' roll.

The other significant pause for thought I experienced since leaving the Academy is that a few years ago I got sick. Very sick.

On the morning of 28 September 2010, I had just dropped the boys off at school when I started coughing. The coughing didn't stop, and within minutes a lot of extremely scary looking blood clots were coming up. It all went very *Witches of Eastwick*. I turned the car around and raced to A&E, where I was promptly quarantined under suspicion of carrying tuberculosis, which was making a resurgence in parts of London.

It was by pure chance that a nurse happened to wander by and recognize my symptoms as a much rarer disease called Weneger's granulomatosis. Since Friedrich Weneger, who discovered the condition, was a particularly evil Nazi concentration camp doctor, the illness often goes by the even less catchy name of vasculitis with polyanginitis and pulmonary embolism.

Whatever they choose to call it, I was very close to death. They opened me up extremely thoroughly in a series of incredibly invasive operations, followed by three months of chemotherapy, and a course of heavy steroids. I am pleased to say, accompanied by a very loud knocking on wood, that it worked. I am now all clear, though very closely monitored. The condition is not curable, but it is manageable.

It was as I was lying in the hospital, with more tubes than I cared to count coming out of my body, that I suddenly realized that my kids were so young that they only really knew me as 'Dad'. I thought that if I was due to check out any time soon, I would quite like them to know about the crazy life I had with the Academy before I became their chauffeur between football matches.

I suppose it brought home to me how lucky I was still to be around at all. Most Thalidomide victims died within weeks of birth, very few made it into later life, and there are only a few hundred of us left in the UK. My friends had been telling me for years that I should write a book about the Academy. So, as I lay there, with the doctors telling me off for cracking jokes with the nurses, I decided I was finally going to write the bloody thing.

I had got out of the Academy at just the right time. All those worrying developments that I had been spying on the horizon in the mid 90s only accelerated and deepened as the decade went on. The endless churn of plastic, identikit pop bands grew oppressively ubiquitous, and the 'MTV effect' ensured that only the blandest, most generic CDs-by-the-tills-at-Tesco rock made it into the charts.

In late-90s Britain, we were made to endure hit single after hit single by the boy band refugee Robbie Williams, and an interminable stream of vacuous Spice Girls knock-off acts. Meanwhile, the American kids somehow got swept up in the manufactured angst of that unmitigated horror known as Nu-Metal. Even hip-hop, a genre that could usually be counted on for at least a bit of conscious anger and innovative production, lost its way. The rap game took a long time to recover from the murders of Tupac Shakur and Biggie Smalls. In the meantime, artists and producers seemed content to tread water, pumping out derivative tracks usually concerning how wealthy they were.

So for several years it was very much a matter of 'keep your head down, and pray for a new Radiohead album'.

But that doesn't fill venues. From a live music perspective, the scene wasn't just dead, it was fossilized.

I couldn't resist a little bit of satisfaction that I seemed to have sold the Academy at exactly the high-water mark, just as the levees broke. The following five years were a wasteland.

Then, of course, the Internet happened.

The record labels were caught asleep at the wheel, and sales plummeted. They'd had it too good for too long and, just like Rank back in the early 80s, had got complacent. That kind of self-satisfied laziness is the undoing of any industry. It wasn't the MP3 that killed the record companies, it was their own utter lack of imagination in how they responded to it.

One positive effect of this radical shift was that, as record sales fell, bands were forced to look for other ways to generate money.

Live music was reborn.

You can't download a great gig. There's no pirating or counterfeiting that electric feeling of an artist connecting with the audience directly in front of them. Suddenly, touring once again became the key. Kids might be stealing your record left, right, and centre, but if they liked it enough, they would still pay for a ticket to see your show.

Rock 'n' roll started to feel vibrant again. Bands like The Strokes and The White Stripes came storming out of America, and the UK responded with its own surge of talent in The Libertines, Razorlight, Franz Ferdinand, and the rest. Once again, the fans seemed interested in, and inspired by, people with guitars singing songs. After the intense musical drudgery of the previous few years, this new wave of rock stars came as a long-awaited liberation.

But the live music industry that these fresh new acts emerged into in the early 2000s was a fundamentally different world from the one that I had had so much fun turning upside down.

In another continuation of the trends that had driven me out of the game, the suits had completely taken over. It was industry-wide, and all pervasive. My mid-90s brainwave had been ahead of its time. Now, it seemed, everyone was part of a PLC. Which meant that everyone now had accountants, lawyers, and shareholders breathing down their necks.

Down in Brixton, Break for the Border had mutated into another corporate entity called the McKenzie Group. But in a pleasing confirmation that my old place on the Stockwell Road was still the best venue around, they quickly transformed into the Academy Music Group. When I had come up with the 'Academy' name, on a cigarette break with Mike Henley all those years before, I had never dreamed that one day there would be an Academy venue in every major town in the country!

Even Vince Power, the most fiercely independent operator I knew, got sucked into the City finance game. He got his fingers burned just as badly as I did. Reportedly, when he wrote his resignation letter from Mean Fiddler, Vince signed off with the line, 'I was never a big PLC fan.' I hear you on that one, Vince! I know the feeling.

Guys like Vince and I were never built for that model of doing business. We were mavericks. We moved too fast, and were too unpredictable, for the boardroom committee types. But now, all the mavericks were getting squeezed out. We may have built this business, but the moneymen were now running the show.

Because even Break for the Border and Mean Fiddler were small fry compared to the real corporate giants taking over the industry.

Nowadays, almost all of UK live music is run through the huge American megacompanies Live Nation or AEG. From their slick offices in Beverly Hills, those guys run the world.

And their game is fundamentally different from how we used to play. In the old days you'd have a venue, a promoter, and an agent. Dealing with those guys may have occasionally been a nightmare, but the division of labour encouraged competition, and kept things fresh.

A company like Live Nation, on the other hand, not only owns almost all the major venues in Britain, including a large stake in Academy Music Group; they also have major interests in agencies, promotion companies, and online ticket retailers. There's no competing with these guys, they're just too big. They sail very close to a horizontal monopoly, and they've got the whole game sewn up.

Ultimately, good luck to them. They're very good at what they do. And really, if they're the ones putting gigs on, then they're to be applauded.

But in my more whimsical moments, I can't help but miss the wildness and creativity of that 80s and 90s scene. We would just think things up and make them happen – even if it was by the skin of our teeth, and with a gun to our heads. It was truly thrilling. That whole creative, romantic way of operating is virtually impossible now. The big boys and their number crunchers would squeeze you out before you even got off the ground. They're just too powerful.

I think that competition keeps people sharp. It makes them take care of their customers. I worry slightly that some of the full-spectrum dominance these giant companies enjoy gets passed down to the punter in terms of their actual experience.

I still manage to get to a fair few gigs. Music hasn't lost any of its power for me. I'm lucky in that I still know enough people that I can always pick up the phone and get on someone's guest list. But I look around at everyone else at the show, think about how much they've paid, and I'm always somewhat horrified.

The days when we would charge a fiver to see UB40 and Simply Red at the Academy, back in 1985, are long gone. And it ain't just inflation.

Now, exactly thirty seconds after the band are offstage, you've got a line of bouncers moving through the crowd, shifting people out the door. It's hard to resist a slight feeling of 'well, we've had your money; now bugger off'.

When you used to hear about a gig, and buy your ticket either from the venue or a tout, you'd know, whatever happened, you were in for a party. Now, you click a button online, get charged an extra booking fee, pay £4 for a pint in a plastic cup, and get booted out before you've had a chance to process the experience. It's less a wild ride into the unknown, and more a flight on easyJet.

It was always the *total experience* of a gig that mattered to me. From the moment a punter saw a poster or held a ticket in their hands, to when they walked out of the venue after the show. I learned it from John Curd. It *all* matters, it should *all* be something special, something out of the run of ordinary life. That's what showbiz is for, isn't it? Beyond that, it's here that the fun, creative part of putting on gigs comes in. If you're just crunching numbers and running bands on and off stage on a conveyer belt, you may as well be selling life insurance.

That's how a lot of us used to think. Guys like Vince Power cared about the details too. But in that way, he and I were really the last of the Mohicans. Vince is still out there fighting the good fight, but when a company like Live Nation owns 90 per cent of the venues in the UK, there's no question about who is going to call the shots.

But, if there's one truth that my Academy adventure taught me, it's that things are cyclical, in music, as in everything else. There will be another wave of creative anarchy soon enough. There always is.

In many ways, these are profoundly exciting times for music. Exciting and, for some, very scary. The Internet really is changing everything. The kind of access and availability to new talent that the technology affords is utterly unprecedented.

The exact ways in which the Web is transforming the industry are as yet unknown. The wheel is still in motion. As much as various pundits will try to convince you that they have the answer to the billion-dollar question 'how is the Internet affecting the music business?', I'll let you in on a secret: *nobody knows*. The technology is too new, and is changing too fast, for the traditional structures to keep up. There are no hard-and-fast rules; people are constantly trying new things. Cyberspace is the Wild West: some are going to lose their scalps: others are going to become very rich indeed.

There is still one aspect of music, though, that no amount of online trickery can change: the gigs. The old equation is still the same. You put a crowd of people in the right space with a great band, and a special kind of magic happens. Beer can help too. There's no replacement for actually being there, for feeling the surge and heat of the crowd.

The most important thing to remember is that music isn't actually about the guys who organize the concerts, or even the guys who flog the records. It's about some kid sitting in their room with a guitar or a laptop and making a song. It's about them turning up to some godforsaken pub, setting up their gear, and playing that song to their mates. And perhaps, finally, it's about them having it sung back to them by 5,000 impassioned fans at the Brixton Academy.

That doesn't change. No matter who runs the venues, who cuts the deals, or who makes the money.

The structures may shift, but the heart remains. There's always that kid out there, hearing a new song and feeling that buzz. His pulse begins to race, his head starts to bounce. No matter what revolutions may shake up 'the biz', that never changes. That's rock 'n' roll.

The other great love of my life that has been completely transformed, while remaining exactly the same, is, of course, Brixton itself.

I walk down the High Street now, through the market, along Coldharbour Lane and Electric Avenue, up the hill and around the prison, and the area is almost unrecognizable from the ghetto I first arrived in aged twenty-three. Back then, Brixton was still disfigured with burned-out buildings from the riots. Now, you can't go and buy a pint of milk without seeing three yoga mats and an organic food shop.

The old edge is definitely still there, though, especially if you know where to look. Scratch the surface only a little, and you'll find out very quickly that Brixton is emphatically still Brixton.

I still see the old faces around the area. Even guys like the Railton Road bunch: now all grown up, legitimate and respected businessmen in the community, or at least as legitimate as any other 'businessmen' in Brixton.

The old guys are usually sat outside a pub, playing dominoes. We always end up having a chat, and a laugh about some long past reggae gig. It's impossible to suppress a wry chuckle as these greying former terrors inevitably begin to complain to me about how 'the youths today have no respect'. Oh boys, if you only knew the havoc you caused me back in the day!

That's how it goes. It's not dissimilar to guys like Vince and me in the music biz. The game stays the same, but the players have entirely changed, and there's a new set of rules. As the new generation comes up, the old guys feel disoriented: in Brixton as in showbiz. The wheel doesn't stop turning for anyone.

And of course, as I walk around Brixton, I pass the Academy.

I always stop to check out who they've got playing, and who's lined up over the next few months. If there's anyone particularly good, maybe I'll even be able to squeeze in a gig between school runs and sports days.

At these moments, it's all too easy to start musing about my life with the Academy, and how it relates to the whole dynamic story of Brixton.

I've lost count of the number of times that I've been chatting to some local character and the second they find out who I am, they suddenly start thanking me, with real fervour, for the crucial role the Academy has played in the redevelopment of the area. At first this was a bit unnerving. Over time it has come to be one of the more deeply satisfying reflections I have on the whole story.

They have a point. It's hard to overstate how down and out Brixton was when we first set up shop and started hiring all the local kids that no one else would even look at. The Academy not only provided a major source of employment, it started attracting crowds who would never otherwise have dreamed of venturing down to the end of the Victoria Line. In a divided era, we provided a rare space for black and white music fans to mix, enjoy themselves, and spend their money in the area.

Beyond that, the Academy was perhaps the first nationally significant symbol that the neighbourhood could wear with pride.

It meant people across the country, and even the world, hearing the word 'Brixton' outside the context of violent crime and race riots.

I've never been one to pay much attention to industry gongs and backslapping awards ceremonies but, for what it's worth, the Academy won 'Best British Venue' in both the *NME* Readers' Poll and the industry mag *Music Week* for something like 20 years running. To get both the popular vote and the nod from the industry insiders is quite an achievement.

There must be hundreds of thousands of people out there whose first visit to Brixton was for a gig or club night at the Academy. The key role we played in transforming Brixton's place in the national conversation is something I think our little gang at the Academy can be quite proud of. That, and putting on the best gigs in town, of course.

But as much as the Academy has put a lot into Brixton, it is nothing compared to what Brixton has given me. SW9 has taught me more than I can say. This neighbourhood is intense. It keeps you guessing. Just when you think you have it figured out, you'll get some shock that will spin you 360 degrees. My entire, 31-years-and-counting experience here has been a profound, life-defining, wild ride. Brixton is an education, that's for damn sure. No boarding school or business course even comes close.

Perhaps Mike Henley was right all those years ago – maybe I was 'off my fucking head'. Somehow, though, between Brixton, me, and all the other wonderful loonies that helped along the way, we found a way to make the madness work, to turn it into something glorious.

So, as I walk past the Academy now and pause for the inevitable moment of reflection, my mind can't help but start spinning on how I set the Academy up; how the Academy has shaped Brixton;

and all the ways in which Brixton has shaped me in return. There's that wheel again.

Perhaps the simplest fact is also the most telling. Brixton is where Pippa, the boys, and I still live. I wouldn't bring up my family anywhere else. It's about as far from the mansions of Lincolnshire, and the spires of Gordonstoun, as you can get without dropping off the island. But after all these years, and after all my adventures, it's the only place I'd think to call *home*.

THANKS

This is a memoir of some pretty wild times. If I've left anyone out, or got anything wrong, please put it down to too many hedonistic late nights. And some names in the text have been changed. In the meantime, massive thanks and respect to:

STAFF
Pat, Johnny, Belinda, Claire, Liz, Angie, Deidre, Louise, Busby, Owalabi, Hazel, John Woodburn, Vince, Angus & Solly, Jason, Dave Seig, Marcus, Gaity, Mike Henley, Pete, Amos, Gello, Sally, Ally, Ros, Derek, Evelyn, Matthew, Dru, Claire & Colin, Percy, John and Natalie, Naphtali and Shirley and Richard Stanley

BOX OFFICE
Sam, Lorna, Fleur, Sian, Florence, Chrissie

SECURITY
Mick Murphy, Big John, Fireman Gary, Pete the Mercenary, Nigel, Chrissie, Mick & Sue and family, Amon & Johnny, Kwami, Maurice and the boys, Ralph, Tony, Richard and Freddie. Messam Show Sec, Top Guard, Camouflage, Vincent and Rats Security

CREWS
Mike, Jim, Josh, Frenchie and his boys, Stage Miracles, Steve Sunderland, Yan at Halo, Dave at Neg Earth, Britannia Row

THE BUSINESS

John Curd, Lillian Marshall, Plum, Bob, Paul, Ray, Simon and all at Metropolis Music, Simon, Rob, Chris and all at SJM, Dave & Alex at Riverman, Tim Parsons at MCP, Bagga John, Harvey Goldsmith, Phil McIntyre and Paul Roberts, Barry Marshall, Rob Hallett, Paul Loasby, John Lennen, Paul Crockford and Paul Darwin and Paul Fenn, Jay Pender, Jeremy Taylor, Graham Ball and Joel Coleman and Westworld Crew, Bob Dog, Yvonne Thompson and Choice FM. Dave Rodigan, Tim Westwood, Norman Jay, Jazzie B and Soul II Soul Crew, Brian, Stephan and Steve from Placebo, Paul Conroy and all at Virgin, Simon Raymond from Cocteau Twins

Barry, Rod, Mike, Scott, Dave, Martin, Pru and all at ITB, John Giddings, John Jackson, Pete Nash, Emma Banks, Dan Silver, Clive Underhill-Smith, Charlie Myatt, Ian Huffam, Steve Strange, Neil Warnock, Solomon Parker, Marlene Tuischi, Rob Prinz, Dave Betteridge, Colin Davie, Jeff Craft, Bob Gold, Barry Marshall, Rob Hallett, Geaff Meall, Rhona Martin, Andy Wooliscroft, Coalition, Steve Strange

ABC

Jeremy, Mark, Roger, Dave, Katy

SPECIAL THANKS

Alex Oldham, Terry Clark, Jim Millar, Bob Scadden, Lynne Franks and Crew, Yvonne, Valerie Smith, Winston Crawely and the 12 Tribes, Dave Mansfield, Lovely Gill Tee and Crew, Andrew Logan an all at Alternative Miss World Crew, Nigel Kotani, Lois Acton & Birdy, Pip Todd-Warmoth. Special thanks and respect to Vince Power

Very special thanks to my family. And, for actually inspiring me to write this book, Joe, Ollie and Sam

Nigel Downs @ O2 Brixton
Tim (Curly) Lyle, and the Edge and Jo Jo @ Livingstone's
Danielle and Peter @ Warrener Stewart
Mike Buggy @ Coutts Bank
Cinema Fumee Crew - Finn, Carden, Matthew and Gary
Official Academy Photographer - Justin Thomas
Frank and all the Templeton Cleaning
Gary and Abacus Recruitment
Lambeth Council – Mike, John, Digby, Reece, Liz Dixon and Heather Rabbatts
Keith – Photographer
Colin Hay – Trower & Hamlins
Simon Vivian - Rakinsons
Az and family for feeding me
Mario @ Mario's for best coffee in Brixton
Chrissie Brown – for endless laughs.
Anna Power and all at Johnson & Alcock
Rebecca Gray and all at Serpent's Tail
Many thanks to Justin Thomas

THANKS AND LOVE ALSO TO:
The Rafaeli family, particularly Barbara for the tireless proof-reading
Vera – my hand in yours
Lou Reed – 'Despite all the amputations, you could just dance to that rock 'n' roll station'

AND SPECIAL THANKS TO SARA OLIVER FOR THE BIG SET-UP

Fiction
World literature
Serpent's Tail Classics
Crime

Non-fiction
Politics & Current Affairs
Music
Biography

Serpent's Tail: Books with Bite!

Visit serpentstail.com today to browse our books, learn more about our authors and events, and for exclusive content, downloads and competitions

---

www.serpentstail.com

Latest News

Author Interviews, Biographies and Q&As

Events

Trade & Media News

Sign up to our newsletter today for exclusive content, interviews and competitions: http://bit.ly/STsubscribe

---

More ways to keep in touch

Twitter @serpentstail

Facebook /serpentstailbooks

Pinterest /serpentstail